KT-407-004

# Curriculum Context

# Curriculum Context

Edited by A.V. Kelly

**Harper & Row, Publishers**
London

Cambridge
Hagerstown
Philadelphia
New York

San Francisco
Mexico City
Sao Paolo
Sydney

First published 1980
Harper & Row Ltd
28 Tavistock Street
London WC2E 7PN



British Library Cataloguing in Publication Data

Curriculum context – (Harper education series).
1. Curriculum planning
I. Kelly, Albert Victor
375'.001 LB1570 79–41761

ISBN 0 06 318148 7 paperback
0 06 318129 0 cased

Typeset by Inforum Ltd, Portsmouth
Printed and bound by A. Wheaton & Co. Ltd, Exeter

# FOREWORD

This book contains the fruits of part of a course provided for a group of students studying Curriculum Theory at Goldsmiths' College. It was the coherence of that course that persuaded us that it could be translated into a worthwhile publication. We believe, therefore, that what is offered here is both a coherent analysis of the context in which curriculum planning and development goes on and a collection of individual contributions of great merit and value in their own right.

A.V. Kelly
London
July 1979

# CONTENTS

# NOTES ON THE CONTRIBUTORS

All the contributors are full-time members of the staff of the Goldsmiths' College School of Education, except Richard Hoggart who is Warden of the college and a member of the School of Education only by adoption. All are members of the Goldsmiths' College Curriculum Study Group.

**A.V. Kelly** is Dean of the School of Education. With a first degree in Philosophy and several years of teaching behind him, most of them spent in a London comprehensive school, he moved into the field of teacher education. His interest in Philosophy quickly developed into a wider interest in the Theory and Practice of Education and, especially, Curriculum Studies. His first books in the field of Education were on mixed-ability teaching; others have followed, including an attempted survey of Curriculum Theory, *The Curriculum: Theory and Practice*.

**Richard Hoggart** is Warden of Goldsmiths' College. Most of his early career was spent in Adult and Higher Education. He is best known, however, nationally and, indeed, internationally, for his work as a writer and broadcaster, particularly in the area of Communication Studies. His seminal work was, of course, *The Uses of Literacy*, which was published in 1957 and had an immediate and profound effect on the development of views about culture in general and working-class culture in particular.

**Geva Blenkin** is a Senior Lecturer in the Department of First School Education. Formerly headteacher of an infant school in the East End of London, her main interest is in adding a curricular perspective to that developmental perspective that has for some time dominated the study of early childhood education. To this end she is currently working on a book on the primary curriculum.

**Meriel Downey** is Deputy Dean of the School of Education. She is also General Editor of the Harper and Row Education Series. A modern linguist and a former teacher of modern languages, she then took a second degree in psychology and began her work in teacher education with this speciality. However, she soon went beyond this to an involvement in the Theory and Practice of Education generally and, particularly, Curriculum Studies, so that, in addition to publishing *Interpersonal Judgements in Education* in 1977, she has struck up a productive partnership with Vic Kelly which has led to the publication of *Moral Education: Theory and Practice* and two editions of *The Theory and Practice of Education: An Introduction*.

**Carol Pudwell** is a Senior Lecturer in the Department of Secondary Education and a former teacher of science in secondary schools. His particular interest is in current developments in the secondary school curriculum, particularly the growth of integrated studies and new forms of assessment and evaluation but he has been widely involved in the work of primary middle schools also.

**Wynne Davies** is Head of the Department of Secondary Education and Senior Tutor to the School of Education. Several years as a teacher of history in a London comprehensive school and, finally, as Head of Upper School have led him to a major interest in the Organization and Administration of Education. He is currently preparing a book in this field and is engaged on research into aspects of local authority control of schools.

**G. Byrne Hill** is Acting Head of the Department of Secondary Education. A former teacher of history in secondary schools, he too spent part of his teaching career in a London comprehensive school. His main interest and involvement in teacher education is with the Theory and Practice of Education, especially at the level of the secondary school, but his particular and abiding interest is in politics in general and the politics of education in particular.

**E.J. Nicholas** is Head of the Department of Postgraduate Secondary

Education. As another former teacher of history in secondary schools and in a college of education, he brings to teacher education an historical viewpoint which, allied to his interest in Comparative Education, provides a particularly useful perspective for a study of the curriculum. He is currently engaged on research into the historical development of curricula in several secondary schools in Middlesex.

# INTRODUCTION

The rapidity with which curriculum change has occurred in the United Kingdom and in the United States in the last twenty years has far exceeded that of any other such period in the history of education, so that the curriculum of most schools today is very different from that of just a few years ago. And this is true however one defines the elusive term 'curriculum'.

Inevitably, this development in curriculum practice has been matched by a similarly rapid growth of curriculum theory. The two have not always advanced in phase. Practical changes have often been made without sufficient attention to relevant theoretical considerations and the theorists have been inclined, on the other hand, to take off from time to time on wild 'ego trips' of academicism. Thus the process of development has been like that of two racehorses going 'nip and tuck' for the line, with first one and then the other inching ahead. However, provided that neither outstrips the other by too great a distance, this is probably the most appropriate and productive model for educational and curricular progress. It is certainly a good model for the relationship between the theory and the practice of education.

Among the most significant features of the development of curriculum practice during this time has been the move towards more considered and deliberate planning and away from the 'unplanned drift' of previous times (Hoyle 1969). Conscious attention to curriculum planning, however, has brought with it an awareness of the many constraints that provide the parameters within which curriculum planning must be undertaken. These can be seen as falling into at least three broad categories.

The first of these contains those limitations that are imposed on curriculum planning by elements in the social context in which the process of education goes on, by the many exigencies of society, by cultural, political, economic and organizational influences, by the pressures of the public examination system and by other demands made on schools that teachers and educationists generally cannot ignore in the planning and execution of their work. No matter how careful and detailed our planning is, nor how sound its theoretical base, these external factors cannot be dismissed.

The second category contains those constraints that arise as a result of our ever-increasing knowledge of education and especially of child development and psychology. For this knowledge, or at least the particular theory or theories we adopt, the school whose principles and tenets we embrace, will clearly influence the decisions we take, not only about how we should set about teaching, but also about the purposes and even the content of our educational provision.

There is a third kind of constraint, however, that is not so readily recognized or acknowledged but whose influence is becoming increasingly apparent from our recent experience of curriculum change and especially from the theoretical development that has accompanied it.

Curriculum theory has now outstripped early attempts to approach or to view it from the separate vantage points of other areas of study, such as philosophy, psychology, sociology and history. It has now become apparent that the adoption of this kind of perspective generates more problems than it solves, since the reconciliation of the often conflicting demands or suggestions of those working in these disparate fields is in itself the major problem of curriculum theory and one to which *ipso facto* no one of these contributory disciplines can provide a solution. In short, as soon as one begins to look at curriculum issues from the collective point of view of all of these disciplines together, one realizes that the central issues of curriculum theory are not historical questions, nor are they scientific questions to which an answer might be provided by psychology or sociology, nor are they questions that require merely the analytical techniques of the philosopher. All of these have their contribution to make to the process but the central issues are such that these disciplines cannot answer either separately or together, since those central issues are questions of value, of choice, of commitment. Without a recognition of this, curriculum theory is but an academic sham and of no help to teachers in their efforts to make fundamental decisions about the curriculum. If curriculum theory is to provide an adequate basis, therefore, for curriculum practice, it must transcend its contributory disciplines and grasp this nettle very firmly.

The third kind of constraint, then, that the development of curriculum theory has brought to our attention is that imposed by a growing awareness of the centrality of issues of value to curriculum planning and the realization that these are not questions to which ready-made answers can be found by any kind of scientific or quasi-scientific exploration.

This book is an attempt to examine all the constraints that create the outer limits within which teachers and curriculum designers in general must work, those factors whose influence on curriculum development may be as strong as, and possibly a good deal stronger than, the most carefully thought out and rational plans.

The main emphasis of the first three chapters is on the last of these kinds of constraint, those created by the system or systems of values within which curriculum planners must work, and especially by the shifts and changes that are constantly taking place within them. Chapter 1 attempts to show some of the major influences on our approach to curriculum planning that have resulted from an awareness of the problematic nature of value questions and the recognition of the plurality of positions that can be and are taken on most such issues. In particular, it attempts to argue that a major consequence of this is that it has become increasingly difficult to define the curriculum in terms either of subject content or of the behavioural changes it is intended to bring about and that we need now to see it in terms of processes. One important result of this which is discussed in some detail is its impact on our thinking about curriculum planning for the less able pupil, since it suggests that we must now acknowledge the existence of many different routes to the common goals of education.

This is a point that is taken up, reasserted and reinforced by Richard Hoggart in Chapter 2, where he examines some of the influences on the curriculum that have derived from the concern which has been displayed both in the United Kingdom and in the United States for the effects of what has been called 'cultural deprivation'. For this is a problem that has been compounded by that same erosion of dogmatism over issues of value. We can no longer claim with confidence that certain kinds of culture are inferior or superior to others and it becomes increasingly difficult to base our curricular decisions on allegiance to any one culture. Yet a commitment to some system of values is central to any process that can properly be termed education, so that it is, indeed, the question of the 'uncertain criteria of deprivation' that needs attention of the kind given here.

The view that we take of culture will be crucial to the view we take of the curriculum and, in Chapter 3, Geva Blenkin argues not only that changes in our views of culture have been important influences on our style of curriculum planning but also that the evoluntionary nature of this process creates its own constraints. The curriculum is not only the product of the cultural history of the society in which it is to be found; it is also, she claims, the product of its own history. Thus, the styles adopted in our early attempts at curriculum planning, especially those of the Schools Council, continue to exercise a major influence and to create major constraints for present-day planning. In particular, the attempts of those associated with these early projects to approach curriculum planning as if it were an exercise in applied science continue to have what is argued to be a detrimental effect on such planning, an effect that is currently influencing even the field of early childhood education which has hitherto been relatively free of such constraints. It is an influence that runs counter to that of the work of the developmental psychologists which has had considerable impact at that level of education and whose importance to educational planning at all levels emerges in Meriel Downey's discussion of psychological influences on the curriculum in Chapter 4.

The dangers and limitations of this kind of scientific approach to curriculum planning are a recurring theme of the first three chapters since they emerge inevitably as soon as we face up to the value questions that educational planning raises. These dangers and limitations are equally exposed, however, when we explore the significance of the work of the developmental psychologists. Both of these points are taken up by Meriel Downey. She begins by drawing attention to the limitations as well as the scope of the psychological contribution and especially its inability to shed any light on issues of value. She then goes on to outline many of the influences on curriculum planning that derive from the growing knowledge of how children learn and develop which has resulted from the researches of psychologists, and she traces the changes in our approach to curriculum and to education in general to which this work has led. She also makes the very important point that different fashions and schools of psychology support and give rise to different models of and approaches to curriculum planning and thus offer different and competing kinds of influence – a point that she illustrates by reference to three curriculum projects.

We then turn to a consideration of the many administrative, economic and political factors that also form an important part of the framework within which we have to work. The next three chapters are devoted to discussions of several particular aspects of these.

In the first of them, Carol Pudwell looks at that well-known source of constraints, the public examination. In considering the use of examinations at many different levels of education over the years since they were first introduced, he shows that, although it has seldom been the intention that they should control the curriculum, this has always been their effect and, moreover, everyone has been aware of this for as long as examinations have been in use. He also stresses the need for continued change and development in our techniques of examining if these are to keep pace with and to promote rather than to inhibit the development of the curriculum and, indeed, of education itself. This discussion highlights the central role of the teacher in curriculum development and thus raises important issues of a political kind, not least those concerned with the degree of control teachers should or can exercise over the curriculum and the extent to which they should be restricted by or accountable to other bodies.

In Chapter 6, Wynne Davies examines some of the subtle features of the control of education and the influences of those bodies that have a share, whether formal or informal, in that control. A survey of the history of the development of publicly provided education in the United Kingdom reveals how there has grown a system in which curricular decisions are the result of a delicate balance of forces formal and informal, lay and professional. These are forces whose origins and strength teachers need to be aware of if their own attempts at curriculum planning are not to upset that balance. The point of balance itself is also subject to periodic shifts and a sensitivity to these is shown to be necessary. It is further argued that current changes both of attitude and of administrative arrangements are leading to such a shift of balance, a major feature of which is an erosion of that control over curricular decisions that teachers had won after a long struggle. This is resulting from increased demands for participation in curricular decisions by other agencies in society and pressures upon teachers for a more direct form of public and political accountability.

It is this question of the role of the state in curriculum development that is taken up by Graham Byrne Hill in Chapter 7. Here he traces the delicate nuances of state influence, as central government attempts to fulfil what are seen as its major duties in respect of the curriculum – to provide a recognized minimum of education for all citizens and to settle and prevent conflict between interest groups – and the ways in which it achieves this through those public bodies to which it delegates its responsibilities in this area. In particular, he argues that the notion of 'democracy as communication' provides a justification of the need for teachers to be accountable and even for the acceptance of a common core to the curriculum, while representative democracy requires that all public services be seen by citizens as being adequately provided. Thus the constraints imposed by government on curriculum planning are viewed not only as inevitable but also as legitimate.

A similar conclusion is reached in Chapter 8, where some of the current problems of curriculum development in the United Kingdom are compared with those of several other countries. Discussion of the role of the state, even the right of the state, in decisions concerning the curriculum can clearly be enhanced and illuminated by a knowledge of what goes on in other states and it is this perspective that Jack Nicholas provides. He sets out to show how such a perspective can make us more critical of and more reflective about our own practices as well as offering deeper insights into what they are and what their effects are likely to be.

In this way, this chapter throws a different but very important light on all those that have gone before. For it picks up many of the points raised by earlier chapters and offers a comparative view of them. Issues such as the effects of competing ideologies which are discussed in Chapter 1, the attempt to achieve educational equality which was explored in Chapters 1 and 2, the conflict of 'progressive' and scientific approaches to educational planning that was one of the subjects of Chapter 3, the view of education as conceptual development that was examined in Chapter 4 and the impact of many features of the administrative and political framework of education that was considered in Chapters 5, 6 and 7 are all touched upon, and the experience of the United Kingdom is thus put into an international context. What emerges is that there is a good deal of tension created by the many competing principles that are to be discerned in English education – in fact, by those very competing ideologies with which we began our discussion. One of those principles is that of teacher autonomy, a point to which we have constantly returned, and the conclusion here is that the experience of other countries also suggests that some erosion of this might be ultimately to the benefit of education.

Thus Chapter 8 rounds off the discussion by drawing together many of the threads of earlier contributions. A brief, concluding chapter attempts to tie these up by picking out some recurrent themes and highlighting the major dilemma that has emerged, that between the freedom of the teacher to attend to the educational needs of each of his pupils and the legitimate pressures and demands for greater external control.

In this way, an attempt has been made to mount a coherent attack on a number of closely interrelated aspects of curriculum development and it has unearthed a number of factors that are inextricably interwoven and, in some cases, also conflicting. Collectively, these factors comprise the context or framework within which all educational planning must occur. However, the context that they create is a confused and tangled one and what emerges from this attempt to consider these factors collectively and individually is how important it is that teachers should be aware of them, not only because they offer constraints on their work, but also because without an understanding of their full implications little satisfactory planning will be achieved.

# CHAPTER ONE

# IDEOLOGICAL CONSTRAINTS ON CURRICULUM PLANNING

**A.V. Kelly**

It was suggested in the Introduction that the attempt to adopt a completely scientific approach to curriculum planning and to the study of the curriculum is misguided and has resulted in serious inadequacies in both. The prime error of this approach is that it mishandles the question of values. For it ignores value issues altogether or it treats such issues as though they can be dealt with in isolation from questions of a scientific or 'factual' kind or, worst of all, it assumes that questions of value can be answered by appeals to scientific evidence. This is now recognized as a serious weakness of the traditional approach to the human sciences generally and we must now acknowledge it as a source of some of the inadequacies of curriculum theory.

This chapter will endeavour to explore some of the implications of this development for current approaches to curriculum planning, some of the ways in which this growing awareness of the centrality of questions of value to the curriculum and of the problematic nature of such questions is leading to important changes in the style of curriculum planning and thus exercising its own subtle influences and controls on such planning.

At one level this development has brought an awareness of those competing ideologies whose influence on the development of the curriculum has been the subject of much recent debate (Young 1971). At another, more general, level, it will be argued, it has led to fundamental changes in our approach to curriculum planning, in the style of such planning. In short, it is my contention that we now set about the planning of the curriculum within a different framework of values and with a different view of values and that this new framework and this new view provide their own constraints and parameters within which we must work.

It will also be argued that these changes have been prompted, or at least promoted, as much by the increased understanding of what education fundamentally consists of which has resulted from the work of people like Richard Peters (1965, 1966) as by any more overtly social or sociological factors. For this work, by offering us criteria by which we can distinguish educational activities from other acts that involve teaching, has provided us with the scope to make distinctions within the work of schools that we were not equipped to make before, has thus offered us greater clarity of perception in certain important areas of curriculum planning and has, as a result, imposed its own constraints by drawing our attention to the fact that some of our practices do not satisfy these criteria.

Three aspects of this work have particular interest and relevance for the case presented here. The first of these is the claim that education must be centrally concerned with the development of those qualities of mind that enable the individual to make critical judgements, to reach informed opinions and, in general, to think for himself. The word 'autonomy' is often used to denote this ability but it is important to appreciate that there is a good deal more to it than is necessarily connoted by that term. A second crucial feature of this analysis is the assertion that for an act of teaching to merit the description of education the teacher must regard it as being of value and must intend that, ultimately if not initially, the pupil will see it in a similar light. The third point, which is closely related to this, is that such value shall be regarded as intrinsic to the activity and shall not be defined by either teacher or pupil in terms of its instrumentality to some extrinsic end or purpose. If these criteria are not met, it is argued, then what is occurring may be instruction or training or socialization or even indoctrination, but it is not education.

This kind of analysis should play a crucial part in the practice of education and of curriculum planning and I hope to show that its effects on our thinking can already be observed in some recent trends in both the theory and the practice of curriculum planning, in short, that it has already begun to create important and necessary constraints for the curriculum planner.

In general, then, the case presented here is that we have begun to attain of late a clearer view of the nature of assertions of value; as a result, we have begun to see how questions of value enter discussions of education and decisions in education; and we have begun to appreciate certain other features of the concept of education and of what it means to provide an education in the full sense. All these things are combining to bring about changes in our view of what constitutes education and are thus having important consequences for curriculum planning; in particular, they are introducting their own kinds of constraint on such planning and we need to be as conscious of the points at which such constraints impinge as we are of the impact of constraints of other kinds.

There are three particular examples of this that this chapter will explore, three areas in which this kind of thinking and the enhanced understanding it has led to have already begun to lead to fundamental changes in our approach to the planning of the curriculum. The first of these is the growing awareness that the issue of values in education, as I have already suggested, is both central to curriculum planning and also highly problematic. The second is the move away from an approach to curriculum planning that begins from the specification of behavioural objectives and the emergence, or perhaps re-emergence, of a 'process' model of curriculum. The third is the change that we are beginning to see in attitudes towards the idea of developing different curricula for different 'types' of child or even different types of mind.

Each of these will be considered in turn and an attempt will be made to demonstrate not only that they are discernible trends in the recent history of curriculum development but also that they are closely interlinked and that they have been prompted, at least in part, by advances in our thinking about both education and values.

## Values and the curriculum

We must begin by noting that it is in part because we have a clearer concept of education that we have become aware of how crucially this problem of values impinges on curriculum planning. For it has become clear that education must be centrally concerned with questions of value. Whatever else education is or is not, there can be little doubt that it must have at its core those things which are thought to be intrinsically valuable (Peters

1965, 1966). To speak of a worthless education would be to involve oneself in a semantic contradiction of a fundamental kind. It is not necessary that other processes which involve teaching, processes like training or instruction, should be concerned with activities or areas of knowledge that are felt to be worthwhile in themselves, but the notion of education itself can never be value-neutral. And schooling in this country is still concerned with education.

It is this central feature of education that creates peculiar and interesting problems for education theory in general and curriculum theory in particular and, indeed, that makes the use of the term 'theory' in the context of education and curriculum different from its use in other contexts. Within the empirical sciences, theories attempt to describe and to explain phenomena; they are also used in the applied field to predict and thus they provide a basis for planning and action. This is also true of the human sciences, although there are special difficulties in the use of theories there as predictive bases for planning. Education theory and curriculum theory must also describe, explain and predict and thus provide a basis for planning and action. However, there can be no educational or curriculum planning without the making of choices and it is for this reason that a further element must be added to the notion of education and curriculum theory, an element that derives from a rather different use of the term 'theory' in non-scientific, political and/or ideological contexts. For in those contexts, the term is used to refer to a particular philosophy, an ideology, a set of values, as when we speak of Marxist theory.

It is this feature of education itself and of education theory that makes a purely scientific approach to it inadequate. For to approach education as if it were just a scientific activity is to ignore that value element that is essential to it and to attempt to set up value-free schemes for curriculum planning is to miss the central point.

This problem is compounded by the recent realization that all the human sciences, upon which education theory draws heavily, are beset by the same difficulty, and that, further, the fact/value distinction is impossible to maintain. No question of value can be resolved without reference to knowledge of a factual kind and, conversely, no 'factual' assertion can be made that does not have built into it certain value assumptions. These two aspects of any human science, therefore, cannot be dealt with in isolation from each other but are inextricably interwoven – especially at the level of action. Since curriculum planning is centrally concerned with action, this is a crucial point for curriculum planners to appreciate.

The nature of the problem becomes immediately apparent if we consider the model of curriculum planning that Denis Lawton offers us (1973). For this model has the great merit of drawing our attention to the fact that an educational curriculum must focus on what is worthwhile and that it must make choices and selections from what is available; but it also reveals the problems that must follow if we assume that this can readily be done and that the answers to such questions of value can be discovered by quasi-scientific means such as through the researches of the philosopher.

If we accept that education is essentially concerned with the transmission of what is intrinsically worthwhile and thus recognize that the focal point of curriculum theory is the question of what falls into that category, it also becomes necessary to acknowledge that to find answers to that question is no easy matter. Not only is the value element in education crucial, it is also highly problematic and it is this that creates particular problems for curriculum planning.

For we are now coming to realize that questions about values are not susceptible to clear-cut or hard and fast solutions; in fact that they are questions to which a number of different solutions can be proposed with equal justification and validity. Richard Peters was right to recognize that the notion of value is conceptually linked to that of education and that it is of the essence of the educative process that it should involve initiation into worthwhile activities (1965, 1966). He was wrong, however, to suggest that it is possible in any final way to identify what these activities are. In the same way, Denis Lawton is wrong to follow that lead and assume that those value issues that are central to the curriculum can be resolved by reference to the work of the philosopher (1973).

For, if one thing is clear from even the most cursory examination of the assertions that are made as a result of this kind of approach, it is that there is no agreement between philosophers on this issue or even on the question of the kind of basis upon which such agreement might be reached. Indeed, it becomes increasingly clear that no such basis could be found. The arguments that are put forward by philosophers in support of qualitative differences between types of knowledge or human activity are very thin, amounting usually to little more than the doubtful claim that philosophers must in some way *qua* philosophers know best. As John Stuart Mill says, 'If the fool, or the pig, are of a different opinion, it is because they only know their own side of the question'. The insubstantial nature of this argument must strengthen rather than weaken Jeremy Bentham's claim that 'push-pin is as good as poetry'. Epistemology can provide no substantive basis for decisions about curriculum content.

Appeals to society or to culture, of the kind that Denis Lawton (1973) would also make, are equally unhelpful (Kelly 1977). For, apart from the ambiguities of the term, it is clear that all developed societies are characterized by the presence within them of several cultures, by their pluralism, by that organic solidarity which 'presupposes a society whose social integration arises out of *differences* between individuals' (Bernstein 1967). This being the case, there is little point in recommending that the curriculum be planned in terms of the culture of society, nor even that it consist of a selection from that culture since, although some basic commonality can be discerned, no one such culture can be identified at a level that would be adequate for curriculum planning, and there are no clear criteria by reference to which such a selection could be made. The nettle of values must be grasped more firmly than that.

Thus the view that the content of the curriculum can be determined in this kind of way has been challenged both by those sociologists who see knowledge not as God-given but as socially constructed, as a 'product of the informal understandings negotiated among members of an organized intellectual collectivity' (Blum 1970), and as a result regard the curriculum as a social system, and by those educationists such as Pat Wilson (1971) who from similar premises insist that the child should have as much right as anyone else to choose his curriculum and who therefore offer criteria such as the interests and the needs of the pupils as the basis for planning.

Both of these claims are founded on the assumption that there can be no objective solutions to issues of value so that any attempt to define or plan the curriculum in terms of its content will involve the imposition of the values of the person or group establishing the definition or doing the planning. And, as John Dewey once told us, any attempt to impose values on pupils in this way is indoctrination.

This is, of course, the main platform of that school of sociology that has recently explored the sociology of knowledge and has come to regard the distribution of knowledge as the major factor in social control (Young 1971). In asserting th subjectivity of all knowledge, these sociologists have overstated their case and perhaps even done it harm, but their major point is made if we accept that their thesis is much stronger in the realm of assertions of value.

For, although there must be some commonality, some agreement on those basic principles that are presupposed by the notion of rationality itself and the possibility of human discourse, the range of interpretation of these principles is so vast that at a very early stage value differences become clearly identifiable. Thus, while, for example, we might be committed in this way to the value of truth telling, there will be wide variations of view concerning what truth consists of and, indeed, what circumstances warrant our dispensing with it.

There will also be some commonality of a contingent kind in every culture, which at the level of basic principles it will be possible to identify, but again differences of interpretation will abound and many views will be held concerning their practical application. Thus, while, for example, it might be claimed that in Western European culture there is universal condemnation of cruelty, there will be important variations in individual interpretations of it and wide disagreement over what such condemnation requires of us in practice. Again, therefore, value differences assert themselves at a very early stage.

The message, then, is simple: we cannot define education or curriculum in terms of specific subjects or a specific subject content without, in so doing, imposing the values implicit in that content on those who are the recipients of it.

The two reactions against this approach that we described above illustrate the two major ways in which the growing awareness of the problematic nature of values in education is influencing our approach to curriculum planning. For, in the first place, it has led to a realization of the strong ideological influences that have been exerted on the curriculum from the aristocratic ideology of traditional education to the more egalitarian or democratic ideology that may be said to be dominant today. We can no longer regard the curriculum as the repository of all that is objectively worthwhile but must see it as the creation of whatever ideology is dominant in society. At the very least, we must recognize that there are strong ideological determinants of the curriculum and that any curriculum will be the product of one or of several such competing ideologies. We must also acknowledge that we have no objective grounds for deciding between these competing ideologies at those points where they are in conflict. There can, for example, no longer be any confident ordering of subjects into a hierarchy of knowledge with, say, the classics at one end and the practical subjects, such as art, woodwork or Physical Education, at the other.

This in turn suggests that the crucial distinction is not between subjects or activities or areas of study but between the levels at which and the manner in which these are handled, that the proper focus for a definition of education is not content but processes, not matter but manner. At root it is this consideration that has led many educationists to claim that education can and should begin from the interests of the pupils (Wilson 1971) or with the commonsense knowledge that they bring into the school with them (Keddie 1971). The important point to grasp about such claims is that if the process is to be truly called education it must not end there. Any area of human experience can be a vehicle for education if it is handled and developed in the light of a clear concept of what education entails. Conversely, it is equally true that the study of any area of human experience and activity can be counter-productive to education if it is not so handled. In short, woodwork can provide a very firm basis for education, as its current transformation into Design and Technology has demonstrated, while a study of the classics, if not properly handled, can be the death of education, as the ghosts of many struggling Latin scholars will readily testify.

Considerations such as these underly the growing objections both to the practice of planning the curriculum in terms of prespecified objectives of a behavioural kind and that of providing radically different curricula for pupils of differing abilities. For the former presupposes or at least leads to a definition of education and curriculum in terms of content and, if it is so defined, it is difficult to see how education can be made available to all pupils regardless of ability. On the other hand, the realization that education has to be defined in terms of its manner and of the processes appropriate to it brings an appreciation of what is required by the demand for education for all and how that ideal might be achieved even with pupils who are not highly gifted academically.

It is to a consideration of these two issues that we now turn.

## A process model of curriculum

The tendency to view education as an instrumental process and to ignore those questions of value that are central to it lies at the heart of the second change in the style of curriculum planning that I want to consider, the move away from an approach based on the prespecification of behavioural objectives and the emergence of what has been called a process model of curriculum (Stenhouse 1975).

Demands on teachers and curriculum planners to make clear prespecifications of their objectives began to be made in the early part of this century in the United States with the work of men such as Franklin Bobbitt (1918) and Werrett Charters (1924), but the movement gained particular momentum during the 1950s and 1960s in both the USA and the UK through the work of Ralph Tyler (1949), D.K. Wheeler (1967) and, of course, Benjamin Bloom and his associates (1956).

The movement was prompted on the one hand by admiration for the job-analysis approach to industrial processes and on the other hand by concern about the vague and unscientific nature of the work of most teachers (Davies 1976). Concern was expressed at the woolly answers most teachers gave when asked about their work and their lack of clarity was attributed to the fact that they had not begun the planning of their work with a clear statement of what it was intended to bring about.

To this was later added the claim that it is an essential characteristic of any rational activity that it should have clear goals so that if education is to have any claim to being a rational activity it must conform to this kind of model (Hirst 1969). The weakness of the traditional approach to education, that most usually associated with the secondary phase, was said to be its obsession with subject content, with examination syllabuses and the like, while that of the 'progressive' school, most usually linked with the primary stage, was its concentration on methods or procedures, on learning by discovery and enquiry methods. Both of these approaches, it was argued, are inadequate, since both fail to commence curriculum construction with a statement and a clarification of their objectives (Hirst 1969).

A further source of support for such an approach has always been the economic consideration that a clear statement of objectives is the quickest way to a proper evaluation of whether the money invested in education is being properly used and, indeed, such evaluation has also been advocated on educational grounds as a tool for the further and continued development of the curriculum (Taba 1962). Thus there emerged the view that the curriculum must be seen as consisting of at least four interrelated elements – objectives, content, procedures and evaluation.

From the outset this movement was closely linked to the behaviourist school of psychology and it was from this source that there emerged the pressures upon teachers not only to be more scientific in their approach to their work but also to do so by prespecifying in behavioural terms what were the intended outcomes of their teaching.

At the level of educational practice, however, these pressures met with little response, despite the fact that in the United Kingdom, for example, throughout the 1960s, as Geva Blenkin shows in Chapter 3, most of the projects sponsored by the Schools Council were heavily biased towards this kind of approach, while teachers and student teachers were continually being asked to state the aims and objectives of their lessons. Secondary schools continued to be concerned mainly with the content of their curricula and primary schools with their 'romantic', 'progressive' concentration on learning processes. Furthermore, individual teachers in both continued to realize, if only intuitively, that the task of education cannot be properly tackled in this way, that the realities of the classroom are far too complex to be reducable to statements of simple, behavioural goals. As a result, no matter how tightly the objectives of any particular project were framed, they soon lost most of their precision when that project reached the individual classroom. This is one area in which teachers have long been ahead of the theoreticians – if not always for the right reasons.

Inevitably, therefore, the approach began to attract criticisms from a number of directions as the theorists produced explanations of what teachers had quite properly sensed through their practice. It came to be realized that, like behaviourist psychology itself, this approach to curriculum planning which it had generated was based on a passive view of man, as a creature whose behaviour one can with justification attempt to modify and would according to certain preconceived purposes. The curriculum model adopted is essentially one that, as we shall see in greater detail in Chapter 4, falls into what some psychologists have called a closed system of learning. It also came to be recognized that this approach places constraints on both teachers an taught that limit the effectiveness of both in the learning situation (James 1968).

What this all adds up to is that this approach to curriculum planning does not square with any viable concept of education. For the concept of education which I am suggesting is now dominant in our thinking about curriculum is one that regards education as a dynamic process and man as an agent who must be active in that process. Moreover, it cannot be reconciled with a view of curriculum planning as an instrumental process designed to achieve ends that are extrinsic to itself. In short, this approach to curriculum planning does not promote those qualities that we suggested earlier are the essential elements of the educative process. It is, in fact, more likely to lead to indoctrination than to education, to behavioural changes unaccompanied by self-direction, to learning of an uncritical kind.

It is also an approach to educational planning that fails to face up to the issues of values. To claim that education can or should be planned in a completely scientific manner is to make one of those fundamental errors to which we referred earlier. For either it is to ignore the problem of values altogether or it is to assume that it is an issue that can be isolated from the other 'factual' elements of curriculum planning or it is to believe that value questions can be answered by reference to scientific data. Most of the exponents of this approach to curriculum planning do in fact make it clear that they set out to be deliberately value-neutral and that it is their intention to offer blueprints or schemes for planning rather than to provide a basis for actual decision making. This kind of approach, however, must founder on the rock of values. For it fails to recognize that one cannot plan any educational activity without being concerned from the outset with questions of its value, that education is an art as well as a science, and that any attempt to ignore that dimension of it will inevitably involve losing its essential ingredient and will be like trying to make a currant bun by baking the bun first and adding the currants later. This, then, is another explanation of why this kind of approach to curriculum planning will not lead to education but again to something nearer to indoctrination.

It further leads to an attempt to define education in terms of its content and this we are also suggesting is no longer tenable. For, although those who have advocated that we begin our curriculum planning with the consideration of our objectives have done so in order to get away from that obsession with content that they found unsatisfactory, their own approach too inevitably focuses on the *what* of education rather than the *how*, on the behavioural changes education is to be concerned to bring about rather than those developments in the manner of thinking, those processes, that we are claiming are the true focus of any educational activity. They have thus lost sight of the fact that the overall ends of education are inevitably greater than the sum either of their prespecified objectives or of its subject contents.

Thus we have of late seen a reaction against this movement, not only in practice but in curriculum theory too. This has taken several forms and several attempts have been made to resolve the dilemma that we seem to be presented with. One such attempt has been to suggest that if the behavioural model is unsatisfactory as a model for educational objectives we must look for a different model (Eisner 1969; Hirst 1975). Another solution is that which has emerged from the practical experience of several projects. We saw earlier that the stated objectives of any project will be modified by teachers in the light of their continuing experiences of the realities of their implementation in their classrooms. Recognizing this and acknowledging that it should be so, those associated with the project in History, Geography and Social Science 8-13 suggested that their objectives should be seen as 'provisional' (Blyth 1974) and the authors of the Nuffield 'A' level Biology project that their objectives should be regarded as 'mutable' (Kelly 1973). Others have suggested that we must not allow any objectives we may begin with to blind us to the possibilities and the attractions of unintended learning outcomes (Hogben 1972). In general, this process has reflected well the claim of Hilda Taba that 'objectives are developmental, representing roads to travel rather than terminal points' (1962, p. 203). The same image is used by Richard Peters when he tells us that, 'To be educated is not to have arrived at a destination; it is to travel with a different view' (1965, p. 110).

However, we still need criteria to refer to when making such modifications and this has led some to suggest that we should begin our curriculum planning with a statement not of it objectives but of the principles that should inform those day-by-day judgements and decisions made by the teachers who will implement it (Stenhouse 1970, 1975; Pring 1973). It has also been suggested that many of the statements of what are called objectives, particularly those offered by many of the Schools Council's projects, appear on analysis to resemble statements of such principles rather than of behavioural objectives (Kelly 1977).

It has been the Humanities Curriculum Project that has pointed the way towards and, indeed, demonstrated the viability of an approach to curriculum planning based on a clear statement of educational principles and a total rejection of prespecified objectives. For it begins from the conviction that any attempt to approach teaching in the area of the humanities with a clear idea of the learning outcomes one intends to promote or produce, the kinds of behavioural change that one intends to bring about, is to be engaged in indoctrination rather than education since it is to deny the right of the individual to respond to what he is presented with in his own way (Stenhouse 1970). Others have argued that the same is true of any area of the curriculum and that the teaching of the sciences too requires an approach which, like scientific method itself, is open to unexpected eventualities (Sockett 1976).

There has thus emerged a model of curriculum that sees the central focus of curriculum as neither objectives nor content but as processes or principles of procedure (Stenhouse 1975). This is a model that, as we shall see in detail in Chapter 3, is very close to that which has shaped the development of the curriculum of the primary school, and this is not surprising when we realize that the philosophy of the primary school has developed from the so-called 'progressive' movement in education which began with the work of early theorists such as Jean-Jacques Rousseau as a revolt against the instrumental approach of traditional education and which took as its central tenet the view that one should view the child as a child and not as a man in the making.

Again, therefore, this development in both the theory and the practice of education can be seen as a direct result of the achievement of a clearer conception of what education is and of those value questions that are central to it. And again this is leading to changes in our approach to curriculum planning, in our style of curriculum planning, that have important implications for and impose their own kinds of constraint on those who are responsible for such planning.

Criticisms of the objectives model of curriculum planning, then, have been based both on the fact that it ignores those issues of value that are central to any decision making in education and that it attempts to view education as an instrumental process that can be defined by reference to short-term goals. It thus fails to recognize that the process of education must be centrally concerned with that which is felt to have intrinsic value. It is also an approach which, by stating in advance its intended learning outcomes, denies the individual the right to respond to what he is offered in his own way and thus to develop that power to think for oneself that is a major part of what it means to be educated, so that it is more likely to lead to indoctrination than to education, or, in less pejorative terms, to what, as we shall see in Chapter 4, some psychologists have called a closed system of learning.

Its fundamental error is that it concentrates on the matter of education rather than on its manner, on *what* is to be taught rather than on *how* children are to learn, and it is this same error that is at the root of the third and final issue that this chapter will examine – the problem of devising appropriate curricular provision for the attainment of educational equality. For, so long as we see education as initiation into certain kinds of subject content, some pupils will always and inevitably be excluded from it.

## Equality and the curriculum

The gradual extension of educational provision for the masses that was the major feature of the development of education in the United Kingdom in the nineteenth century and the early part of the twentieth century cannot be seen as evidence of a desire to provide everyone with an education in the full sense of the term or, to put it into the context of the time, to offer in the elementary school the same form of education as was available in the public and grammar schools. In fact, it was prompted much more clearly and overtly by the economic need to create an efficient workforce and to promote social cohesion by achieving law and order at the lowest possible price (Gordon and Lawton 1978).

Thus there emerged two broad traditions, well summed up in the words of Robert Lowe in 1867:

> The lower classes ought to be educated to discharge the duties cast upon them. They should also be educated that they may appreciate and defer to a higher cultivation when they meet it: and the higher classes ought to be educated in a very different manner, in order that they may exhibit to the lower classes that higher education to which, if it were shown to them, they would bow and defer (Lowe 1867, p. 32; Gordon and Lawton 1978, p. 121).

Clearly the place in which this dichotomy was most apparent was in the curricula of the different schools.

Nor was there any significant change when the focus shifted from elementary to secondary education with the Education Act of 1902. For, although opportunities were increased for brighter pupils from poor homes to gain access to secondary education, this continued to be seen as essentially different from that provided by the elementary schools, whose purpose, as defined in the Code for Public Elementary Schools of 1904, 'is to form and strengthen the character and to develop the intelligence of the children entrusted to it, and to make the best use of the school years available, in assisting both boys and girls, according to their different needs, to fit themselves, practically as well as intellectually, for the work of life' (Curtis 1948, p. 324). Again, this difference was reflected in the curricula offered by the different schools.

It is with the emergence of the idea of secondary education for all and the expression given to that ideal by the Hadow Report of 1926 that we see the first suggestions that an attempt might be made to offer all pupils something that might be regarded as having a truly educational value rather than a merely utilitarian function. The Report does recommend the organization of secondary education in separate schools with separate curricula, and in doing so it reiterates the earlier view that the new 'modern' form of secondary education would differ from the older form and 'would be characterised by a practical and realistic rather than by an academic bias' (Curtis 1948, p. 348). 'There is no question that among the pupils of the new post-primary schools the desire and the ability to do and to make, to learn from concrete things and situations, will be more widely diffused than the desire and the ability to acquire book-knowledge and to master generalizations and abstract ideas' (Hadow 1926). It also expresses fear lest the modern school should become an inferior kind of secondary school and suggests that, in order to avoid this and to achieve what was later to be called 'parity of esteem', such schools should not attempt to ape the academic approach and curriculum of the grammar school. However, it takes us some way beyond the rather simplistic idea that this can involve no more than a basic mechanical training and evinces a genuine desire to do more for these pupils than merely to socialize them. For it goes on to claim that 'for many children the attainment of skill in some form of practical work in science, handwork, or the domestic arts may be a stimulus to higher intellectual effort', and that, moreover, 'apart from the question of stimulus, boys and girls with the types of interests we have in view can grasp concepts through practical work much more easily than by devoting long periods to the abstract study of ideas' (Hadow 1926).

It would thus seem fair to suggest that the Report was feeling its way towards some kind of concept of education and that it was the lack of such a concept that was responsible not only for its own failure to make this kind of point clearly and with force but also for the fact that attempts to implement its recommendations in the schools led to a perpetuation of the dichotomy between the academic and the practical forms of secondary curriculum and to a reinforcement of the view of the latter as inferior to the former, in fact, to the continuation of the practice of making available one curriculum that offered an education and another that did not.

Nothing that emerged in the 1930s or 1940s from the Spens Report (1938), from that of the Norwood Committee (1943) or even from the 1944 Education Act itself with its demand for 'education for all according to age, aptitude and ability' did anything to erode this view of the need for clearly differentiated curricula, although the advent of the notion of technical education did introduce a third type of curriculum. Even where comprehensive secondary schools were established as a result of the permissiveness of the 1944 Act, different forms of curriculum continued to be offered within them and the secondary modern schools were at this time positively discouraged from offering to any of their pupils a curriculum comparable to that of their grammar school neighbours, a feature of their existence at that time which is reflected most clearly in their inability to use public money to enter any of their pupils for public examinations.

The advent of the Certificate of Secondary Education examinations in the early 1960s as a result of the recommendations of the Beloe Report (1960) might be seen as a step forward but it must also be seen as emphasizing the distinction and as doing so in the wrong way. For the tentative suggestion of Hadow that we should look for different routes to the same goal of conceptual development had still not been taken up and the institution of the CSE, as a public examination at a lower level than the GCE, only served to emphasize that we had still not grasped the notion of education for all. For the differences made manifest by the arrival of the CSE were not only differences in subjects, syllabuses, approach and modes of assessment; they were also differences of status and level.

This distinction was further confirmed by and hardened as a result of the publication of the Newsom Report in 1963. Its title, 'Half Our Future', offered the wrong kind of emotive appeal and clearly illustrates the continuing view that the needs of this half of our future must be considered and catered for in total separation, and even isolation, from those of the other half. It offers us four key words for the curriculum for pupils of average and below-average abilities – 'practical, realistic, vocational, choice' (para. 317); it emphasizes the need for personal and social development; and it advises us to resist external pressures 'to extend public examinations to pupils for whom they are inappropriate, or over an excessively large part of the programme for any pupil' (p. xvii). It thus adds its weight to the continuing tradition of separate curricula.

However, like the Hadow Report, it contains flashes of a view of education that goes beyond this. In particular, although emphasizing the role of practical subjects in an appropriate curriculum for such pupils, it tells us that these subjects are 'not to be an ivory tower in which our boys and girls take refuge, or are shut up because they are not good at words and ideas' (para. 320), and goes on to claim that 'Taught properly, they should be one of the major ways by which ordinary boys and girls find they have ideas to express and acquire the words to express them' (para. 320).

Again, however, although groping towards a concept of education, the Report did not attain such a concept sufficiently clearly and, as a result, its own lack of understanding was reflected in the subsequent practical implementation of what were seen as its main recommendations. For, inspired by the general tenor of its suggestions and in some trepidation about the likely effects of its proposal for the raising of the school leaving age to 16+, most schools immediately set up 'Newsom courses', established 'Newsom classes' and even began to speak of their 'Newsom children'. The effect of this was again to harden these distinctions.

The same factors influenced the early thinking of many of the projects sponsored by the Schools Council which was established in 1964 to guide the development of curricula and examinations in schools and especially to help schools and teachers to prepare for the raising of the school leaving age. This kind of brief inevitably resulted in its main attentions being directed at the needs of pupils of average and below-average abilities, and it was encouraged in this by the comparative ease with which curriculum change and innovation could be achieved in this area.

It began, however, by taking the line that was implicit, even if uncritically and unanalytically so, in both the Hadow and Newsom Reports and asserting that a curriculum that has as its focus those practical subjects that both Hadow and Newsom had recommended need not involve cutting its pupils off from the ability to handle ideas and concepts and to think for themselves. Thus Working Paper No. 2, *Raising the School Leaving Age: A comparative programme of research and development* (Schools Council 1965), one of the best documents to emerge from the Schools Council on any subject, defined as 'the distinctive task of secondary education' 'to help the pupils make the judgements, or choices, which will determine the use they make of whatever capacities their parents, their school and their environment have enabled them to develop' (para. 39). It speaks too of 'the possibility of helping the pupils who are the concern of this paper to enter the world of ideas, to use powers of reason, and to acquire even the beginnings of mature judgement' (para. 40), and tells us that 'they will be left prisoners of their own experience if the teacher cannot find a way of so enlarging their vision and understanding that they come to see value for themselves in gaining some understanding of Man's total experience, and with it some capacity to contribute to its further enlargement' (para. 47). 'What is at issue is, therefore, the bringing of the best traditional view of what constitutes a liberal education within the grasp of ordinary people' (para. 48). Thus there can be seen to be emerging precisely that concept of education that Hadow and Newsom had been groping towards and with it a clearer notion of what is involved in education for all. Allied to this was the conviction that the extra year at school would provide more scope for achieving universal education if we were prepared to challenge some of the underlying assumptions of the traditional approaches to the education of less able pupils.

The impact of this, however, was soon diminished. We have already noted that the interpretation placed by the schools and the teachers on the recommendations of the Newsom Report was very different and that they had immediately rushed into the creation of a curriculum quite different from that provided for brighter pupils. Indeed, Working Paper No. 2 itself admitted that the concept of education it offered might 'seem to contradict the experience of many teachers. Indeed it may carry an almost revolutionary ring to some' (para. 40). That ring proved to be too revolutionary, so that not only did the practice of schools fall short of its ideals, the ideals themselves soon came to be watered down to the point where they dissolved completely.

This is apparent from even a cursory glance at the Council's next publication in this field, Working Paper No. 11, *Society and the Young School Leaver: A humanities programme in preparation for the raising of the school leaving age*. For there is little evidence here of any attempt to challenge the traditional view of the needs of these pupils or to bring within their grasp 'the best traditional view of what constitutes a liberal education'. The emphasis is again on vocational subjects, on relevance and enquiry, on social science courses, on 'education for citizenship' and 'tuition in living' (para. 13), and, although it is clearly the aim to ensure that the approach never becomes too narrow, the ideals of Working Paper No. 2 have receded some distance. This becomes especially apparent when one looks at those things that the authors feel are fundamental and common characteristics of all work in the humanities with such pupils. The first of these is the pupil's 'personal needs related to the present' (para. 50); the second his 'social needs' (para. 51); only third comes 'some measure of intellectual extension so that he can begin to comprehend the complexity and totality of man's civilization and environment' (para. 52), and even the wording of that has a ring of somewhat forced optimism to it.

This interpretation of the philosophy of the Working Paper is reinforced by an examination of the suggestions it makes for the development of pupils' enquiries. It offers four examples of such enquiries, the most notable of which is the notorious enquiry into the mysteries of 'The 97 Bus'. For it is quite clear that the purpose of these enquiries is to do no more than to help such pupils to learn about their immediate environment, to consider only those elements in it that are directly relevant to their lives and to gain only the kind of understanding of it that will enable them to cope with it. At no point are they seen as starting points for a genuine broadening of horizons. The furthest the proposal for the enquiry into the 97 bus goes in this direction, for example, is to include among its purposes 'To bring out other social problems, e.g. of conveying people to work, shops and entertainment centres' (p. 64). Nevertheless, this Working Paper was certainly more in tune with what the schools had begun to do after the decision had been taken to raise the school leaving age, and it has been the starting point for a number of projects, particularly in the sphere of social studies, that have been beamed at pupils of average and below-average abilities.

Thus it would seem that the main effect of the work of the Schools

Council has been to reinforce the traditional view that separate curricula are needed for different types of pupil and, although one can see some excuses for this in, for example, the raising of the school leaving age and the ossification of the traditional grammar school curriculum, it is an effect that must be recognized as militating against the aim of educational equality.

This approach to curriculum planning has been the source of a number of problems. It is within the curriculum for the less able pupil that most of the curriculum development of recent years has occurred and there have been at least two important results of this. For, in the first place, both new subjects, such as moral education, social education and integrated studies, and new approaches to traditional subjects, such as that developed within the Geography for the Young School Leaver project, because they have been devised for inclusion in the 'inferior' version of curriculum, have come to be regarded as of low status. For the same reason, those pupils who have had time of Plato, whose system of education was carefully planned to educate of such progress as has been made in the development of the curriculum. Thus both have been disadvantaged. 'The lower ability groups have suffered from social adjustment courses, low status knowledge which is unexamined and therefore restricts occupational choice; whilst most aspiring to higher education would benefit from the erosion of some subject boundaries, the introduction of more active methods of learning and the use of relevance as one criterion for selection content' (Schofield 1977, p. 36).

This is a feature of curriculum planning that has also contributed to that educational inequality the evidence for which was massively provided by the Early Leaving (1954) and Crowther (1959) Reports and which a further twenty years have done little to erode. For it quickly became apparent that a major source of this inequality is the use of selection procedures within the education system, procedures which even at their most efficient could not achieve the impossible task that was set them. We have, however, been slower to appreciate that the heart of the problem is that pupils once selected by these procedures embark on different curricula and it is this that makes subsequent adjustment by transfer between schools or streams more or less impossible. Thus the endemic inefficiencies of the selection procedures have been compounded by the development of differentiated curricula, so that, having sought the source of educational inequality in the home, in the organization of the school system and in the internal organization of the schools, we are now beginning to realize that it is more likely to be found in our approach to curriculum planning.

An even more serious criticism of this approach to the curriculum is that it has led not only to a denial of equality of educational opportunity to large numbers of pupils but that it has also led to a denial of education itself. For it will be clear that what we have been identifying as the practice of many schools is an approach to curriculum planning that attempts to educate only one select group of pupils while continuing to 'gentle' the others. This process in the modern jargon is called 'socialization', but it is essentially the same. Its roots go back well beyond the nineteenth century, at least to the time of Plato, whose system of education was carefully planned to educate the 'men of gold' to think, to choose and to rule, while training the 'men of silver and bronze' to accept the judgements of their betters and to obey them. There are still, of course, those who recommend this approach to schooling (Bantock 1968, 1971), an acceptance of the existence of two or more different levels of culture within society, a 'high culture' and a 'low culture', an 'upper class' culture and a 'folk' culture, which need to be catered for within our schools by the generation of different curricula. It is important, however, to be clear about what such an approach entails. For it entails reinforcing the social divisions that do exist by the stratification of knowledge (Young 1971); it entails using knowledge as a means of social control (Young 1971); and it entails trapping individuals in the culture into which they were born (White 1968, 1973), so that they become, in the words that Richard Hoggart uses in Chapter 2, 'trapped in the cycle of their deprivation'. In short, it represents a failure to appreciate what is implied by the expression 'education for all', since it involves providing for a large section of the population a form of indoctrination rather than education and, if one can say this without sounding emotive, denying them a basic human right. It also indicates a failure to recognize that advanced industrial societies require an educated rather than a trained workforce.

It is the contention here, however, not only that we ought to move away from this kind of ideology but that there are signs that such a movement is already under way and that the somewhat unformed gropings towards a clearer concept of education which can be detected in both Hadow and Newsom are beginning to have some impact.

Some of the earliest indications of this can be seen in the work of what later came to be known as the Goldsmiths' College Curriculum Laboratory, under the direction of Charity James. Established initially to provide courses for senior teachers in preparation for the raising of the school leaving age, it quickly realized that the curriculum for those pupils who would be directly affected by this change should not be planned separately and in isolation from the curriculum as a whole. As the report of its First

Pilot Course for Experienced Teachers, *The Role of the School in a Changing Society*, (Goldsmiths' College 1965) tells us, 'Some of the most urgent questions which all Secondary schools are having to ask themselves just now are about the total pattern of the curriculum for *all* their pupils' (p. 27). Furthermore, in looking at the curriculum as a whole, the report lists among what it sees as the major features of the curriculum that it must be 'appropriate to interests and development of pupils, but using these as launching pads, not pillows, introducing new interests, preparing for new kinds of knowing and thinking' (p. 26), 'cumulative, in terms of concepts, areas of experience, types of activity' (p. 27) and 'personal, in that teacher and pupil recognise that individuals contribute differently, according to their different capacities and dispositions, and there is no-one who is culturally deprived in the sense of being unable to contribute to the culture, and in the sense that although the subject matter may not be the self, it will contribute to self-knowledge' (p. 27). These are some of the principles that underlay that approach to education that came to be known as Interdisciplinary Enquiry (IDE) and that was taken up and developed by a number of schools that were associated with the Goldsmiths' College Curriculum Laboratory.

The same kind of stance was adopted from the outset by the team associated with the Humanities Curriculum Project, which, although given the same brief as most Schools Council projects and asked to 'extend the range of choice open to teachers working in the humanities with adolescents of average and below average ability' (Schools Council 1970, pp. 5-6), nevertheless took the view of Working Paper No. 2 and decided that such pupils should be stretched as much as possible, that what they were offered should be 'justifiable as being educationally worthwhile' (Schools Council 1970, p. 6), that the main purpose of this should be to promote the ability to make informed, critical and personal judgements, and, in short, that every attempt should be made to provide them with an education in the full meaning of the term.

One result of this approach has been that the materials generated by the project have been such as to be suitable for work with pupils of all abilities, so that they have been used as effectively with sixth formers as with those for whom they were originally designed.

A similar experience has befallen the Geography for the Young School Leaver project, in that the approach to the teaching of geography which it advocated to meet what it felt were the needs of pupils of average and below-average abilities has been adopted by the Southern Examination

Board for its 'O' level GCE syllabus, so that that approach and the materials developed in conjunction with it have been made available to pupils of all abilities.

It is developments such as these that seem to represent the beginnings of a move away from the elementary tradition in our approach to the curriculum for pupils of this kind and the gathering momentum of this movement is reflected in the development of the idea of comprehensive education, the rapid spread of mixed-ability classes in the early years of secondary schooling and some of the arguments currently being advanced in favour of a common curriculum.

It is important to realize, however, that none of these developments will achieve their purpose unless we are clear about their underlying principles and recognize that the idea of education for all does not imply that all should have the same content to their education but that the principles upon which everyone's education is founded should be common. Variations in subjects, in syllabuses, in content and in the methods we adopt can be justified, but once we accept the view that we can begin with different aims or principles in planning a curriculum for certain categories of pupil, we have abrogated the principle of education for all. What was wrong with the 97 bus project was not that it does not provide an adequate and justifiable starting point for education; it was that the suggested execution of it was such as to ensure that pupils would never progress beyond its terminus.

It is my contention, therefore, that a trend away from the tradition of differentiated curricula can be discerned in the recent theory and practice of curriculum planning and, further, that that trend has been eased by the emergence of a clearer concept of education and a better understanding of the issue of values, which is enabling us to grasp more firmly those ideals that the Hadow and Newsom Reports were groping for. In particular, it is enabling us to see that an approach to the curriculum that sees it as, for some pupils, solely a means to an end is unsatisfactory in that it entails denying them access to the pursuit of knowledge for its own sake which is at the heart of what it means to be educated, and ultimately denying them also the right to think for themselves.

It is at this point that the threads of my argument may be seen to come together. For it is my contention that this growing awareness of the problematic nature of value questions and the implications of that for curriculum planning is leading us to appreciate the inadequacies both of the objectives approach to such planning and of the generation of different curricula for pupils of differing abilities, where such curricula are defined in terms both of a differentiated content and different underlying principles. A clearer concept of education and a greater appreciation of the difficulties surrounding the issue of values that is central to it are leading to a realization that education must be seen as a process, as the development of what Richard Hoggart in Chapter 2 calls certain 'capacities', and that it cannot be defined either in terms of objectives that are extrinsic to it or in terms of subject content. As a result we are beginning to see that it is a realistic goal for all or most of our pupils and not just for those who appear to be capable of coping with a curriculum that is focused on 'academic' subjects. As we noted above, what is wrong with the project on the 97 bus is not that it cannot be a vehicle (the pun is unintentional) for education but that the recommended treatment of it was such as to render it inadequate as such a vehicle. This is the key to the issue of differentiated curricula and equality of educational opportunity towards which we suggested earlier Hadow, Newsom and, especially, Working Paper No. 2 were groping, and its ultimate source is a clearer concept of education.

Such a process model of curriculum, of course, itself assumes a certain view of values. However, the central feature of the view it assumes is that commonality of values which we referred to earlier. For the values it assumes are of that kind which we argued are based on the notion of rationality itself and the requirements of human discourse. The model does not support any particular subject content whose value assumptions can be seen to be problematic, but merely asserts the right of the individual to be initiated into that rationality and human discourse in such a way as to widen his range of choices and to enable him to live as an autonomous individual.

It can be argued, of course, that this represents a particular ideology derived from a particular kind of epistemology and, as Jack Nicholas reveals in Chapter 8, it is not an ideology that is universally accepted since, as he shows there, different epistemological positions give rise to different ideologies. We might, however, turn to the second kind of commonality of values, the second source of shared values, that we argued for earlier and claim that such a view of rationality and education, if not God-given, is widely accepted in Western European society in a way that particular interpretations of it are not. It is in this direction, therefore, that a solution to the problem of values and the curriculum lies.

Every curriculum will reinforce particular attitudes and values, but it is important to realize that, if we can accept a definition of curriculum in terms of processes and cease to be dogmatic in the controversial areas of particular subject content, we may hope to create a curriculum that establishes or reinforces those values that can be shown to be part of that commonality of beliefs which can be discerned throughout society. At the very least, if we adopt this approach, we are less likely to run the risk of allowing any particular ideology or ideologies to predominate.

## Summary and conclusions

It has been the contention of this chapter that ideological constraints on curriculum planning are as important and as influential as constraints of any other kind. Indeed, they may well be more so in that they are less easily identified and understood. It has also been the contention that a clearer concept of education, especially in respect of its value components, is enabling us both to appreciate rather better than was once the case the kinds of influence these constraints have and also to understand some of the major ways in which they are currently affecting our approach to curriculum planning. In particular, it has been suggested that they are leading to the view that education must be defined in terms of processes rather than either objectives or content and that, once it is so defined, the full meaning of that egalitarian ideology to which the schools of the United Kingdom are committed becomes more apparent in respect not only of its theory but, more importantly, of its practice too.

## CHAPTER TWO

# THE UNCERTAIN CRITERIA OF DEPRIVATION*

**Richard Hoggart**

During the last fifteen to twenty years there has taken place, in both the United Kingdom and North America, a continuous debate about 'cultural deprivation' and its implications for education. There are interesting differences in the way the debate has been conducted on each side of the Atlantic and it would be worthwhile to examine them, but for several reasons I will not try to do that. Instead I will try to lay out the main lines of the debate, indicate some differences between the British and North American approaches, and offer a non-specialist's view on its implications.

By the 'cultural deprivation' theory at its purest children from certain kinds of home (those of the poor, blacks, Indians, immigrants) are regarded as cut off from certain essential social and linguistic experiences and so as at an educational disadvantage. They are trapped in the 'cycle of deprivation' and are at best 'empty vessels' when they enter the classroom, at worst locked into restricting forms of behaviour and expression. It is difficult to

*First presented at a conference on literacy at the University of Edmonton, Alberta, in October 1976, and subsequently published in E.J. King (ed.) (1978), *Education for Uncertainty*, Sage Publications.

pick up a British book from the sixties concerned with education and society which does not, directly or implicitly, take up a position on this very large theory. I will recall only a couple of names at this point; first J.M.B. Douglas, whose *The Home and the School* (1964) nicely captures the nature and force of these preoccupations as they were felt a dozen years ago. One of the most outstanding among British names is that of Basil Berstein. Professor Bernstein has by now a substantial weight of published work to his credit. But his reputation was originally founded, fifteen or so years ago, on a few highly suggestive and widely influential papers. What was chiefly taken from him at that time, and applied in different ways, was the notion of 'restricted' and 'elaborated' codes of discourse.

A restricted code is seen as confining its user to the concrete, the immediate, the metaphorical speech of the here and now; whereas an elaborated code gives access to rationality, shows language in use as the bearer of the grounds of meaning. Bernstein himself says that these early concepts have been misunderstood and misused. They certainly fed the debate in ways he seems not to have intended. Some people took him as suggesting that the duty of schools was to persuade children to deny the language of their background and learn the elaborated code of – and here we come to the inevitable social-class element in British debate – the middle class. Such people tended to equate the use of a restricted code with the condition of being culturally deprived.

Bernstein has denied the accuracy and regretted the oversimplification of these interpretations, has insisted that he does not identify the use of a restricted code with the condition of cultural deprivation and that he thinks schools should change their approach rather than reject and try to erase the local languages of the children in their care. This whole debate, so far as it has centred on arguments about Bernstein – and these particular arguments have been an important part of the British debate – can be found well and critically discussed in the booklet *Language and Class: a Critical Look at the Theories of Basil Bernstein* (1972) by Harold Rosen.

It follows from the 'cultural deprivation' theory that compensatory action should be taken on behalf of children so situated, that there should be 'positive discrimination' in their favour, that whereas the financing of schools in areas of deprivation tends at present to be lower than that of the schools which train those about to enter university, the balance should be shifted; the state should intervene to give such deprived children some of the advantages enjoyed by children from stable, comfortable and literate homes. A typical book inspired by this outlook is that by Clegg and Megson called *Children in Distress* (1968). That book, incidentally, is a Penguin paperback and it is worth saying at this point that the list of very cheap paperbacks issued by Penguin on this whole debate is an impressive one.

Above all, the Plowden Report (1967) on *Children and their Primary Schools*, named after the Chairman of the Committee which produced it, calls up the spirit of that part of the decade. One can most conveniently see something of what it inspired by following the fortunes of the experimental projects in what it proposed should be called Educational Priority Areas; and again Penguins have some relevant titles, such as Eric Midwinter's account of the Liverpool project (1972).

The reaction against the purer forms of cultural deprivation theory was political, social and educational. The basically political reaction can conveniently be gauged from the collection of essays edited by Nell Keddie with the title *Tinker, Tailer: the Myth of Cultural Deprivation* (1973). Central to this reaction is the argument that what any particular society at any particular time calls 'knowledge' is what the dominant 'estates' of that society choose to call knowledge. It follows that what are called the 'fundamental educational values' by which the disadvantaged are tested and found to be wanting are not fundamental or objective at all but rather the culturally determined values of the dominant sectors of a society, and in the British case of the dominant middle class. They play back their own answers to their own questions; their tests are circular and self-validating (as some old style IQ tests, we now see, so blatantly were). The educational process is therefore shaped so as to enforce the consensus values of our particular type of capitalist society; and the mass media, perhaps even more insistently than the education system, reinforce the sense that this world is immutable, objectively out there, rather than a historical and contingent man-made structure. Hence, it is 'The Hidden Curriculum' of the schools rather than the explicit list of subjects taught which one should analyse more thoroughly. The hidden curriculum is that pattern of assumptions which is carried, day in day out, by the sanctions of the school, by these actions and attitudes which are encouraged and praised and those which are discouraged and frowned on; it is recognizable as much by what it omits as by its positive acts, it is as much implicit as explicit; and it is carried at least as much by tones of voice in the teacher as by statements.

On this view – and it provides a salutary shift of balance – the 'cultural deprivation' theory, if it is too simply conceived, blames on the shortcomings of the home ills which arise much more from both the shortsightedness of the teachers themselves and from the whole drive of society, its use and misuse of the educational system. Whenever I read this part of the debate I am reminded of the traditional role of the British '1902 Act' grammar schools. I mean the schools set up by the local municipality to cater for the brighter children from homes where there was no money to pay for a grammar school education. As one of the 'scholarship winners' from a very poor district, I went to such a school along with others – though not many; only two or three classes were taken in each year from a catchment area of a good few thousand – from either similarly poor backgrounds or, at the highest, from genteel skilled-craftsmen backgrounds. I owe a lot to that school and in particular to a couple of individual teachers, a master and a mistess, who thought they detected talent which should be specially encouraged. But there was no doubt that the school saw itself as called to make us into minor, lower-middle class professionals. Which meant in most cases that the brighter among us were expected to become teachers and the very brightest perhaps to go to university for our teacher training rather than to a mere teachers' training college. There was an insistent pressure, no less strong from being only partly conscious in the minds of the teachers, to cut us off from the culture of the streets to which we returned each night and to offer us the prospect of suburban living on the other side of town.

It was an extraordinarily all-embracing atmosphere. It has been described in more than one novel but David Storey's new novel *Saville* (1976) captures as well as any book I have read the spirit of such schools, on their good sides as well as their bad. That spirit is by no means dead. Let me give one small example. I know of a girl who, not all that long ago, was transplanted from Yorkshire to the Midlands. She was twelve years old and therefore had to change grammar schools. Reading aloud in class during her early weeks there she said 'bath' with the short Yorkshire 'a'. She was stopped and told that that wasn't a 'proper' pronunciation, that the proper pronunciation had a long 'a', 'bāth'. The objection to this sort of thing is not so much that the correction was ill-founded, though certainly few who have given any thought to linguistic practice in the last ten years or so think any longer that there is a 'proper' pronunciation in such cases. The objection is much more that, to the young girl concerned (and in Britain we learn to read such signs from a very early age), the rebuke was a snobbish one; she was being rebuked for not employing the accepted genteel southern forms of pronunciation encouraged in that Midlands city grammar school.

So, though one can certainly learn the bases of the intellectual life and be well-trained in certain ways at any reasonably good British grammar school, and though one may well – if one is bright – be taken up and pushed along by one's teacher, I think it fair to say that all in all the British local authority grammar schools did an inadequate job in assessing and responding to their own socio-cultural position and therefore to their best possible roles. This is one reason among several why I welcome the movement towards comprehensive education in Britain.

The reaction against the simpler forms of cultural deprivation theory also takes a social and cultural form. Here, it is argued that what are called deprived groups can be, if we know how to listen to them, culturally as rich and complex as the dominant, defining middle class. In Britain three books, all of which appeared towards the end of the sixties, probably did much to reinforce this response even though no one of them was specifically a contribution to educational thinking. I have in mind Raymond Williams' *Culture and Society* (1958) together with what is really a companion volume, *The Long Revolution* (1961), E.P. Thompson's *The Making of the English Working Class* (1963) and my own *The Uses of Literacy* (1957). It is worth noticing, incidentally, for a small instance of the way a change in opinion gathers force from several directions at once, that though we all three knew each other and knew we were writing sizeable books, though we all spent the heart of the fifties in writing them, though we were all in the same field of work (evening classes for adults sponsored by the universities which employed us, and given up to a hundred miles from base); yet we did not discuss the books before they appeared and so had no prior knowledge of the similarities in the impulses behind them, of the complementarities or the differences.

Raymond Williams gave greater depth to the concept of 'the working classes' in itself. In this connection, I always think first of the way in which he argued that the imaginative creativity of working-class people expressed itself not in the practice of the high arts (what access did they have?) as in the creation of institutions (the co-ops, the unions, the friendly societies and clubs, etc., etc.) which themselves embodied and practised a subtle and humane conception of the relations between people. Edward Thompson's book is a magisterial account of the struggles and achievements of the English working class over the immense and painful transition from an agricultural to an industrial economy. Since, even at grammar schools, we tended to be offered a view of English history which stressed the imperial achievement by 'great men' and left 'the workers' in the wings – the people of England who have not spoken yet, but are presumed ready to come forward and die in battle if suitably officered – Edward Thompson's and Raymond Williams' writings were powerful correctives for those teachers and others who wished to face them. My own book was neither an essay in cultural analysis nor an historical study; but its efforts to describe, from within as it were, the texture of urban working-class life in the thirties added to what was offered by the other two.

From books such as the above and rather similar later work in England came the argument that working-class culture and working-class language were more complex than we had been used to assume. In the United States this position has more recently been carried very much further in the remarkable work of Labov (1972, 1977). I suppose it is an indication of both the greater resources and the greater commitment to long-term and intensive field work among American scholars that, to the best of my knowledge, no one in Britain has produced anything approaching Labov's work in its scope and sustained application. Bernstein's work (1973, 1974, 1976) is now considerable in size but its empirical base does not compare with Labov's: it is much more theoretic and abstract. For the rest, the typical British production here is represented by that shelf of red Penguin paperbacks, most of them fairly small and most of them arguing energetically for one view or another. Labov and his team did long studies of the speech habits of their chosen subjects. His analysis, done in great detail from recordings, of the speech of urban black youths does more than any other single work I know to destroy the argument that social deprivation inevitably connotes also verbal deprivation. It is not simply that Labov is showing that the speech of such people may be strong in, for example, concrete metaphors. That would fit some English views, where it is readily agreed that working-class speech may be racy, down-to-earth, and full of vivid images, but where it is also assumed that that speech lacks the capacity to handle abstractions. What Labov shows is that this urban black speech, once we have learned how to interpret it (by not trying to read it as though it were an aberrant form of grammatically exact middle-class or 'educated' speech), can handle complex concepts very effectively indeed – especially about relationships and roles and the world outside their own local area, as seen by those youths.

On a less impressively extended scale but still very usefully there are also such works as John Holt's *How Children Fail* (1969), especially where he analyses subtleties in classroom behaviour among 'deprived' children and especially the subtlety of the roles they can adopt towards teachers, subtleties which most teachers do not notice. Similarly, Jane Torrey writes interestingly on the subtleties of non-standard language in 'Illiteracy in the Ghetto' which is contained in Nell Keddie's *Tinker, Tailor* (1973).

Coming in from yet another angle, some people have argued that discussions which stress the verbal deprivation of socially deprived people often have behind them the unspoken assumption that more favoured social groups normally have a capacity for live discourse which is to be emulated, or even that most middle-class homes are centres for conversations which habitually deploy complex arguments. But in fact – they continue – the speech of such people, whether in Britain or North America, is often bland and blunted, and shows no sign of becoming less so. The number of those who can handle language publicly in a lively way whilst also managing the exposition of ideas is limited, and no single class or profession seems to have a special hold on the capacity . . . especially not national trade union leaders, who often seem – as they climb to the top – to believe they have to make their language more and more polysyllabically redudant and periphrastic; nor especially politicians who between them exhibit far more kinds of bad rhetoric than of good speech.

I always remember in this connection two experiences of my own. One was a reply I had from the Public Relations department of a big American airline, in answer to a well-merited complaint couched in economical and unambiguous terms. It began: 'We are privileged to have shared your thoughts on the customer-efficacity of our service . . .' The other occasion was in a remote Scottish village grocer's. A travelling salesman from Glasgow poured out for quite a while to the shopkeeper a well-rehearsed sales talk about special offers and reductions, all in the boneless persuasive language of the advertising and promotions business. In the end the elderly grocer cut him short and said simply: 'Young man, give me no more of your inducements. Show me your list of goods and I will tell you what I will buy.' There is only one word of more than one syllable in that utterance, and that word rings of Biblical morality.

All this kind of analysis is clearly useful so long as teachers take heed of it and of its implications for their own practice. Teachers *should* have a better understanding of the relations between current assumptions about education, about modes of teaching and about their society's dominant drives. They should aim for a more inward knowledge of the lives and cultures of their pupils. They would thus have a fuller knowledge of their own positions as mediators between society and the family, between young people in deprived situations and the larger society outside. They should have tried to think through all this web of issues much more than most teachers have done so far. I am arguing throughout this paper that an important and interesting debate about fundamental educational purposes has been going on in Britain and in North America over the last fifteen years or so. The main lines of that debate can be followed for the expenditure, in Britain, of a few pounds a year on paperbacks. But the majority of teachers, or for that matter the majority of senior civil servants or of politicians, hardly know that the debate has been and is still taking place.

I have so far sketched in, very briefly, the basic case for cultural and linguistic deprivation; and I have also briefly put the objections to the simpler forms of that view, objections which may be political or cultural or linguistic. Those objections have done something to discourage a simplistic attitude in those who hold too unqualified a version of the idea of cultural deprivation. People may not be 'as daft as they look' to an outsider who cannot interpret the inwardness of their habits and language. Still, there are ditches on both sides of this road. If we pull away from the ditch of an oversimplified neo-paternalism we had better take care not to drop into the ditch of reductive identification with what we see as a rich working-class culture. That is its own kind of romanticism. Working-class people, even the most deprived, can be verbally more skilful than we have been used to thinking; their ways may be as dignified and humane as those of the genteel.

Nevertheless, there are many people from deprived homes whose language shows no trace of traditional vigour, who are indeed locked into restricting forms of speech, who have virtually no command of language for activities outside the home or neighbourhood, of those types of speech which will allow them to move with reasonable effectiveness through the public situations – elections, applications for public assistance, medical needs, educational questions, shopping itself day-by-day – which complex societies increasingly present to all of us. They are not used to handling concepts even in their own kinds of speech; they are neither numerate nor really literate. Their lives do not give them the opportunity or the habit of planning forward, of making long-term choices between options. Their children seem therefore destined to become the new hinds of late twentieth-century industrial society.

Since those societies are massively committed to keeping most people quiet, consumers of its palliatives, these people are at the tail end of a continuous process. They can scarcely read – except for that simplified stuff which is meant to make them buy and buy; they do not discuss, in any recognizable sense of the word; instead, they face an almost nonstop stream of simplified opinionation designed to fix them in certain prejudices. These are the people at the very bottom of the social body and they need all the help that can be given them, all the informed help; or they will remain trapped in the cycle of their deprivation.

I put this so strongly because some of those who have reacted against the purer forms of cultural deprivation theory and have insisted on the possible richness of working-class culture are in danger of themselves falling into a new noble savage myth. The wastage of human beings in our society is still great. We are right to think that the aim of education should not be to destroy working-class culture and substitute for it a universal lower-middle-class culture. But these are not the only options. People do have a right to be offered, to the tops of their bents, what all those of us who engage in educational debates have and value, a grasp of the public use of language which is the essential tool for understanding our own situations and the nature of our society better, and for deciding what we can do to improve matters. To wish less for people is implicitly to hand them over even more firmly to the new social controllers, the low-level mass-persuaders.

Between these who plan their educational aims in the light of a strongly held theory of cultural deprivation, and those who oppose that position on political grounds or in defence of continuing working-class values there is a third educational position; or, rather, two different kinds of third position. The first begins by arguing that the conclusions which can be legitimately drawn from discussions about culture and class in relation to education, interesting and important though they may be, are essentially tactical rather than strategic. An understanding of the strengths of working-class culture and of the powers and limits of its available language may well effect the way teachers set about their work, help to define starting points, suggest qualities to connect with and build upon; and all that can be useful. But such knowledge does not in itself define what is to be done, does not provide basic educational aims; it provides rather the frame within which non-contingent educational aims are to be pursued. This is, again, a very bare version of a complex position and misses much of its intricacy; but it does not seriously distort it.

People with this point of view are likely to go on to argue that a primary attention to cultural considerations produces the risk of 'levelling down' in educational aims, of asking less from children than, differently approached, they are capable of giving. One interesting offshoot of this position is to be seen in the London 'Right to Learn' group who are concerned with the fact that, in their view, the current debate has induced in many teachers in poor areas an unduly low expectation of what their pupils are capable of, and hence unjustifiably low educational aspirations for them.

At its most central point, this position argues that there are still basic educational aims which are not altered by the social conditions of pupils, that these basic aims are to introduce pupils to a common core of intellectual and imaginative values beyond those of a particular historical consensus. There are variants of this general idea. Hardly anyone is more serious about basic educational aims than G.H. Bantock; but he does make specific aims largely dependent on his social judgements about the educability of different groups within society, and from this posits different educational purposes for each, according to their presumed levels of intelligence (Bantock 1968, 1971).

Those who hold to the idea of a common core of intellectual and imaginative values, no doubt affected by but not determined by particular circumstances, are not, it is important to say, necessarily arguing that there is a 'body of knowledge' out there, a sort of bundle of mental baggage which every child should take with him on his journey through school. That is an inert approach. The current debate in the United Kingdom about the pros and cons of a 'core curriculum' is bound to throw up this set of arguments. A recurring British educational nightmare is that some government will try to impose a system ('like that in France' we say) in which all children of a certain age are said (falsely) at a certain time of day to be studying the same set books, acquiring the same items of information. I do not think the more thoughtful of the proponents of a 'core curriculum' are suggesting this at all. They are much more nearly arguing for an education which aims to offer all children the opportunity to develop certain valuable intellectual and imaginative *capacities*; and they recognize that – depending upon a child's social and cultural background, and much else – there is more than one route to acquiring those capacities. I imagine that this is what Raymond Williams has in mind when he argues for a common culture, but one which can best be acquired by starting from strong and differentiated social experiences.

It is important to stress again the value of starting and indeed the absolute need to start from *where people are*. This is always a double process; it is partly an understanding of what pupils or students are really saying and so of the texture of their lives, the better to understand the connections which can be made and developed from; it is partly a process of self-examination by the teacher, and this is quite a difficult process in which we strip ourselves of the protection given by those academic or pedagogic styles which give us the edge over members of the class. I mean styles in language, in presentation of material and in virtually all aspects of our own comportment. If we do undertake that process we will be constantly surprised by how far people can go in perception; people who, faced with the more usual methods of teaching, appear stupid, silent or morose. Freire is a valuable corrective here. Again, such a book as Holt's *How Children Fail* (1969) is very valuable also. I remember, in particular, from that book a description of a mathematics lesson by C. Gattegno in which a severely retarded boy, through Gattegno's most imaginative understanding of the necessary interplay between him and a good teacher, was brought to *see* how a mathematical process works, and of the boy's delight when he had seen.

My own first thirteen professional years were spent teaching adults, few of whom had any academic background, in the evenings. I started by in effect giving these groups, of a dozen or so, hour-long lectures of the sort I had myself been given at university; then, in the second hour, I told them we would have 'the discussion'. Of course, the discussions were dead and I had to do most of the talking. I had given them no purchase on the material, no way of bringing to bear their emerging interests and abilities; I had set up the whole business in safe terms, safe for me but not for them since they could not play that game without learning the rules and conventions within which I had decided it would operate. Naturally, that procedure was discarded very quickly, once I began to see how important it was for the students to be able to use their own languages, to set their own paces, to move outwards from their own experiences and their own modes of coping with their experience into the world of, say, a great novel. I deliberately say 'great' because an erroneous way of 'starting where the students are' is to offer to adult classes simplified texts, second-line literature with an obvious social commitment, or to be so consistently encouraging that any comment by any member of a class – no matter how mistaken it may really be – is greeted as a most interesting insight. Once again, we owe it to other people to let them be taxed and challenged by great literature in the way we always claim we ourselves are. The tutor is not only trying to see further into people's potential capacities; he is also the representative of intellectual standards and must therefore, if necessary by a rigorously Socratic approach, try to encourage his students to face what they may not want to face, to slowly start to disembarrass themselves of prejudices, sentimentality and the rest.

The other form of this third position is more radical than the one I have just described and finds the first form too narrowly intellectual, if not downright academic. It too, however, begins by rejecting as inadequate a major concentration of interest on social-class differences in educational thinking. It regards such a concentration as over-rigid, two-dimensional. It starts from the major problems of the present day and from the view that these problems affect us all, whatever our social class or level of prosperity. It argues, therefore, that education must aim above all not just to introduce us to intellectual values but to *human* values and to the massive contemporary challenges to those values – challenges often made in the name of the intellect, of rationality, of 'common sense'. Here, a whole range of names comes to mind, most of them American: Illich, of course, (1971a, 1971b) and also Paul Goodman, whose *Compulsory Miseducation* (1962) is as good an introduction as any to what this general point of view finds wanting in the present educational system, and what it would put in its place.

On this view most school procedures and syllabuses are out of date, academic in the limiting sense, *subject-bound*. These people too would start from the concrete, from situations in the 'real' lives of pupils. They would shape teaching around issues which bear upon their pupils day-by-day, but which they at present see only in an immediate, on-the-pulses way, without having the tools with which to make larger sense of what is happening to them. Thus teaching would be 'theme' not 'subject' centred, and would try to keep in place all the time both intellectual and imaginative issues; it would be centred on the whole individual and his life experiences, not on an abstract idea of the 'trained mind' in a narrower sense. It would deal with issues in the environment – the pressures of urban life on the individual and the family, the role of the mass media, racism, the increasing gap between the developed and the underdeveloped world (I say 'underdeveloped' and would in some instances say 'undeveloped' rather than using the United Nations' preferred word 'developing' – which is a verbal cosmetic). All this can lead to some exciting and inspiring new teaching. But, like all new modes, it can be unwisely used. That is why, I guess, the 'Right to Learn' group insist that much teaching in Britain which is inspired by this outlook is sloppy, without intellectual or imaginative backbone, and that there is still a case for teaching the major intellectual disciplines as we have habitually known them.

It is time to sum up. The debate I have been describing has had some considerable achievements. Above all, it has offered teachers and others the opportunity to take a more open and diverse view of class/culture differences and so of children's possibilities. It offers a more pluralistic and richer set of approaches than were assumed in, for example, those local grammar schools I described much earlier. It discourages us from seeking to iron out, in the name of 'proper' educational and social standards, social and cultural differences which are still important, not necessarily divisive, and together contribute to the still quite rich fabric of British social life. The recognition of these varied values, not only in educational terms but in all aspects of culture, is one of the better products of the years since the early sixties.

I do not think the most radical holders of views on the relations between educational systems and authority will see anything like the changes they want. This is partly because they will not be likely to carry with them more than a minority even of the left wing in politics, partly because on the whole open societies do not take such giant radical leaps (neither of these characteristics is necessarily or wholly a matter of selfishness among the powerful), and partly because their case is not wholly sustainable; it has a lot of truth in it, but is not completely true.

Meanwhile, there are some rules of thumb which need holding on to firmly. One I have already more than hinted at: that, in spite of all the pros and cons of the debate about where the blame for educational insufficiency lies, there are some children who need special extra provision and care. Another is that, whatever the limitations of some old-established educational attitudes towards class, manners and language, not all middle-class attitudes are bad nor even the bad ones unique to the middle classes; conversely, and even when we have recognized the hitherto insufficiently recognized virtues of working-class life, not all working-class habits are good nor are even the good ones unique to working-class people. These are simple enough assertions but sometimes they need to be made.

If this seems doubtful, let me give you only one example from many. A contemporary book on education and class in Britain discusses the advice given by a headmaster that his pupils donate some of their pocket money to good causes and take up voluntary work on behalf of needy members of the community. Having quoted the headmaster, the author says:

> It is possible to read this passage as giving some substance to [the view] that schools attempt to foist dubious middle-class values on the poor.

Let us adopt the careful insurance policy phrasing and comment:

> It is possible to read this passage as an expression of the headmaster's belief that whatever your social class and whatever your opportunities in life it is good to help the poor, the sick and the old.

We are not told where the author stands, and presumably he does not actually know where the headmaster stands. Maybe the headmaster had thought through the matter of values and socially-conditioned behaviour further than the book's author seems to assume.

Even more complicated is the wide, undifferentiated sea of total relativism, the reluctance to recognize that some values, attitudes, habits may be morally preferable to others. Here is a distinguished writer on modern educational theory putting one toe into the shallower waters of that sea: he is grappling with the matter of value judgements:

> It is at least possible that some kinds of knowledge are superior in some meaningful way to other kinds of knowledge.

Note the similarly cautious phrasing of this passage with that quoted just above. But if, and in spite of all the pitfalls, people engaged in education do not think that some kinds of knowledge *are* superior in some meaningful way to others then on what criteria can they devise a syllabus in any subject?

I suppose the far end of this line is the position taken by some teachers, on their being convinced that there is no point in making their pupils – from deprived homes – merely marginally numerate and literate (which is all that present conditions sometimes seem to make possible) since they seem then more securely trained to be the obedient helots of a corrupt society. Better to let them be as they are, since they will inevitably spend their days on the worst kind of routine work, work which demands nothing seriously numerate or literate from them. Why should they be only partially trained, trained only so far as to bind them more securely?

There is something in the basic analysis, but the conclusions from it are deeply mistaken. It *is* wrong for teachers to be satisfied to train children to be just sufficiently literate as to accept, but not literate enough to challenge, some of the dominant values of open commercial democracies. But the teacher's response should be to increase the pressure on all sides to get them through to a fuller literacy and numeracy, to help them stand up better on their own feet as articulate, critical, judging human beings. To do that, drawing on all we know of their backgrounds and all we know of the values of intellectual life, is the best single aim any of us could set ourselves. To do less than that is a sort of betrayal of them as humans, and of the intellectual life itself. With such an aim at its heart, the debate about culture, class, language and education could begin to find its proper focus.

## CHAPTER THREE

# THE INFLUENCE OF INITIAL STYLES OF CURRICULUM DEVELOPMENT

**Geva Blenkin**

It is well known that the most recent generation of British teachers has worked through the most rapid period of curriculum development in the history of state education. Innovation and dissemination are today terms in common usage in educational circles and it is readily conceded at every level in the discussion about the curriculum, from the Secretary of State for Education to the class teacher and from the radical left to the Black Paper writers, that the 'unplanned drift' of earlier work in schools is no longer satisfactory (Hoyle 1969) and that planned curriculum changes and the speedy spread of information about the best of these planned changes is the way forward in the development of curriculum in general and hence the most important way to raise the quality of each child's educational experience in particular. The fundamental message in educational circles during the past two decades, therefore, has been that the curriculum in our schools – and the planned development of this curriculum – holds the key to educational success.

The purpose of this discussion is to examine the early attempts at curriculum development in Britain during the 1960s. These developments are now of historical significance and an understanding of the climate which led curriculum planners in a particular direction during this period can shed light on many of the dilemmas and problems which face educators today. For the styles adopted by those responsible for curriculum planning and innovation at that time continue to influence approaches today.

There were, of course, many changes to be applauded in this period of rapid development of curriculum and in many cases much was achieved by teachers in raising the quality of education and widening the experiences of pupils in our schools. There were also readily identifiable constraints which not only tempered the excesses of some developments of the curriculum but also at times led to disillusionment and frustration on the part of some teachers who had worked hard to realize developments. Indeed these external constraints – notably those of a political and administrative kind – have usually been offered by teachers as the main cause of any failure that has occurred. The examination system in the secondary school and the unfavourable pupil/teacher ratio in the primary school are two obvious examples.

What is less easy for educators to concede, however, is that the planned curriculum development itself can offer a serious constraint, not least on teachers' thinking about the way that worthwhile development can occur. Like all questions of an educational kind, the question of what constitutes curriculum development raises complex issues which are both interdisciplinary in nature and coloured by the views of those engaged in that development. In other words, it is equally justifiable, if somewhat more uncomfortable, to claim that it was the changes attempted by curriculum planners, and in particular the styles of those changes, or the models of curriculum development that were proposed and often adopted, that themselves contributed to more subtle forms of constraint on teachers' thinking and hence on their work.

In their enthusiasm to engage in planned changes, educators in many spheres – nationally, locally and at school level – adopted, somewhat uncritically, during this period, styles of development that have left a residue of thinking in teachers' minds about the nature of curriculum and how it can be changed. It is this residue which has become legitimized by the early official attempts at curriculum development and which now jeopardizes any worthwhile curriculum development in the future. It is also, however, the seemingly rational nature of early curriculum development that led to its legitimization in teachers' minds and hence to the fact that it has become a most persistent constraint on future development. In this sense the carefully planned curriculum of the sixties was as adrift as the unplanned work of earlier times.

In an attempt to clarify this contention, I hope to show that many teachers, regardless of the age group with which they are concerned, have, in the past, been misled by planning theorists, advisers and others into accepting a particular view of what constitutes the curriculum and how it is developed. By briefly examining the styles of the early planned curriculum development in Britain, I hope also to clarify the sources of these particular styles and, in doing so, to show both why they were influential and why they are less appropriate than they at first seemed.

In doing this it will be necessary to make some references to background influences which have been discussed more thoroughly in several other chapters. In the setting of this discussion, however, the focus will be directed towards an examination of how policy was shaped by particular theories and views and the resultant curriculum planning that occurred.

It will be argued that an understanding of the directions taken in the 1960s hinges largely on two fundamental factors, and these will be discussed in turn. The first is a historical perspective. Of particular importance here is an understanding of how the values in our society have, in the past, had an influence on the organization of schooling and how these values not only manifested themselves in the ways in which schools came to be administered but also influenced the views of educators and coloured the decisions that they made in providing for and planning the educational programme. To provide a framework for this point, one important analysis of the pressures on the educational system in Britain from its inception will be examined – that of Raymond Williams (1961). Using Williams' analysis it will be shown that curriculum development was seen as essential and accepted by every influential sector of society as such, and it will also be argued that the developments that occurred were almost inevitably if not exclusively along one course.

The second fundamental factor to be examined will be the developments in curriculum planning which were taking place abroad, and the effects that these developments were to have on work in this country. Of paramount importance here are the ideas of American educators – particularly those who hold Utopian views of curriculum planning and development. British educators have always studied with interest the developments taking place in the United States of America but they have also tended to be more eclectic and diffuse about their approach to their work. With the establishment of the Schools Council, however, and with the urgent calls for planned innovation, a venue was established in Britain for a more systematic and deliberate approach to planning. It was, therefore, the climate of the 1960s that provided an avenue for the direct influence of the work of some Americans as can be seen particularly from the styles and approaches of early national curriculum projects.

Finally, and in the light of these two fundamental factors, some curriculum developments that occurred during this period in one sector of the education system will be examined – that of early childhood education. The work undertaken with very young children has tended in the past to be ignored in general discussions about curriculum development. For the purposes of this discussion, however, it serves as an excellent example for three main reasons. Firstly, there has always been a minimum of the more obvious external constraints in this sector of schooling. Secondly, and, it could be argued, largely as a result of this, a tradition had evolved by the 1960s which could be seen as distinct from the traditions in other sectors, especially with regard to curriculum development, and lessons of a more general educational kind might be learned from this tradition. Thirdly, this separate tradition of curriculum development has been placed under threat recently and it will be argued that one reason for this has been the constraining effects on teachers' thinking of the general directions taken by early attempts at curriculum development in Britain in this and in other sectors of the education system.

## Sources of values and early curriculum development: one analysis

It is a cliché and an oversimplication to describe Britain as a 'class-ridden' society. Nonetheless the simplistic stratification generated by opinions about different social classes is basic to the way children have been viewed and is still one of the most decisive factors in the way our schools are organized, the way children within them are treated, and the way the curriculum in its wider sense is structured, as we saw in Chapter 1. If we remain in doubt about this assertion we can now make reference to work such as that of Becker (1952) in Chicago and the ensuing research carried out in Britain and America which attempted to identify the sources of the school failure of a disproportinate number of working-class children. We should also note that the causes of this failure were first sought outside the schooling system. The time of the flourishing interest in curriculum development in the 1960s also corresponded with the emerging attempts on the part of the schools to compensate for the supposed disadvantages of children from lower socio-economic groups. It was a decade later that attention was given to the effects that teachers' attitudes had on pupils' progress (Downey 1977) and studies such as those of Fuchs (1968) and Rist (1970) which pointed to the schooling system itself, and in particular the attitudes to pupils and the values held of them by teachers, as a major source of this failure, were not available to the curriculum planners of the early 1960s.

What was emerging by the early 1960s, however, was a new interest in the description and analysis of the life style and values of the working class whose culture had been largely ignored in discussions of what is of value in our society. Important among this work is that of Raymond Williams, who set out to trace historically the effects of political and social change on the cultural values of the whole of British society. One aspect of his analysis concerns the effects of these values on the system of education (Williams 1961, chapter 1, part 2).

Williams argues that it was the long debate on educational provision for the working class in Britain in the nineteenth century that gave shape to our present view of the purposes of education and was a major source of reference for the kinds of institution that should be established to cater for these purposes. He identifies two main strands throughout this debate – the idea of education for all and the definition of a liberal education (Williams 1961). He argues that two major pressures – those caused by changing industrial needs and those caused by the emergence of the democratic principle – drew attention increasingly throughout the century to the educational neglect of the majority of people. It became increasingly clear that the majority were not passively accepting their lot, and three broad stances were adopted by those who sought a resolution to this neglect.

First Williams identifies 'the industrial trainers' who dominated the nineteenth-century debate. In pursuing arguments for a schooling system that was responsive to the changing economic needs, they defined education 'in terms of future adult work, with the parallel clause of teaching the required social character – habits of regularity, "self discipline", obedience and trained effort' (Williams 1961, p. 162). 'The industrial trainers', therefore, saw education for the majority simply as a means towards industrial efficiency and the 'gentling of the masses' and, as we saw in Chapter 1, their views dominated educational planning in the United Kingdom for a long time.

Two kinds of objection were made to this narrowly instrumental view of education. On the one hand there were those who argued from a more traditional stance that 'man's spiritual health depended on a kind of education which was more than a training for some specialized work' (Williams 1961, p. 162). Williams identifies these as 'the old humanists' and points out that, despite the fact that they were élitist in the sense that they were often deeply opposed to the democratic principle, their concept of education was more 'liberal', 'humane' or 'cultural' than that of 'the industrial trainers'.

On the other hand there were those who were deeply committed to the view that 'men had a natural human right to be educated, and that any good society depended on governments accepting this principle as their duty' (Williams 1961, p. 162). These he identifies as 'the public educators', and they were broadly those who responded to notions of democracy and, by implication, an educated rather than a trained workforce.

Williams concedes that his analysis is an over-simplification and that viewpoints merged in debate as alliances were made in response to particular circumstances (the long controversy over science and technical education, for example), but he also argues that the three distinctive views were still being expressed in the 1950s in discussions about education and its purposes. He argues further that, although 'the industrial trainers' were more obviously dominant at the turn of the century and that the trend in theory at least in the twentieth century has led to the gradual dominance of 'the public educators', a cursory examination of the present system reveals, again as we saw in Chapter 1, that it is still deeply influenced by the conflicting claims of all three viewpoints and that there is an inevitability about these conflicting stances influencing the values of individuals (including teachers) who are part of a society which defines its social classes with such rigidity.

Williams views the achievements of primary education with more optimism, for he claims that it is here that the influences of 'the public educators' have been most effective. He argues that, 'in primary education, a notable expansion of the curriculum is perhaps the century's major achievement' (Williams 1961, p. 165), and we will return to this point later in the discussion.

He draws attention to the fact, however, that by 1960 the educational system was still far short of the principle that he would wish to establish, that is, 'what a member of an educated and participating democracy needs'. (Williams 1961, p. 169). Although the first half of the twentieth century saw provision established for schools for all, this provision was made within the now well-established views of educability. He illustrates this point by showing how provision was made for the new class of skilled professionals required to meet new needs within society, professionals who were drawn largely from the lower social groups. Selection was based on merit defined by the use of tests and other devices to ascertain levels of intelligence of pupils. As a result, by 1960, although the selection procedures themselves were undergoing criticism, the British educational system placed major emphasis on the processes of sorting and grading, based now on views of ability rather than on social origin. The meritocratic rather than democratic principle penetrated thinking about education at every level. 'How else,' he asks, 'can we explain the very odd principle . . . that those who are slowest to learn should have the shortest time in which to learn, while those who learn quickly will be able to extend the process for as much as seven years beyond them?' (Williams 1961, pp. 167–168).

In summary, he argues that, although the rhetoric by 1960 was close to that of 'the public educators', the reality showed that judgements were made about children more often in accordance with the instrumental views of 'the industrial trainers' and the élitist views of 'the old humanists'.

As was also seen in Chapter 1, this is reflected in and confirmed both by the official recommendations made in reports such as the Crowther Report (1959) and the Newsom Report (1963) – both from the Central Advisory Council for Education – and by the earliest projects undertaken by the Schools Council for Curriculum and Examinations which was founded in 1964. The Schools Council used as its terms of reference for both its organization and the generation of its first projects the problems identified in earlier reports (Schools Council 1974a). Indeed, what characterized the Schools Council's early work was the largeness of its ambitions and the idealism with which these ambitions were expressed which contrasted strongly with the conservatism of its constitutional structure (committees were defined by age ranges and subject specialisms already existing in schools) and the way in which it tackled issues within the parameters of the problems defined in the above reports. There were no attempts to gain a more overall perspective on curriculum theory, and curriculum matters were defined either within existing content areas (the early work in the teaching of English, for example) or as perceived problems of some urgency, such as the work in preparation for the raising of the school leaving age, which was largely aimed at solving the problem of the average and below-average children whose schooling was to be extended.

For these reasons the Schools Council's early work merits the severe criticisms of writers such as M.F.D. Young (1971). Although, again as we saw in Chapter 1, Working Paper No. 2, *Raising the School Leaving Age* (1965), expressed the ideals of 'the public educators', the values implicit in Working Paper No. 11, *Society and the Young School Leaver* (1967), which was attempting to resolve a particular problem, reflected much more the conventional values in operation.

It could equally well be argued that the Schools Council, in providing a platform for debate and in collecting evidence from national curriculum development projects, also gave scope for ideas to change at the level of national debate, and in this way new approaches have evolved as a result of early mistakes. What is worrying, however, is the teachers' response to the early work. For the Schools Council's work was both a reflection of and reflected back the values held by teachers in the early 1960s, both in relation to curriculum content and to categories of pupil, again as was argued in some detail in Chapter 1. Thus, at a time of great interest in matters relating to curriculum, the teacher representation on the Schools Council sought innovation within the established view of the curriculum. Conventional values were, therefore, reinforced rather than questioned.

It has thus become clear through the use of one historical analysis of British culture and its effects on the educational system that the values implicit in early attempts at curriculum development in the 1960s – certainly those of national bodies such as the Schools Council – were the same values which had been demonstrated throughout the long debate on the principles which should guide the establishment of state education for all. In other words, the curriculum and its development was still being viewed in relation to three broad categories: academic education, technical training and utilitarian schooling. An overview of the function of education, and egalitarian principles related to this, tended to be expressed at too theoretical and idealistic a level and thus was distant from the practice in schools and from the teachers, who were naturally more conscious of the more pressing instrumental demands being made upon them from such sources as industrialists and academics.

Those involved in planning the work in schools were not challenged to make a reappraisal of the attitudes they demonstrated to pupils of different social origins. The idealism of the democratic principle was also set aside when the first national curriculum projects were embarked upon. Curriculum issues were defined narrowly and conventionally. Selection of curriculum areas worthy of detailed consideration seemed to be either restricted within existing subject frameworks (science in the primary schools, for example) or based on what teachers and others thought were the pressing needs at the time. (How to cope with and contain the reluctant fifteen-year-old at school coloured much of the Schools Council's early work.)

The opportunity for a truly fresh look at the implications for educational provision for all was missed, not least by those involved within the teaching profession. Although these values came to be questioned a decade later, many teachers were by then even more confirmed in their opinions about the curriculum and its development as a result of early definitions of what was at issue.

As was argued at the start, however, this important question of the impact of cultural values is one of two fundamental considerations to be clarified if we are to understand the direction taken by early curriculum development. The other dimension is that of the planning styles or models of development that were adopted.

## American influences on early curriculum planning

It has been shown that decisions were made quickly – and somewhat uncritically – about the nature of the curriculum and the aspects of it that required development. Questions still had to be answered, however, about how these developments would be planned and executed. There is every indication from material produced at the time that this dimension was afforded much more serious and direct attention.

As was pointed out earlier, dissatisfaction was being expressed at every level about the haphazard and formless way in which curriculum matters were dealt with. This undoubtedly had been one important reason for the Ministry of Education's sudden active interest in the curriculum and its development.

Reflecting on this period, Becher and Maclure (1978) show how by 1960 the Ministry was expressing interest in 'a heuristic style' of planning – an interdisciplinary approach which pooled the expertise of academics, technicians and other specialist planners. This kind of approach to planning the curriculum had proved to be popular in North America in the 1950s and had been successful in Britain when applied to school buildings by the development group within the Ministry's Architects and Building Branch. Becher and Maclure express the thinking behind this interest on the part of the Ministry, when they say, 'if school design shapes the activities which take place within the school, it shapes the curriculum; if it shapes the curriculum, should not this be subject to systematic development techniques as other aspects of school design and technology might be?' (Becher and Maclure 1978, p. 61). They go on to argue that the Curriculum Study Group of the early 1960s, from which the Schools Council emerged was 'consciously modelled on that which had transformed the approach to school building' (Becher and Maclure 1978, p. 61).

The beginning of an interest in this 'heuristic' or 'utopian' approach to planning in education is usually traced to the success of Russian technology and the American response to the launching of the first Sputnik in the mid 1950s. It is true to say that the impact of this event popularized such techniques, but again we must note that the thinking which led to this seemingly rational and comprehensive approach to curriculum planning had been developing during most of the twentieth century. It was a scientific methodology that was being developed in fields related to education that gradually led educationists themselves – especially in America – to believe in a scientific solution to the problem of analysis of the curriculum and teacher preparation and to look with optimism to science for the key to many of the problems of implementing loosely expressed educational doctrines.

Movements in this direction began with an interest in causal explanations of man's behaviour and learning, an approach which had much in common with the physical and natural sciences. This point will be developed more fully in Chapter 4 but it is worth noting here that this kind of approach was also based on a particular view of man, which was influential also in the development of the major theories of learning. It should be further noted that 'causal explanations of man's behaviour give an impression of a rather passive, machine-like creature, who is at the mercy of all sorts of forces pushing him along' (Downey and Kelly 1975, p. 53; 1979, p. 81).

A good example of the kind of work that was being developed in related fields at the beginning of the century and which came to influence educationists was that of Frederick Taylor and his colleagues, who attempted to discover the most efficient methods of working in industry by systematically observing the nature of work. Their intention was to eliminate activities that were inefficient and wasteful and, by doing so, to improve both conditions of work and productivity (Davies 1976). Taylor's approach put stress on analysis, method and content, and he worked on the assumption that a single optimum solution could be found. This was an early demonstration of the application of scientific method to the serious study of human performance and achievement.

It was an approach that had immediate impact on industrial planning through job-analysis and systems methods. It was the success in industry that caused it to be adopted by the Architects and Building Branch, and hence led to the Ministry's interest in the 'heuristic' style of planning the curriculum, mentioned earlier. The approach had also been developed in the field of psychology and by the 1940s behavioural psychologists were an important and influential group in America.

It was in the late 1940s that the idea of objectives as a factor central to the debate on curriculum development and methodology was revived. This came with the publication in 1949 of Tyler's *Basic Principles of Curriculum and Instruction*, a small book which was intended as an outline of 'one way of viewing an instructional programme as a functional instrument of education' (Tyler 1971, p.1).

It should be stated that this work did not have immediate impact either in America or in Britain. Popham (1969) shows that both this important work and the later classic work of Benjamin Bloom and his colleagues provoked, at first, only a mild flutter of interest among educators. The impact upon curriculum planners was not felt until the 1960s in Britain.

As was shown in Chapter 1, this scientific mode of planning gained impetus through the work of early large-scale projects of the Schools Council. It was also shown that, far from being a value-neutral approach to planning, as Tyler and others claimed, it came under severe criticism because of its particular view of the educational process and the particular values that it assumed. Despite the flaws in planning of this kind, and despite the fact that an objectives approach can be shown to be anti-educational, if one's concept of an educational enterprise includes an active learner engaged in an intrinsically worthwhile activity which leads him to unintended but worthwhile outcomes, in the setting of this discussion it is important to note that the impact of the objectives approach on general views of curriculum planning has been profound and persistent.

It is true to say that this general approach has been abandoned by many, if not all, of those engaged in large-scale curriculum projects. This is partly due to the experience of project teams who tried to apply it and partly due to the severe and convincing criticisms made of it. The change of direction taken by those engaged in the development of science in the primary schools for the Schools Council is evidence of this. The Science 5–13 project team, as we shall see again in Chapter 4, began their work with a careful pre-specification of objectives in learning science, but later project teams moved from this to a looser approach which focused attention on the processes involved in learning science rather than the end-states to be achieved.

There is no doubt, however, that the general approach has outlived its criticism and has become part of the wider interpretation of what curriculum planning means. It is now commonplace, especially in primary schools, as will be shown later, for teachers to be expected to state the aims and objectives of the activities planned for children. This narrow view of planning can also be seen in the records that are kept of children, the demands made upon teachers by their employers and the textbooks and schemes (especially in the area of mathematics) that teachers choose to use with children.

The success of the objectives approach to planning seems due to two factors. Firstly, there is a remarkable degree of consensus, and therefore plausibility, in the behaviourists' view that objectives need to be formulated and how this should be done. Attention is diverted from uncomfortable and difficult questions of value and from the intangibles in the process of learning, and converges on prespecifying outcomes within already defined skills and content areas. Secondly, their approach works in as far as it provides a tool that can be used in curriculum development. Its seemingly rational, straightforward and scientific style is, therefore, attractive to teachers and administrators alike, who had been in the past unsure of the worth of their work. The situation has also been compounded by demands from outside the teaching profession that the education system should be made more accountable, and teachers have sought, or been encouraged to seek, security in this cost-effective approach to planning and assessment. Thirdly, as will be explained in greater detail in Chapter 4, it received support from the work of the behavioural psychologists, whose influence on education has been quite widespread and far-reaching.

Having been encouraged to adopt the objectives approach for these reasons and having found some security in applying the approach, however loosely, it is understandable that teachers have tended to resist more diffuse and demanding styles of curriculum planning. The objectives approach, therefore, has proved to be one persistent American influence on curriculum planning.

One other North American influence on planning is worthy of mention, and that is one which stems more directly from the urgency of the American response to the success of Russian technology. The 'progressive' tradition in America, which had stemmed largely from the work developed by John Dewey, was already in decline by the 1950s and those promoting a 'discipline-centred' education (many of them, as Becher and Maclure (1978) point out, leading university scientists) rapidly gained ground in their challenge to the approaches to curriculum development in American schools.

The American solution was again to turn to academic specialists to provide planned changes. Worthy of mention here is the distinguished gathering of specialists at the Woods Hole Conference in 1959, which included leading scientists, linguists and others from subject departments of American universities as well as leading psychologists. Fundamental to the thinking of the members of this conference was the now famous notion that 'any subject can be taught effectively in some intellectually honest form to any child at any stage of development' (Bruner 1960a, p. 33). It was the American attempt at realizing this notion that influenced curriculum planners in Britain. The style was again on a large scale and depended on academic experts within disciplines (notably the sciences) to structure the knowledge and expert planners and psychologists to relate this knowledge structure to the child's level of learning. It was intended that, having engaged experts to resolve the 'structure' and 'readiness' issues, the teacher's task would be simply to implement the curriculum development.

Two important consequences followed from this approach. The teacher was not afforded any particular expertise and was encouraged to be passive and to look elsewhere for expert guidance both in the structuring of what should be learned and the pacing of when learning should occur. The teacher was also encouraged to develop curriculum in schools within the subject specialisms defined by (and unquestioned by) university departments. In both instances, focus was diverted from the particular contribution of the teacher in the classroom to curriculum planning, and teachers were encouraged in the belief that solutions to curriculum problems could be provided for them by outside experts.

The optimism of this approach, however, was infectious and similar moves began to be made in Britain by teachers, academics and industrialists, again largely in the realm of science teaching (Becher and Maclure 1978). One important result was the funding of a science curriculum programme by the Nuffield Foundation which was later followed by the sponsoring of other projects within subject specialisms by the same foundation. This tradition was adopted by the Schools Council, who, in doing so, severely limited the possibility of engaging in a more comprehensive view of either curriculum planning or, perhaps more significantly, teacher development. The pattern of curriculum development was, therefore, severely limited to individual developments within the strict confines of subject areas, and teachers, in turn, were led to associate curriculum development with programmes developed for these areas and produced by subject specialists.

The issues that were identified, therefore, were problems related to content. Even in the field of early childhood education, where teachers specialized in education itself and were not accorded subject specialist skills, the same influence can be discerned.

Thus the American influence on curriculum planning can be summarized as Utopian in style, and can be seen both in the desire for a clearer prespecification of the educational enterprise (the objectives model of planning) and in the belief that subject specialists can resolve the problems of planning for the teacher by structuring knowledge and relating this structure to the child's level of understanding.

Although, as was shown in Chapter 1, the later national developments of the 1970s have consciously tried to change these planning styles and although much of the ensuing debate, at a theoretical level at least, about the curriculum has stressed the anti-educational nature of early attempts at curriculum development, as was argued at the beginning of this chapter, the early developments themselves now constrain the practice of teachers in schools. It remains to examine briefly, therefore, the impact of these early attempts at curriculum development on present-day thinking about the curriculum, as it is revealed by developments in one particular field, that of early childhood education.

## The impact on early childhood education

As was suggested in the introduction to this chapter, there are three main reasons why an examination of recent directions taken by teachers concerned with the education of very young children offers an opportunity to assess the impact of these more subtle and persistent constraints on curriculum development. The first and most obvious one is that there is a minimum of the external political, academic and administrative constraints on the teachers working in this sector of schooling. The second is that a 'progressive' tradition has thus been freer to develop in this area of education than elsewhere. The third is the commitment to the notion of active learning that is an essential ingredient of that tradition. Each of these we must briefly consider in turn.

Throughout the history of state education in Britain, the education of children under seven years of age has been directly controlled by externally devised examinations for a period of ten years only (1861–1871). This is not to say that external constraints have had no impact. The required activities of the junior schools ('payment-by-results', scholarships, 11+ examinations etc.) and the widespread belief that the teaching of basic skills is wholly the responsibility of the teacher of the very young child, have created constraints which have led to two clearly definable approaches – 'the elementary' and 'the progressive' traditions (Blyth 1965). The former, which is still the most widespread in practice, has always been related closely to the more instrumental traditions of schooling. The latter, however, has taken full advantage of the absence of obvious constraints.

For a century it has been possible for educators to develop work at this stage with a degree of freedom that has been denied in all other stages of the school system. Not surprisingly, therefore, some of the teachers working with young children and most of those responsible for their training (including the inspectorate responsible for early childhood education at a local and national level) have pioneered innovatory activities. It is this informal, progressive tradition, well established by 1960, that Williams claims comes closest to the democratic ideal. It is also the tradition that has been influential in shaping the view of education held by most teachers of young children and in this sense has come to be the mainstream influence on the planning of work in nursery and infant schools – an influence which led to a unique approach in the schooling system and which leads to the second main reason for using this sector to illustrate the points made earlier in the discussion. It is important, therefore, to set out the recurring themes in this mainstream view.

The first commitment is to the idea of social reform. Early educational experiences are not only seen as intrinsically worthwhile, but the right kinds of experiences are also seen to affect positively the child's subsequent school success. Thus, much attention is paid to the child's adjustment to and response to the school's environment. Dearden argues that it is 'relational' aims, aims which provide a context where education is possible, which characterize this commitment. What is learned in schools, therefore, is of less importance than the attitude to learning that is developed and so planning avoids being 'prescriptive of content' (Dearden 1976).

The next commitment is to the freedom for children to learn in flexible, benevolent, child-centred environments. The classic expression of this commitment came in the Hadow Report of 1931: 'We are of the opinion that the curriculum of the Primary School is to be thought of in terms of activity and experience, rather than of knowledge to be acquired and facts to be stored' (Hadow 1931, p. 93). In the later Plowden Report, some effort was made to develop this statement, and it was argued that 'We certainly would not wish to undervalue knowledge and facts, but facts are best retained when they are used and understood, when right attitudes to learning are created, when children learn to learn. Instruction in many primary schools continues to bewilder children because it outruns their experience' (Plowden 1967, para. 529, p. 195).

This more open approach had a profound effect on curriculum planning for the early years of schooling, and the stress on the child's total experience and individualized approaches to teaching led to a more flexible organization of time, content and grouping. The Plowden Report made reference to an integrated curriculum; during recent years the flexible use of time began to be referred to as 'the integrated day'; and children were not only unstreamed, but 'vertical' or 'family' groupings became commonplace.

The flavour of this informal approach, which was designed to allow the individual child the maximum possible amount of freedom in his learning in school, is captured well in the description of an American visitor: 'open education is a way of thinking about children, about learning and about knowledge. . . . The curriculum is open to choices by adults and by children as a function of the interests of children. The curriculum is the dependent variable – dependent on the child – rather than the independent variable upon which the child must depend' (Walton 1971, p.10).

Related to the commitment to freedom to learn in an active way and at the child's own pace is a third influence in traditional thinking: this is a belief in childhood as a unique, precious and critical period for effective development. One consequence of this belief was that opportunities were given to children to play and explore the environment freely. Again, the Plowden Report devotes much time to defending the child's 'need' for play and the general theme is that 'this distinction between work and play is false, possibly throughout life, certainly in the Primary school. . . . In play, children gradually develop concepts of causal relationships, the power to discriminate, to make judgements, to analyse and synthesize, to imagine and to formulate' (Plowden 1967, para. 523, p. 193).

In general, therefore, the mainstream thinking by the 1960s about early childhood education placed stress on the active nature of the child. Early experiences were seen as vital to later development. Informal, individualized learning was organized where possible and the curriculum, which was approached from the child's viewpoint, was undifferentiated and avoided conventional subject categories. Skills learning was developed in accordance with the needs of individuals and coincidentally with and supportive of other kinds of learning.

The advocates of this general approach attached importance to the manner and processes of education and were criticized as being somewhat reticent about stating aims. In their defence, however, they argued that aims tended to be external to the processes being developed and encouraged instrumentalism by diverting attention from the child. The members of the Plowden Committee, who saw these as good reasons for avoiding planning in accordance with statements of aims, also advised, however, that decisions concerning the planning of curriculum should be made within individual schools and also that teachers should be supported and advised so that 'the decisions taken in schools spring from the best available knowledge and are not dictated by habit and convention' (Plowden 1967, para. 507, p. 188).

It was claimed at the beginning of this chapter that this tradition held within it approaches to education and curriculum planning that are of general interest and, before moving to the third reason for examining this section of the schooling system, it is worth indicating these more clearly. By the 1960s, mainstream approaches to planning in this sector of schooling incorporated many of the elements of both a process model of planning and a school-based view of curriculum development. Admittedly, the rationale for the approach was expressed in loose, romantic terms which were rightly criticized. The approach had also been developed by teachers who were not restricted in their thinking by either examinations or particular subject specialisms. This enabled them to evolve a more comprehensive approach which focused on the quality of the child's experience and the processes that would enhance this experience. This led in turn to a more unified view of curriculum which raised issues that did not focus exclusively on one element of the planning process.

It is also worth adding that the direction of curriculum development advocated by the mid-1960s was that teachers needed to be aided in their own development as the quality of curriculum development hinged on the abilities of individual teachers and their overall understanding of the processes of education. This contrasted sharply with the recommendations in other sectors which focused largely on content and subject specialisms. This point again entered general theoretical discussions much later in the 1970s, when research began to indicate that the teacher's attitudes, values and understandings had a powerful impact on children's performance in school.

Finally it remains to examine the impact of the thinking that resulted from early curriculum planning on the work engaged in recently by teachers of very young children. It was argued in the introduction to this chapter that the mainstream approach, described above, has been placed under threat and a major reason for this has been the constraining effects of this thinking. These constraints are many and various, but for the purposes of this discussion three aspects can be cited.

The first relates to the impact of the values implicit in the social-class structure of British society. It was shown earlier that the cultural values that are generally held will influence the values of teachers working within the society. This may explain the paradox that teachers who had developed a tradition of valuing the individual contribution of each child began to predict and explain educational failure in terms of supposed deficiencies – usually language deficiencies – of categories of pupils. This led to the surprising willingness of nursery and infant teachers to participate in the now maligned 'compensatory' programmes. It also led to the strong recommendations in the Plowden Report for 'positive discrimination' in favour of children who are 'most severely handicapped by home conditions' (Plowden 1967, para. 174, p. 66), and these recommendations being interpreted as a need to combat supposed cultural and linguistic rather than physical poverty. As a result of this, early intervention programmes were introduced in schools and even nursery teachers began to view certain children, a significant proportion of whom were from lower socio-economic groups, as in need of compensatory education.

A second change of direction stems from this. Many of the language programmes that were introduced at this time were based on similar projects that had been developed in North America and were therefore overtly behavioural. Although these simplistic language programmes were rejected by British teachers, the objectives approach to planning had more influence in other spheres. Worth noting again in this respect is the table of objectives constructed by the Schools Council's Science 5–13 project team (Schools Council 1972). The project team justified their objectives approach to planning by saying that 'working with objectives takes some of the insecurity out of discovery situations' and that 'objectives have a value in encouraging progression in work' (Schools Council 1972, p. 26).

Similarly, in a recent book on pre-school education, McCreesh and Maher claim that they are in line with modern curriculum practice, when they propose that those concerned with the teaching of pre-school children should have clearly thought-out aims and objectives (McCreesh and Maher 1976, p. 34).

These two statements, selected from a profusion of examples that are available, are of particular interest as they illustrate two adaptations of the objectives approach to planning. The Science 5–13 project team have seen their use of objectives as the key to rational curriculum planning on a large scale. Objectives are used as a hopeful alternative to haphazard, ill-considered innovation, and this is largely in line with the British adaptation of the approach. McCreesh and Maher, however, come closer to a strict behavioural approach, more common in America. Although the authors concede that teachers and other adults concerned with planning work for the preschool child must have scope to formulate their own priorities when stating aims and objectives, they are very specific about techniques for achieving the objectives they feel to be important, and they put stress on the end results.

It is also interesting to note that, as was shown earlier, although the large-scale project teams have sought other, more productive models, the preoccupation with stating aims and objectives has become a persistent influence on teachers' thinking, especially in terms of the kinds of record-keeping systems that are now being used by teachers. These are usually clear statements of behaviour changes, and tangible results are looked for rather than indications of processes that are being developed.

Finally, through a belief in the structuring of knowledge in terms of existing content areas there has been a tendency recently on the part of teachers of very young children to see curriculum development in terms of subject specialisms – especially those specialisms defined by scientists and mathematicians. This view of the nature of curriculum is understandable when teachers of young children, far from being encouraged to develop their own special understandings, are seen as non-specialists. It has led, however, to an undermining of their confidence, and many have begun to look to subject programmes, again usually constructed in behavioural terms, in order to develop work in certain content areas. They have also been reinforced in the view that curriculum developments need to occur in fragmented, subject-based areas.

The three chosen examples all point to an increased tendency on the part of teachers, advisers and others concerned with early childhood education to move away from their earlier view of education as a subtle and complex process, and to plan for a more reductionist enterprise, which amounts to little more than the training of children in order to achieve measurable results. They illustrate, in fact, the theme that has recurred throughout this discussion, namely, that the styles, values and approaches initially adopted for curriculum planning can gain credibility in teachers' minds and can therefore be self-perpetuating and continue to exercise their own constraints on subsequent planning, even to the extent of drawing teachers away from what may be a more satisfactory model for educational planning and one which, as was argued in Chapter 1, may even be gaining ground in other sectors of the education system.

## Summary and conclusions

Through examining the values and styles adopted in early attempts at curriculum planning in the 1960s, it has been shown that, in addition to the more obvious external constraints, teachers themselves can be misled into adopting approaches to their work with children that can prove harmful to educational planning. In this way persistent and subtle constraints have been placed on future curriculum development by teachers themselves, either through the judgements they make of children, the curriculum models they adopt or the view they hold of the nature of curriculum. Although theoretical discussion has shown serious deficiencies in early curriculum development, these styles can be seen to continue to influence the practice of curriculum planning at all levels of the schooling system.

CHAPTER FOUR

# THE PSYCHOLOGICAL BACKGROUND TO CURRICULUM PLANNING

**Meriel Downey**

## The nature of the psychological contribution

'Psychologists know plenty about learning; educators know the probems of the schools. If only we could get them together to talk to each other, most of our problems would be solved' (Hilgard 1964, p. 404). This facile statement is quoted by Hilgard in his discussion of theories of learning and instruction as one of the many half-truths that abound about the links between education and psychology. Indeed, as he suggests, what is needed is collaboration in terms of long-term investigations, rather than discussions of a more informal nature designed to put education to rights, as the statement implies. Before any such investigations are launched, however, we need to ask what kinds of educational problem might be solved by drawing upon psychological research. Our present concern with curriculum planning raises questions about the kind of positive contribution that psychology can make to curriculum issues and also the limits placed upon planning by characteristics of the people involved, both teachers and pupils.

Psychology, according to Taylor (1968), should have something to tell us about 'populations, processes and products' or, in other words, teachers and pupils, learning strategies and outcomes in relation to curriculum. Whichever view of learning or development we take, it is clear that we are far more enlightened now about teachers and pupils as individuals than when universal education was introduced in the 1870s. We recognize children as active, self-aware, creative beings who are endowed with feelings, emotions and thoughts, and who are capable of learning to make moral choices. This emphasis on the individual is due partly to the work of Freud which stimulated wide-ranging research on personality structure and development, drawing attention to the uniqueness of each individual, the significance of unconscious processes, and the long-lasting effects of early childhood experiences. Studies of child and human development raised questions about the importance of early emotional attachments for subsequent mental health and social adjustment (Eriksen 1950; Bowlby 1950). The work of Piaget and his followers on cognitive growth threw new light on stages of development, different rates of growth and readiness for learning. In addition, studies of social psychology have made valuable contributions to our knowledge of group dynamics and have provided a background for more recent work on classroom interaction (Delamont 1976). We have been made aware of differences in cognitive mode by the work of Guildford (1950), Torrance (1964), Kagan (1967), for example, so that we no longer expect all children to learn in the same way and feel encouraged to explore different teaching strategies suited to the children's different learning styles (Bennett 1976).

When we turn to the processes that Taylor refers to, we find that much of the work carried out by psychologists on learning processes springs from learning theory built up from animal and carefully controlled laboratory experiments. Such theory has led to a general proposition that learning involves a change in behaviour, and indeed, as we have seen in earlier chapters, Tyler (1949) claimed that the function of the curriculum was to bring about desirable changes in behaviour and that the purpose of the curriculum was to provide the kind of *control* that would direct a pupil's learning to worthwhile ends. The emphasis placed by much learning theory upon training, repetition and practice has led to a tendency to analyse learning tasks so that components can be presented to pupils in the most effective way for learning (Bloom 1965; Skinner 1968). However, as we shall show later, it is clearly not possible to extrapolate from work done in the laboratory to all human learning. Since animals are far less complex than humans, much of their learning is a matter of reinforcement and repetition; critical judgement and understanding are not part of their repertoire.

Similarly, much of the work done on human learning under laboratory conditions has deliberately eliminated those very factors that are important in school learning, namely past experience, previous associations, differences in interpretation. Furthermore, when theorists such as Tyler talk about directing pupils' learning to worthwhile ends or about desirable changes in behaviour, it is clear from the start that psychology cannot help us to decide what is desirable or worthwhile. As a largely empirical discipline, it cannot settle matters of value, which, as was argued in Chapter 1, are of crucial importance to curriculum planning.

A psychological perspective on the products of learning can contribute towards our understanding of the development of intelligence, although there is so far little consensus on its nature. This perspective throws light also on ways in which children acquire attitudes, beliefs and values, and helps us to appreciate the importance of interpersonal relationships. Above all it claims to help assess and measure what children have learned, though not all learning can be evaluated within a psychometric framework.

Clearly, as we have already implied, psychology cannot help us to decide what to teach or to justify why we teach what we do, since these are value-related matters. Further limitations must be recognized when attempts are made to apply findings of experimental psychology or to adhere too closely to a psychometric framework in trying to assess what children have learned.

Hilgard (1964), in his plea for systematic research designed to illuminate learning processes, outlines a continuum of six steps ranging from pure to applied studies. His first three stages include investigations under laboratory conditions of animal and human learning with no relevance to school learning at all. The next stage however, although still laboratory-based, includes studies of programmed learning or simulated classroom conditions with a teacher specially trained by the experimenter to operate according to instructions. Results of such experiments can then be tried out, he says, in a normal classroom and techniques modified accordingly until finally manuals and textbooks can be prepared so that any teacher anywhere can make use of them and adopt the teaching strategies carefully worked out under controlled conditions. Although this approach sounds highly mechanistic and as such must be very suspect to many teachers today, there is no doubt that some useful and practical guidelines have been derived from such work. We know, for example, that long periods of time spent on the same task without a break result in psychological fatigue and less effective learning, or to use the technical terms, that massed practice is inferior to spaced practice. This is particularly applicable to the acquisition of skills such as reading, using tools and machines or playing a musical instrument, where formerly children were forced to apply themselves for hours on end. However, the organization of learning and the learning processes themselves are far too complex for specific teaching or learning strategies to be applied and practised according to a fixed model. Such an approach must necessarily neglect individual learning styles, differences in cognitive mode and social interaction in learning, not to mention the personality make-up of both teachers and learners.

## Development of psychological influences from the late nineteenth century

### *Formal discipline and connectionism*

In a discussion of the kinds of contribution made by psychology to curriculum planning, it will be interesting to trace its influence over the past eighty years or so. Towards the turn of the century, the doctrine of formal discipline, derived from nineteenth-century faculty psychology, still held sway. The main tenet of this doctrine was that any kind of mental practice improved memory, just as regular exercise of the muscles strengthens them for physical skills. Thus children were forced or cajoled into learning reams of verse or chunks of the Bible off by heart in the firm belief that such mental exercise would make them better able to learn other, quite unrelated material. In public schools the learning of classical languages, or at any rate the recitation of declensions of nouns and conjugations of verbs, was thought to be valuable discipline for the mind. This heavy emphasis upon drill, repetition and rote learning was still at the basis of most learning in elementary schools at the time of the notorious payment by results system. Teachers carefully drilled their unfortunate pupils in chanting tables, spouting poems and learning lists of unrelated facts to impress visiting inspectors. Right answers to predictable questions were the hallmark of satisfactory teaching and learning.

It was Thorndike, one of the first to write on educational psychology, who destroyed the myth of formal discipline. For him, learning was not simply a matter of repetition but, instead, of establishing meaningful connections between the items to be learned. 'Learning is connecting; and teaching is the arrangement of situations which will lead to desirable bonds and make them satisfying' (1913, p. 20) was one of his general rules for education. The teacher's task then was to 'exercise and reward desirable connections, punish undesirable connections' (1913, p. 20), a recommendation later to become known as the law of effect. What constituted a desirable connection was a matter of social utility – a prevailing doctrine at that time in the USA where Thorndike practised. He left decisions about curriculum content to others and concentrated upon methods of organizing what others had decreed should be learnt. Thorndike continued to concern himself with matters of teaching and learning and later in his career (1932–1933) revised the law of effect, by assigning greater weight to reward than punishment, thus heralding behaviourist views such as those of Skinner with which we are more familiar today. The effect of a minor punishment for making an undesirable connection (that is, giving a wrong answer) was intended to encourage the learner to try something else until he was eventually rewarded. Thus the gradual establishment of correct responses would eliminate incorrect ones. This, in Thorndike's view, constituted active learning as opposed to the passive recitation or repetition of faculty psychology.

### *Behaviourist theories*

Skinner's influence has been widespread both in the USA and in this country. His theory of learning is based on operant conditioning techniques which have reward or positive reinforcement as their cornerstone. Efficient learning, which, in his view, rests on appropriate reinforcement schedules, takes place when the learner is rewarded for making a correct response. However, since the reward must be immediate in order to have the desired effect, much valuable learning time in school is wasted, he claims, because teachers are poor reinforcers. They are naturally unable to supply immediate reward to each child for each correct answer. Skinner's criticism (1959) is that teachers are very often inefficient because they spend too much time attempting to redesign the curriculum instead of learning how to employ 'available engineering techniques which would efficiently build the interests and instil the knowledge which are the goals of education'.

He thus calls for a technology of teaching to replace these inefficient methods and claims that teachers would benefit from the kind of help offered by a scientific analysis of behaviour. He suggests that just as animals learn as a result of tangible rewards in the form of food or drink, humans in their everyday behaviour learn 'because they are reinforced for what they have seen and heard, just as a newspaper reporter notes and remembers things he sees because he is paid for reporting them' (1965, p. 81). Children in school should be encouraged to explore and ask questions, he concedes, but it does not follow that they will learn and remember what they discover unless they are suitably reinforced at the appropriate time. Teaching may thus be defined, he maintains, as an arrangement of contingencies of reinforcement designed to change pupils' behaviour. Skinner himself advocated the use of programmed learning in schools as an effective way of ensuring that each correct response a child makes is reinforced immediately by the book or machine. The teacher is thus released to supervise the whole class, each of whom can work at his own rate. Individual differences in rate of progress are thus catered for and no child need feel at a loss because of absence from school.

Like Thorndike, Skinner claims that his techniques encourage children to take an active part in their own learning, since everyone is forced to produce or develop an answer himself rather than sitting passively waiting for a classmate to do so. Content however must remain teacher-directed and the teacher's main task is to structure the material so that learning can proceed in very small steps and small items of information can be reinforced one at a time. Mastering a body of knowledge consists largely in producing a large number of correct responses to logically related sequences of questions that constitute the subject matter. Carroll (1963), Bloom (1965) and Homme (1966) have suggested techniques of learning that basically rest on Skinner's techniques. These will be discussed later in a comparison of two essentially different approaches to curriculum planning and structure.

### *Influence of social psychology*

At the same time as teaching styles in the USA were being influenced by Skinner's procedures, other influences of a different nature were beginning to have an impact on educational practice. Social psychology with its concern with group dynamics, leadership style, role playing, attitudes and prejudice, to name some of the major areas, emerged in the late 1940s in the USA. Studies initiated by Adorno, Sanford and Frenkel-Brunswik (1950), amongst others, of the authoritarian personality stemmed from an underlying anxiety about violent anti-semitic attitudes in particular and ethnocentrism in general.

Their analysis of authoritarian characteristics, manifested by rigidity of thought and action, dislike and fear of change, respect for status and emphasis on conformity and obedience, led other investigators to examine the effects on children of authoritarian child-rearing practices and teaching styles. The study by Lippitt and White (1945) of authoritarian, democratic and laissez-faire leadership styles was soon to become famous and for years was quoted in support of more cooperation and collaboration between teachers and pupils than had traditionally been the case. An authoritarian classroom style, it was claimed, was likely to make children work harder and behave better while the teacher was present, but failed to engender the sort of social climate in which children became absorbed in their work for its own sake. Its emphasis upon competition rather than cooperation produced animosity amongst children, revealed as soon as the teacher had to leave the classroom. However, since the original study was carried out with groups of boys voluntarily attending extracurricular activities, its findings could not be applied to normal classroom conditions. What happens in an artificially created situation with its careful control of variables does not necessarily occur in real life contexts with so many unpredictable elements.

Anderson and Brewer (1945) set out to observe the effects of similar leadership patterns on nursery school children. Their observations showed that with a democratic or socially integrative teacher, children were on the whole relaxed and friendly, showing an interest in their school activities. Those working with a dominative or authoritarian teacher were likely to be over-submissive, yet aggressive and uncooperative when left on their own.

These early attempts to examine the influence of teacher type on children led eventually to more systematic and sophisticated studies of classroom interaction (Delamont 1976; Downey and Kelly 1979) which were to become an important element in curriculum development and innovation. Walker and Adelman (1975) initiated the Ford Teaching Project in 1973 in order to monitor the practices of forty teachers in fourteen East Anglian schools who were attempting to use enquiry/discovery methods in connection with the Humanities Curriculum Project. Observation revealed that the kind of curriculum development envisaged by the Stenhouse team, where the teacher was to act as neutral chairman so that pupils could no longer rely on him as a source of information, was impossible unless teachers and pupils learned to adopt new roles and a new pattern of interaction emerged.

## *Theories of cognitive development: Piaget and Bruner*

However, by far the most powerful influence on educational thinking in general, with some impact on curriculum planning, comes from the work of

Piaget and Bruner on children's intellectual development. Piaget's main concern was to explore the growth of intelligence and to establish how a child is able to learn. Whereas the behaviourist approach focused on learning processes, Piaget emphasized the child's *capacity* to learn. His detailed studies of the stages through which a child passes towards intellectual/cognitive maturity consistently reveal his interest in processes rather than products of thought. He distinguishes between action-derived and environmentally-derived knowledge in that the former is non-specific and can develop only over a period of time during which the child's experience and interaction with his environment are broadened. It is thus that he learns concepts of time, space and conservation, for example, none of which he could learn on an isolated occasion, nor could he be taught them directly. Environmentally-derived knowledge, on the other hand, includes the learning of names or of specific facts which can be taught. But Piaget claims that the true learning of facts or names presupposes that learning of the first kind has already taken place: a child can learn that he lives ten miles from London and properly understand it only if he already has some notion of distance and space and understands what it means to use place names.

Writing of the application of psychology to education, he himself points out that it is becoming increasingly important for teaching methods to be adapted to the ways in which children's thought processes develop. He strikes a rather pessimistic note when he writes, 'as regards the development and actual building up of thinking processes, modern education still adheres to an empiricism and opportunism bearing a closer resemblance to seventeenth-century medicine than to that of our day' (Piaget 1973, p. 61). However, most teachers and educators are now well aware of the importance of developing children's powers of thought and many now recognize three main principles that emerge from Piaget's work on intellectual development and have importance and relevance for educational practice.

Firstly, learning has to be an active process, because true knowledge is a construction from within. This is reflected in the emphasis on active learning and on enquiry and discovery techniques found particularly in primary schools today. The teacher's task, within this context, is not to transmit ready-made knowledge to children, but to help them to develop their own understanding by guiding their experience and encouraging them to check for themselves what they think they have learned, rather than to expect answers from the teacher.

Related to this is a second principle derived from Piaget's work which shows that thought is rooted in action rather than in language. Concrete experience as the basis of thinking cannot be supplanted. Although language and speech are important to express thinking, they cannot take the place of active experience and, as research has shown (for example, Sinclair de Zwart 1967), learning the appropriate term so that the right answer can be supplied cannot accelerate the development of thought processes. Experience of a varied kind enables a child to come to grips with inconsistencies within his own thinking and as a result to proceed to a more complex operational stage.

The importance of social interaction, particularly amongst children of similar cognitive levels, provides the third principle that emerges from Piaget's investigation. Whereas an adult is usually clear about what is at stake in a problem and can readily provide the child with an answer, a clash of convictions amongst children who are all in a state of cognitive uncertainty can lead them to think and question more carefully because the onus is on them to resolve the conflict which faces them. Thus they are helped to move out of their own egocentricity not by an adult who knows the way to go but by a peer who, being equally uncertain, can pose some crucial questions, thus unwittingly prompting one who is at a transition stage to move further.

Bruner too sees learning in terms of intellectual or cognitive growth. Learning in his view is a means of mastering an immensely complicated environment – too complex to cope with unless the individual, as a young child, begins to develop strategies to bring it within his reach. Cognitive growth can be conceived as the development of a capacity for simplifying the environment by various ways of representing reality to oneself. Although he does not suggest a stage theory of development, as does Piaget, Bruner stresses the importance and logic of mastering some skills before proceeding to other more complex ones. The young child, for instance, learns first of all to cope with his world through action, then through images and pictures and eventually by symbolic means, mainly by the use of language. Bruner calls these ways of understanding the world 'modes of representation': enactive, iconic and symbolic modes.

At the enactive stage, the young child learns about his environment by looking, walking and climbing; touching, tasting and smelling. All his learning proceeds in context; at this point he cannot learn by being told or taught out of context. Exploration and free play provide him with optimal opportunities for learning of this kind since he can discover actively for himself what objects are like, how they work, how his own body moves and so on. In time he is freed from the immediacy of direct action by using images, models and pictures, or by pretending and imagining himself in situations other than those of reality. Eventually he is released further from the concrete by the use of language which enables him to transcend the immediate. Language offers him a means not only of representing experience but also of transforming it. For instance, as well as being able to deal with the past and the future, he can also handle the possible or the hypothetical. Instead of exploring his world only in action, he now has the greater flexibility of exploring it in thought.

Like Piaget's theory of cognitive growth, Bruner's also stresses the importance of action and direct experience, especially in the early years. But because he does not embrace a theory which rests so heavily upon maturational or biological facts, he attaches greater importance to the role of experience in furthering cognitive growth. Traces of all three modes of representation are present in children by the time they come to school and one of the functions of the school is to provide means of promoting intellectual development deliberately. 'Experience has shown that it is worth the effort to provide the growing child with problems that tempt him into next stages of development', he writes (1960, p. 39). It is not so much interaction with cognitive equals that helps to promote this growth as the presence of a complexity model, that is, someone who has already mastered more complicated skills and strategies, be it peer or adult, and who can thus act as a competence model to be emulated. One task of the school is to find ways of converting what is known by man into a form capable of being mastered by a beginner. When Bruner writes that 'any subject can be taught effectively in some intellectually honest form to any child at any stage of development' (1960a, p. 33), he means that, provided what is to be learned is available to children in a mode that is within their reach, they will be able to make sense of it.

Whereas Piaget's ideas were largely taken by others and applied to educational practice, Bruner himself deliberately set out to outline a theory of instruction and to develop ideas upon which a curriculum could be based. Such ideas will be discussed more fully later on.

## Contrasting models of curriculum planning

After this brief historical outline of some of the main ways in which psychological thinking has affected educational practice, we can now examine more closely how different curricular models have been supported by psychological theory and research.

Pask and Lewis (1972), adopting a systemic approach to curriculum design, isolate four main preconditions for designing a curriculum strategy. The features that determine the nature of a curriculum model are, firstly, the degree and type of learner-teacher communication; secondly, the nature of the learner, namely whether he is on the whole an active problem-solver or a passive answer-giver; coupled with this is the role of the teacher who can be either an instructor and controller of learning or a guide and co-learner; and, finally, the nature of the subject matter itself which can either be largely predetermined or completely open-ended. Using these criteria as a guide, they discuss three approaches which fall largely into a closed system category: Skinner's behaviourist shaping scheme (1968); Homme's reinforcement menu scheme (1966); and Gagné's scheme of guided discovery (1965). Open systems of learning they style 'conversational' learning.

Let us then consider closed and open systems as our two main curriculum paradigms and examine the nature of psychological support that sustains each.

A closed system necessarily implies prespecified behavioural objectives that set out precisely what pupils should finally have achieved. Some of the difficulties associated with this approach have already been discussed in Chapters 1 and 3. Bloom's notion of mastery learning (1965) provides a clear example and can, he claims, be applied to any part of the curriculum involving sequential learning, such as mathematics and language learning. It can also be applied to subjects requiring closed or convergent thinking, including science, history, mathematics and languages, because, in his view, it is relatively simple to define standards of achievement in these areas. Although he nowhere clearly defines mastery learning, he claims that a high level of mastery can be achieved by as many as 95 per cent of learners, given sufficient time, effective teaching strategies and learning conditions. Success of this kind provides the individual with a sense of adequacy and achievement, encouraging a positive self-concept and favourable attitudes towards school.

Skinner's approach (1965, 1968) also implies the setting of clearly defined objectives, since all content, which eventually is broken down into small units to be learned, must be teacher-selected. Notions of reinforcement and reward are typical of a closed system approach. Skinner (1965) calls for a technology of teaching to replace what he sees as ineffective reinforcement techniques employed by teachers. Teachers need the kind of help offered by scientific analysis of behaviour which sees learning as brought about by carefully controlled conditions where every correct move or response is positively rewarded. Teaching he sees as an arrangement of contingencies of reinforcement under which behaviour can be controlled or shaped in the desired direction, that is, that pupils learn what the teacher or curriculum planner has preordained. To those educators adopting a more open view of learning this must smack of manipulation or even bargaining and, as such, is seen by them as educationally undesirable. However, Skinner is at any rate using reinforcement in the sense of providing the learner with feedback about his progress or knowledge of results

Homme's use of the notion of incentives in learning is even more suggestive of bribery. His reinforcement menu scheme (1966) consists in offering children a reward of their own choice, such as running around in the playground, firing popguns or pushing the teacher along in a chair, in return for work successfully completed. Emphasis is solely on getting children to do what is required of them with little regard for the consequences of inducing in them the idea that learning is worth doing only if there is a reward to follow. And such rewards, being quite extraneous to the learning task, must in any case surely be of dubious value.

Learning within this framework is a linear, cumulative process; content can be sequentially arranged as Skinner advocates, and types of learning hierarchically ordered. Gagné (1965) specifies eight different types of learning, proceeding from the learning of simple S–R bonds and culminating in the mastering of concepts or principles which equip the learner to solve problems. Not until the lower orders of the hierarchy have been mastered can the learner move on to more complex ones, so that, if learning is to proceed systematically, careful attention must be paid to prerequisites at every level. Children cannot be expected to solve geometrical problems, for example, until they have grasped relevant geometrical principles; and these can only be understood once concepts such as angle, line or bisection have been acquired. In Gagné's view, learning is defined in terms of observable performances; the teacher or curriculum planner using specialized knowledge of the psychology of learning as well as knowledge about a subject area must structure the learning conditions and material so that pupils are taken through the steps in the appropriate order as set out in Gagné's hierarchy.

Whereas learning according to the approaches of Skinner, Bloom and Homme remains almost entirely under teacher control, Gagné sees the pupil eventually as a problem-solver, albeit within a restricted framework. He accepts the notion of guided discovery, whereby pupils discover for themselves concepts and principles. But the concepts and principles as well

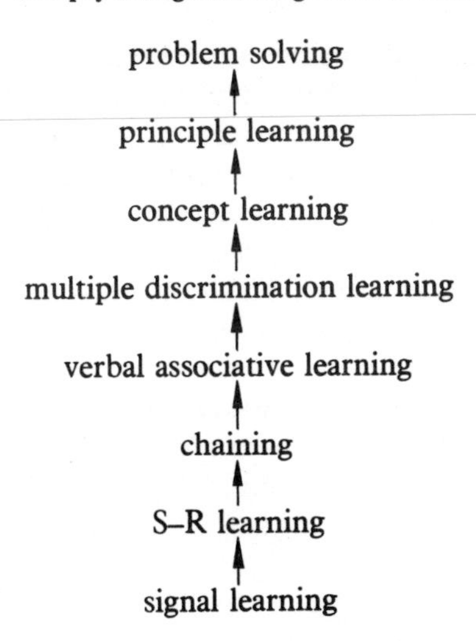


as the steps towards their discovery are carefully planned by the teacher, so that there is minimum risk of making a false move. None of these approaches attaches any significance to learning from one's own mistakes and logical errors.

Recent studies of classroom language suggest that on this model, teacher-pupil communication is limited largely to questions posed by the teacher who expects clearly defined answers, often of the one-word variety, from pupils. Flanders' interaction analysis (1971) showed that teachers generally speak for two-thirds of the time and that roughly two-thirds of this time is spent in telling, instructing and asking closed questions. As a result, pupils tend to use what Barnes (1976) calls 'final draft' language in which to present the answers they hope the teacher expects and thus are not required to reveal how they reached their conclusions. One-way communication operates between teacher and pupil, with very little room for dialogue or multi-channel communication between those involved in the learning enterprise.

An open system of learning takes a different view of the learner and his educational environment from the one we have just been describing. Objectives are not prespecified because, as Wickens (1974) puts it, there is a constant state of disequilibrium in response to the changing interests and achievements of pupils. Learning is no longer seen as a linear process, since individuals can digress and explore lines of enquiry that arouse their curiosity. Curriculum content is not preordained since individual interests are likely to go beyond any boundaries determined by a specific subject area. This does not mean to say that content is totally open or that anything counts as valid learning. What it does imply, as in Bruner's MACOS which focuses on the study of man, is that there is no prespecified material that learners can reproduce as evidence of learning. Thus the teacher is not one who shapes children's behaviour and directs their learning but is seen as a guide, a catalyst or a co-learner. The learner is ideally not only an active problem-solver but also a problem-setter: he learns to recognize what constitutes a problem and pursues it for its own sake, displaying what Berlyne (1960) termed epistemic curiosity. Communication between pupils and teacher and amongst pupils is flexible, so that frequently questions are genuine ones to which even the teacher does not know the answer. Incentives are not offered as rewards for work done, but instead, understanding, problem solving, the satisfaction of curiosity and mastery are considered to be self-rewarding (Bruner 1966).

Learning through active involvement which is essential for the development of cognitive powers through which experience is organized is thus a main feature of this model. Whereas the emphasis in a closed system tends to be on the learning of facts or propositional knowledge which can be objectively assessed, an open system stresses activity, involvement and the learning of procedures. Bruner (1960) claims that any area of knowledge can be translated into the enactive mode, so that children need not learn physics or geography, for instance, by noting and regurgitating facts they have been told; instead he prefers to talk of *doing* physics or geography by experimentation and observation, not only in the classroom but also outside in the broader environment. The learning of both practical and intellectual skills germane to a particular area of enquiry is thus important so that, instead of learning isolated fragments of information or single performances, overall competence is built up. Bruner (1966) compares learning to be skilful with a body of knowledge to mastering a language and its rules of syntax. Whereas mastery learning in Bloom's sense seemed to imply committing to memory a body of facts, for Bruner it means attaining competence of a kind that is transferable to other types of learning.

Discovery and exploration are regarded as important means of learning, provided that children are given some guidance in helping them to appreciate the significance of what they are discovering and to apply their newly established knowledge to other situations. Adult guidance serves to draw a child's attention to inconsistencies in his thinking, to compatibilities between the new and the familiar and to ways in which he can use his own capacity to solve problems (Bruner 1961). Adult guidance too is important in enabling a child to learn from his own mistakes. To have the chance to make mistakes and to learn from them can be highly instructive, since this is part of the educative process that continues long after the end of formal schooling.

This scheme then suggests an emphasis on the importance of teaching children to discover, to explore and to think for themselves. It encourages them to be partly responsible for their own learning; intrinsic motivation, resting on the child's own curiosity and sense of wonder, is at a premium; individual differences in capacities and interest are to be exploited.

However, it is often invidious to compare and contrast two systems as if there were no compatibility at all between them, considering the features of one to be totally acceptable while those of the other are to be rejected out of hand. Ausubel (1963) makes some attempt at a synthesis. He points out that active learning through direct experience can often be meaningless, especially if it is too unstructured. Learning needs to be consolidated by constant practice, which necessarily involves repetition and is helped by reinforcement or reward on the part of the teacher so that pupils know they are on the right path. Failure to provide sufficient practice impedes the adequate mastery of basic skills in mathematics or reading for instance, as Gagné (1965) makes clear in his hierarchical model of learning. Any curriculum planner clearly needs to consider seriously which elements of each model can best serve the particular area of knowledge with which he is concerned so that true benefit is derived from the theory and the research of learning theorists and developmental psychologists.

## Some current curriculum projects

It will be useful, as a conclusion to this chapter, to look at the psychological foundations of three current curriculum projects. The Schools Council's Science 5–13 project (1972) is particularly interesting in that it is based on a Piagetian notion of stages of development but at the same time embraces an objectives model. The research team distinguished three main stages of intellectual development in the children for whom the project was designed:

1a Transition from intuitive to concrete operations
1b Early stages of concrete operations
2 Later stages of concrete operations
3 Transition to stage of abstract thinking or formal operations

Then, starting from the general aim of science teaching, which is to develop an enquiring mind and a scientific approach to problems (or, in Bruner's terms, learning the skills of science), they arrived firstly at eight broad aims, each of which was further worked out into more detailed objectives considered appropriate to each developmental stage. For example, with the broad aim of developing basic concepts and logical thinking in science, a child at stage 1a would be expected to develop an 'awareness of the meaning of words which describe various types of quantity' (Schools Council 1972, p. 62). A child at stage 3 much later on should develop the 'ability to formulate hypotheses not dependent upon direct observation' (ibid.).

The project team argued that such objectives would help teachers to structure their work sequentially, taking into account pupils' stages of development, yet at the same time the insecurity of working completely within a discovery context would be reduced. And although the objectives are clearly defined, the need for flexibility is stressed so that spontaneous responses and suggestions on the part of the learners are not ignored. This project is perhaps one of the best examples of a combination of features from learning theory, with its emphasis upon objectives, and developmental psychology, which stresses the importance of cognitive stages.

Bruner's MACOS (Man–A Course Of Study) is a social-science based curriculum designed mainly for the 8–13 age range. The study of man constitutes the main content of the course and questions are posed about man's nature as a species and the forces that shape his humanity. Three broad questions recur throughout the project:

> What is human about human beings?
>
> How did they get that way?
>
> How can they be made more so?

The subject matter thus includes empirical issues, such as comparative data derived from a study of the herring gull, the salmon, the baboon family and the Netsilik Eskimo, but also issues of value. As such, the content is speculative, since it embraces no clear-cut body of information which can be transmitted to pupils by instructional techniques. The broad aims of the project centre around the processes of learning rather than the products, and include teaching children the skills of enquiry; helping them to develop methods of observation and research; encouraging them to reflect on their own experiences; and helping them to use original source material and to evaluate it critically.

Clearly, with aims of this kind there can be no prespecified objectives, since the whole idea is based upon the notion that knowledge is speculative and that therefore what pupils derive from the material cannot be determined in advance. The project illustrates Bruner's claim that anything can be taught to children at any stage of development and exemplifies a spiral curriculum. In this case, the basic themes of adaptation, learning and aggression return again and again to be reconsidered in the light of children's modes of understanding. Enactive, iconic and symbolic modes are used as ways of understanding, experiencing and interpreting the material. The teacher must see himself in the role of co-learner but must at the same time accept responsibility for his pupils' learning in helping them to acquire the skills of enquiry discussed earlier, and also to understand the nature of value issues.

The Schools Council's project in Moral Education, *Lifeline* (McPhail 1972), is an interesting example of a project that curiously falls short of its own ideals in that it lacks the firm psychological underpinning which could give it considerable strength. The overall general aim of the programme is to further pupils' moral understanding and moral conduct by helping them to adopt a considerate style of life. Its underlying philosophy is that the basic form of moral motivation lies in treating others with consideration, since this will not only prove intrinsically rewarding, but will also result in one's being treated similarly by others. The programme is planned to cover a five-year course for pupils of eleven–sixteen and published material is graded according to the needs of pupils of different ages and stages of development.

However, although this is one of the main attractions of the Lifeline project, and McPhail himself claims that one of the major criteria to be used in deciding which material to select is the stage of development which pupils have reached, the research team gives no guidance on how teachers can recognize a pupil's stage of development or readiness for certain types of moral argument. Unlike Kohlberg (1966), McPhail does not make clear the importance of the *quality* of moral argument used, if it is to lead to progress towards a more advanced stage of moral reasoning. To have linked the programme with Kohlberg's findings relating to a stage theory of moral development would have strengthened the psychological basis of the project considerably. On the other hand, however, McPhail's confidence that moral development will follow from group discussion amongst pupils might rest on Piaget's belief in the importance of the peer group for any kind of intellectual development. But if this is the case, it is nowhere explicitly stated. The aims and materials of the project could very easily lend themselves to a spiral curriculum approach, as advocated by Bruner, since moral issues are introduced over and over again to match children's levels of understanding. In addition, a variety of learning techniques is suggested, including role play, socio-drama, discussion, writing and even painting and drawing – all very reminiscent of Bruner's three modes of understanding.

Although this is not openly acknowledged, the Lifeline project seems to rest on a learning theory approach to moral development, in that reward and reinforcement play a significant part. One of the main reasons for treating others with consideration, McPhail argues, is that we tend to receive social approval from others which in itself is rewarding. Similarly, failure to treat others with consideration may result in unpleasant consequences, which, like any other kinds of negative reinforcement, are to be avoided. However, to base a theory of moral learning upon notions of reward and punishment raises serious questions, since the ensuing moral conduct might be merely a matter of expediency.

It seems strange that so much psychological theory and research at present available has apparently been overlooked in relation to this project. Reference to the work of Piaget, Bruner and Kohlberg would have provided the project with the firm psychological basis that it needs.

## Summary and conclusions

This chapter first of all discussed the kinds of contribution that can be made by psychology to curriculum planning and suggested that these lie mainly in the area of teaching methods and learning processes, taking into account the nature of children's intellectual development.

A brief outline of the history of psychological influences showed how teachers and educators have been influenced by theories and research which developed and made an impact upon practice from the late nineteenth century to the present day.

Two models of curriculum planning were then compared and contrasted with reference to the kind of psychological theory and evidence that lend them support. Finally, several current curriculum projects were briefly examined and the kind of psychological foundations upon which they are based were discussed.

# CHAPTER FIVE

# EXAMINATIONS AND THE SCHOOL CURRICULUM

**Carol Pudwell**

To most people, both within the teaching profession and outside, public examinations probably seem the greatest single influence on the school curriculum and on children's education. Some regard them as highly desirable, feeling that they assess as impartially and objectively as possible the achievements of pupils. Others see them as mere inconveniences which we all have to put up with in our schooling, as 'unnecessary necessities' which are just a part of the system and which society seems to expect us to undertake. For these people, examinations are not really central or essential to education, but, since they exist, pupils ought to be taught to do as well as they can in them. Yet others are strongly opposed to examinations, as being anti- or non-educational or as being concerned with mere utilitarian aspects of schooling such as selection and grading. All these groups have different views of examinations, but all have criticisms of them which need to be looked at and discussed.

## Criticisms of examinations

Claims are made, especially by teachers, but also by parents, employers and pupils themselves, that examinations *determine* what shall be included in syllabuses, that they prescribe certain sorts of content which, by implication, restrict study to those particular aspects only and thus inhibit wider investigation. Although matters 'beyond the pale' are often deemed to be of far greater interest and educational value than many in the syllabuses, any incursions into them are either ruthlessly stopped or are decried as red herrings to be quickly netted in order for the main work to be continued. This view suggests that some of the really educational aspects of courses and subjects are not examined at all, or, because of the imputed nature of examinations, cannot be assessed in any case. Questions arising at this point concern the proper limits of examinations, and their place in a wider concept of assessment in education.

Another kind of claim asserts that examinations determine not only the content of curricula but also the methods of teaching and learning. Teachers and pupils tend to play the 'examinations game' wherein emphasis is given to skills in spotting the 'right' questions; to learning, almost by rote, appropriate, stock answers; to unimaginative styles of teaching, learning, and revision; to teachers divining what topics to leave out of the syllabuses and what are 'sure to come up to this year'; or, if the whole syllabuses are covered, to relentless cramming of bread-and-butter information. The schoolchild's view of history offered in '1066 and All That' is an amusing and pathetic reminder of the worst excesses of these methods. Many students, especially at 'O' level, say that if they try to think for themselves (usually an alleged objective of teachers), they are dissuaded by their teachers who suggest that the examiners want straightforward, down-to-earth answers. (If only those particular teachers were aware that an examiner's heart leaps with pleasure when he does come across an 'original' answer where the student is really trying to use his own knowledge and understanding to tackle a problem!)

A further objection is that standards of examinations are not consistent or comparable throughout the country, that different examinations boards vary in their assessments of students' work. Critics here also say that examinations are not objective enough, but rely too much on the personal evaluations of the markers, especially in essay-type answers in non-science subjects. They go on to claim that terminal or postcourse examinations are not necessarily suitable for all students, many of whom find the stress of coping with two or three papers to be done in limited time too great to do themselves justice. Such examinations are said to put too great a store on memory and speed. Then again, various incidental factors are said to have a bearing on individual students' performances, such that some are unfairly, if unwittingly penalized. These might include slow or untidy handwriting, poor spelling and grammar, a clumsy style and so on, as well as physical things like the heat or cold in the examination hall, or a bout of hay fever.

A further concern is that different kinds of examinations for different 'types' of students, particularly the GCE 'O' level and the CSE, do not have equal esteem in people's eyes, and that they are also educationally and socially divisive. On the other hand, proposals for a common examination or examination system for students of 16+ years, which have been made in response to certain aspects of comprehensive education and mixed-ability teaching, have been queried on the grounds of their being incapable of assessing such a wide range of attainment as the top 60 per cent of those students.

This raises the very basic question of what examinations are for. Many people are not clear about the purposes of examinations, whether they are for selection and prediction, or whether they are to assess levels of attainment. Indeed, it is interesting to observe how frequently examinations devised for one purpose have eventually been used for quite a different function.

A final criticism, one which underlies all the others, is that teachers have little or no part in the control of the examinations, but have merely to teach what the examiners prescribe in their syllabuses. This affects notions of teacher autonomy, of teachers' professionalism and of their accountability. Teachers worry that examinations restrict their freedom, and that central supervision of examinations by the examinations boards and the Schools Council adds to this constraint. They are concerned, too, that some subjects are harder than others and that only the 'brightest' students should be allowed to enter for examinations in them. Opposed to this, however, is the fear that subjects are only regarded as of worthwhile status if they have an examination connected with them, and, indeed, that the teachers themselves are only of acceptable status if their subjects are examinable and if they teach examinations classes. We must not forget, though, that many teachers have used external examinations and their promise of social currency as a means of discipline and control in groups of youngsters who might not otherwise be so amenable.

Having outlined some of the main criticisms of public examinations, it is necessary to discuss them more fully with a view not only to clarifying them but also to offering an argument that examinations can and should be seen as an essential element in the concept of education itself. Together with this is the notion of placing the *teacher* more centrally in the whole field of curriculum and examinations.

## Analysis of the criticisms

### *Restrictions on the content of curricula*

The first point, that examinations determine the curricula in schools and that examining authorities effectively control these curricula, can be seen to have a history going back to before the beginnings of state education.

As for the schools (originally the private schools and later the secondary schools), the story of examinations began in earnest in the middle of the nineteenth century, and right from the outset the inherent dangers of the examination system were realized. For it could be claimed that the curricula in public and endowed schools were directly and closely influenced by entrance examinations to the universities. There was, too, a clearly obvious backlash into the preparatory school curriculum whose main *raison d'être* was to enable the boys of thirteen years of age to succeed in the very demanding standards of the entrance scholarships at the public schools (later popularly known as 'The Common Entrance') (Montgomery 1965).

The examinations directly affected the content of the syllabuses taught in schools in that, by effectively prescribing what would be examined, they encouraged the teachers to cover only or mainly those particular elements of their subjects. Not only did this limit the teaching syllabuses in the subjects, but it also limited the curriculum as a whole since non-examined subjects were either not included or were of low status and given little time on the timetables. Pattison, in evidence given to the Taunton Commission in 1868, alleged that the key problem was that of the great influence (almost control) on schools being exercised by outside organizations such as the Civil Service Commissioners and the Council for Military Education whose interests were not necessarily in line with the educational aims of the schools. He said that 'the school follows the examination, and not the examination the school' (Taunton Commission 1868, vol. 5, p. 952) – a cry we have heard many times since then. Other contributors to the Taunton Report spoke of these examinations as being a 'blight on education' by making teachers teach for the examinations rather than what was good for the pupils, since these examinations were concerned with narrowly specialized professions (e.g., the army, the civil service, medicine), whereas the schools were interested in providing a 'general' education to suit a wider variety of middle-class occupations (Taunton Commission 1868, vol. 4). By this time a great many boys were, in fact, leaving the schools to attend the many 'crammers' (still a flourishing institution to this day), because the examinations had become so competitive.

Between the best public school sector and the parish elementary school sector, the 'middle-class schools', as they were called, formed a rather amorphous mass. Their standards and aims varied very greatly, with many being not as good as some of the elementary national schools, so that the middle classes became wary of the success of the inspected, tax-supported education of the elementary sector and began to look for ways of improving the standards of their own schools. To improve the standards required the establishment of a common device for measuring standards, and for organizing the implementation of the device. Following a local venture in the west of England in 1857, the universities of Oxford and Cambridge instituted in 1858 the first of their 'local examinations', which were organized to test the boys in the middle-class schools. The 'good general education' of the universities was being brought into the schools and examined by the universities. The teachers in the schools now had a standard, albeit externally imposed, to work towards, thus giving confidence to themselves, their charges, the parents, and the professional and commercial world outside.

The universities also had regulations for 'matriculation' or admittance to them, which served to limit and confine the curricula in schools. During the first half of the twentieth century the First Examination (or School Certificate) at sixteen years was introduced and developed, with a Second, or Higher School Certificate Examination at eighteen years. The School Certificates were offered in a wider range of subjects or groups of subjects than the Matriculation Certificates, but they became used as equivalent to matriculation qualifications in that certain groups of subjects at 'credit' standard were accepted. These examinations had considerable impact on schools in the curricula they followed. The Higher School Certificate, for example, required students to elect to study in *one* of three groups of subjects, together with a subsidiary subject from outside that group. From these earliest times, then, the universities exerted a most powerful influence on what was taught in school.

In the elementary school sector a well-known, even notorious, influence of examinations on curricula was that which resulted from the 'Revised Code' of 1861. Money from rates and taxes had to be seen to be soundly 'invested'. Payment was to be on a 'capitation' basis wherein grants were based on the regular attendance of individual children and on their ability to pass six 'standards' in the three Rs (reading, writing, and reckoning). Inspectors from a middle- and upper-class tradition were laying down the standards and curriculum of the elementary schools in the lower-class tradition. This kind of influence amounting to control of the education of children in one large social group by people in another, smaller group has been the subject of serious and heated debate in recent years (Young 1971). The elementary school teachers concentrated merely on training, by rote methods, their pupils to pass the minimum levels required. This system of 'payment by results', as Matthew Arnold called it in 1867, had a deadening effect on curriculum, on teaching and learning methods and on morale in the schools, yet it continued in use for at least thirty years.

After 1902, elementary schools came under pressure to prepare pupils for the 'scholarship' examinations for free places in the new secondary grammar schools. Later, after 1944, the '11+' examination became the means for selecting primary school children for the secondary grammar and the secondary modern schools. The 'backwash' effect of this on the primary school is well known, in that the schools were often almost 'forcing' institutions, coaching as many pupils as possible to 'pass' for the grammar schools. Instead of being a device merely to *select* children for their appropriate secondary school, it became regarded as a *competitive* examination.

Much more could be said about this point of the examinations restricting the curriculum, but enough has been said so far to show that restriction has often been the *effect* rather than the *purpose* of examinations. From being a device to give direction and standards to the nineteenth-century middle-class schools, and for raising standards of entry to universities and professions, examinations became regarded by schools as more or less their entire curriculum. From being statements of what content was to be *examined*, the syllabus became interpreted by teachers as the only content to be *taught* in schools.

To bring the discussion up to date we can refer to some government reports on education which have commented on examinations. The Consultative Committee on the Education of the Adolescent, 1926 (The Hadow Committee), although the majority of witnesses disliked, on educational grounds, external examinations for children under sixteen years, because they restricted the curriculum and because children were not considered mature enough, nevertheless proposed a new examination for fifteen-year-olds in the higher elementary schools (or secondary moderns as they were to be called). The leaving age was then fourteen years, so the examination was to be partly a device to encourage youngsters to stay on at school to benefit from longer education. The proposed examination was to be optional and to be widened to include less literary, 'non-academic' subjects. A point, to be taken up later, was that the examination was to be designed by teachers for their own children, and the whole thing organized locally. The implementation of these proposals was delayed because of the economic stringencies of the 1930s and then the intervention of the Second World War. However, a report in 1930 by the Joint Committee of the Association of Education Committees and the National Union of Teachers, whilst approving of *internal* school certificates signed by the headteacher and the local director of education (another proposal of the Hadow Committee for those leaving school at fourteen years), disapproved of external examinations. They claimed that not only would an optional or voluntary examination become compulsory in practice as a result of public pressure, but also that examinations had a detrimental effect on curriculum (Montgomery 1965).

The Consultative Committee on Secondary Education in 1938 (The Spens Committee) saw the School Certificate Examination as inhibiting curriculum change, and also recommended the abolition of the subject groupings in order to free the choices of subjects chosen by the candidates. Again the war intervened, but a wartime committee of the Examinations Council, appointed by the president of the Board of Education, considered both examinations and the secondary school curriculum. Their report, the Norwood Report of 1943, made several radical proposals for peacetime education. The examinations were to be 'subject'- rather than 'group'-based, enabling both freer choice of subjects and the possibility of some children getting a certificate in only one or two subjects, their levels of performance to be recorded on the certificate. The intention was to phase out eventually and completely the external examination in favour of making all examining at 16+ an internal matter for schools. The committee felt that the possession of a certificate was no longer the mark of a 'good general education', hence their advocacy of also including school records and reports in the examination certificate.

A report of the Secondary School Examinations Council in 1947 took the Norwood proposals further. A General Certificate of Education (GCE) would replace the School Certificate, with the 'group' requirements removed and with the possibility of acquiring a certificate in only one subject. But the standard was to be raised at both Ordinary and Advanced levels with, for example, the old 'credit' standard of the School Certificate becoming the pass standard of 'O' level. The 'O' level was intended primarily as a means for judging the suitability of pupils for further study in sixth forms and its use for public purposes would be as part of a comprehensive leaving certificate. Eventually the 'O' level would disappear or become merely part of the schools' internal assessment machinery. It was also planned as a 16+ examination which was aimed at allowing the opportunity of developing full five-year secondary courses. But the 'O' level did not disappear because universities redefined their matriculation requirements to include three 'O' level passes and two 'A' level passes in the specified subjects of English language, mathematics or an approved science subject, and a foreign language. Once again the universities were, in effect, 'calling the tune'.

At 18+ the 'A' level was also seen as a *qualifying* examination for university education, but it became regarded later in practice as a *competitive* examination, as a result of pressure for university places, with the result that grades of pass were introduced. Originally it was only at Scholarship level that competition was envisaged as a means for awarding State Scholarships.

The GCE was introduced in 1951, and within a couple of years the 'A' level had become graded and used for selection purposes, whilst moves were afoot to lower the minimum age for entry to 'O' level. This resulted in cramming a five-year course into four years to the detriment of the course and the pupils. In many grammar schools 'express' streams were put through the mill to take 'O' level a year early. A few of the most able survived well, and did 'A' level courses with flying colours. Many, though, were intellectually spent, besides being emotionally and socially too immature to cope with sixth-form work.

The presumed 'parity of esteem' of the secondary modern and the secondary grammar schools was not evident as the postwar years advanced. During the 1950s the modern schools were looking for new directions as well as feeling the pressures from parents and pupils to enter pupils for external examinations. Many were already sitting examinations set by such bodies as the Royal Society of Arts and the College of Preceptors, but it was the prospect of the GCE 'O' level which gave people the incentive and motivation to stay on at school for a year beyond the then current leaving age of fifteen years and to have the opportunity of gaining the more highly regarded certificate. In 1955 and 1957 the Minister turned down the proposals to extend 'O' level to secondary modern schools on the grounds of their being too demanding and inappropriate, as well as having a bad effect on the whole school curriculum and organization. The interests of the mass of the pupils might suffer for those of the few. However, hundreds of modern schools were already teaching some pupils for 'O' level subjects even though the parents had to pay the examination fees (5,500 from modern schools in 1954, and 16,787 in 1958) (Montgomery 1965). The Minister was in a quandary, though, in that he did not want to be seen to deny modern school pupils the opportunity of taking the GCE because of the inadequacies of the 11+ selection processes.

The committee reporting in 1960 on 'Secondary School Examinations other than the GCE' (The Beloe Report) pointed to the same danger that had been noted a century earlier – that of the examinations moulding and directing the curriculum.

> 'The examination dictates the curriculum and cannot do otherwise; it confines experiment, limits free choice of subject, hampers treatment of subjects, encourages wrong values in the classroom.' We have heard these warnings reiterated, in terms of their own experience and judgement, by teachers, by educational administrators, and not least by the [Secondary School Examinations] Council's expert subject advisers. (The Beloe Report 1960, p. 23, para. 77).

The Beloe Committee complained of the narrowness of existing examination syllabuses and, whilst bearing in mind their warning quoted above, made suggestions for a more appropriate examination for the 40 per cent of pupils below the 20 per cent sitting for GCE 'O' level. Like the GCE, the proposed Certificate of Secondary Education (CSE) was to be a 'subject' examination. In order to try to avoid its becoming a paler version of the GCE, new approaches to examining were to be developed, especially in subjects usually restricted to modern schools. The examining was to be in the hands of teachers and organized by regional boards (now fourteen in number). The new steps were to help to overcome as much as possible the 'dictation' of the curriculum by the examination, by encouraging the teachers to assess what *they* had taught in their schools. Their own *teaching* syllabuses were to be drawn on for examination purposes, rather than the other way round. In 1963 a report of the Central Advisory Council for Education (England), *Half Our Future* (The Newsom Report), gave tentative support to the Beloe proposals.

More recently, from 1968 until now, the Schools Council for Curriculum and Examinations, which replaced the former Secondary Schools Examinations Council in 1964, has spent a great deal of time, money and energy in devising different kinds of examinations for secondary schools. A Common Examination at 16+ (Schools Council 1975b) has, perhaps, met with greater acceptance in principle than have proposals for examinations at 18+

(first mooted as Qualifying and Further Levels – 'Q and F' – and subsequently as Normal and Further Levels – 'N and F'). These examination proposals have not only been responses to developments in educational thinking and organization, such as comprehensivization and all-ability classes, and to the 'new sixth' form with wider aspirations than the traditional 'sixth', but have also attempted to influence the curriculum. At the 18+ level the 'N and F' recommendations have been a response to calls for broadening the sixth-form curriculum and for delaying specialization until as late as possible, by advocating a five-subject curriculum, with university entrance requirements as three 'N' level and two 'F' level passes. At the same time it is said that these proposals will not detract from the students' opportunities of studying their subjects in depth. The detailed arguments expressed in Working Paper 60 (1978b) claim that 'although F-level covers less content it is just as demanding as A-level' and though F-level occupies less timetable time than A-level, that 'loss of one-quarter of the time given to an A-level does not mean the loss of one-quarter of the content of A-level . . . [because] . . . the small and homogeneous F-level groups may be able to achieve a great deal in the time allotted to them'. Pilot surveys reported in Working Paper 60 and in Examinations Bulletin 38 (1978a) indicate that students would select 'N and F' subjects from a wider field than at 'A' level so that there would be less tendency to choose only or mainly from the 'sciences' or the 'arts', for example, but from these and other groups of subjects.

Interested parties have recently sent in their views on the 'N and F' proposals to the Schools Council before it gives its final report to the Secretary of State for Education and Science. From preliminary comments one senses that they have more opposers than supporters. Universities are concerned that the narrower syllabuses at 'F' level might necessitate a lengthening of first-degree courses and a need for more taught MA/MSc courses in order to maintain their standards. Such a move would be too costly and unwelcome. Some faculties might require three 'F' level passes, whilst many students might well take four 'F' levels in order to compete for places. (This may be offset by the considerable decrease which is forecast for the next decade in the numbers of young people of undergraduate age.) A *Daily Telegraph* report says that the National Association of Head Teachers (NAHT), representing two-thirds of all state schools, has asked for the continuance of 'A' levels 'for all pupils for whom they are suitable'. At the same time it is alleged that 'vociferous opposition against scrapping A-levels has flowed in from the heads of both state and public schools, senior secondary school teachers, university chiefs and industrialists' (*Daily Telegraph* 2 April 1979). In the same newspaper report it was remarked that the Secretary of State, who had previously supported 'N and F', has now said that the government under Labour would not abolish 'A' levels in the future. At the same time, though, there seems to be much more support for the proposed Certificate of Extended Education (CEE) for those members of the 'new sixth' who do not aspire to 'A' level and university education. It would be set for seventeen-year-olds on a broadly based curriculum and would probably attract those who had previously acquired the CSE.

It must not be forgotten in all this that public examinations have adapted to changing needs and, in certain ways, have contributed to and facilitated curriculum development. T.S. Wyatt, a former secretary of a GCE examining board, says:

> . . . existing [examination] syllabuses undergo continuous modification or are discarded in favour of newer approaches and new subjects are regularly introduced. In recent years the syllabuses of all the science subjects have been radically revised to take account of new developments, those in mathematics have been expanded by the provision of alternatives for pupils taught on the 'modern method', those in geography have been substantially modified in accordance with new approaches and those in the domestic subjects have been overhauled to provide for scientific and sociological study as it applies to matters affecting the family. At the same time a large variety of new subjects has been brought in to meet the needs of the schools (Wyatt 1975, p. 102).

Wyatt has listed twenty-four 'A' level subjects and thirty-eight (Mode 1) syllabuses which have been introduced by GCE boards since 1960. At the same time some examining boards have responded to developments in schools of integrated courses, in humanities and sciences for instance, and others have awarded 'multiple certificates' for such courses. Suggestions for changing the examination syllabuses and for introducing new ones come from different sources, such as teachers' professional and subject associations, individual teachers or groups of teachers, from the boards themselves, and from the sponsors and planners of new curriculum projects, including the Schools Council (which is responsible for both curriculum and examinations development) and, formerly, the Nuffield Foundation (Wyatt 1975).

### *Constraints on the methods of teaching and learning*

References to 'new approaches' brings us to the second main source of criticism of examinations, namely, that they limit the methods of teaching and learning in schools and inhibit the development of more creative or imaginative approaches. As has been hinted already, this criticism has also had a long history. The charge of their encouraging rote learning of the minimal or basic facts to the exclusion of much else is bred partly out of ignorance, partly from tradition and partly from certain difficulties in examination techniques. Because most examinations require written papers which are done privately and marked secretly elsewhere, people claim that they are not clear what the examiners are looking for. Many do not read the chief examiners' reports which frequently contain pleas for more adventurous approaches to answering questions or to bringing in evidence of wider understanding. Or, if they do read them, they continue to 'play safe' by not encouraging their pupils to be more original. Teachers, pupils and parents also have past records to support them in knowing that the mainstream, safe way gets pupils an adequate pass; the 'high-fliers' survive anyway.

Another aspect of this is the cynicism of many people, in schools and out, about the role of examinations. They see them as purely instrumental to other ends than education, and have adopted the attitude that these external ends ('getting a good job', selection of the fittest, winning in the competitive stakes and so on) are really the only worthwhile objectives. For these people, who include, perhaps, the majority of pupils, learning in schools is undertaken in order to pass examinations. Could it be that this attitude reflects a traditional authoritarianism in many schools where an unquestioning acceptance of externally 'imposed' syllabuses is common? Perhaps the newer generation of teachers, who are becoming better qualified and educated, will be able to counteract this cynical negativism and to bring to the mass of pupils the excitement and enlightening quality which learning can have, where examinations *reflect* the courses taught and the educational aims inherent in them.

Several of the new courses have responded to a more educational view of school curricula and of the examinations devised to accompany them. A good example is that of the Nuffield Science Project in the 1960s, where pupils were to learn to be scientific rather than to be memorizers of scientific information. 'Discovery' and 'enquiry' were to be the key concepts in the learning strategies, which necessitated a different role for the teachers and a different kind of relationship between them and their pupils. In the Nuffield Chemistry Introduction and Guide was written:

> . . . teachers seek to encourage lively enquiry, understanding, and an ability to interpret evidence. . . . [There is] need for more people with scientific training

> and with critical attitude of mind, [and this] has become a matter of national concern. . . .
>
> Our proposals . . . are four.
>
> (a) Pupils should gain an understanding that lasts throughout their lives of what it means to approach a problem scientifically. . . . They must be given opportunities to observe and explore so that they develop disciplined imaginative thinking. . . .
>
> (b) Which ideas are discussed, how they are presented, what materials and techniques are used to demonstrate them, depend on the level of development reached by the pupils . . . [and] must reflect up-to-date thought. . . .
>
> (c) Examination marks . . . must be awarded chiefly for intellectual and manipulative skills, understanding, and a lively critical mind.
>
> (d) The teaching profession already possesses an imaginative outlook, wide experience, and a sympathetic understanding of pupils' needs and interests. (Halliwell 1966).

Another notable curriculum development was the Humanities Curriculum Project under the direction of Lawrence Stenhouse (1967–1972) where materials as 'evidence' in pupils' enquiries are chosen as the direction of enquiry warrants, and where open-endedness is a hallmark of learning. Again we note that the Schools Council Integrated Studies Project centred at Keele University (1968–1972) pointed out that 'schools have to view "subjects" as modes of enquiry, rather than bodies of information' (Bolam 1971). Project Technology also reemphasized the curriculum of the subjects in that field in such a way as to encourage enquiry methods. The *teaching* syllabuses tend to dwell on modes of enquiry and on the main areas of experience the teachers consider it worthwhile for their pupils to explore, rather than on statements of specific facts to be learned. Courses centred on enquiry and discovery methods develop as they progress so that, in a way, the syllabuses are retrospective statements of what happened rather than prescribed plans of work (Schools Council 1975a).

These and other curriculum developments, with a new view of content, aims and methods, pose fresh problems of assessment. S.J. Eggleston has given us a timely warning that traditional concepts of examining may be deleterious for these new approaches and has advised us that a revision and development of new examination methods could support and enhance the further growth of these more educationally founded courses (Eggleston 1973).

D. Holly (1973) has been somewhat discouraging in suggesting that those ideals of pupil enquiry, and of learning as being an exciting discovery of various ways of understanding the world, are not yet available to the mass of our pupils. The new relationships required between teachers and pupils are more readily adopted by those in public schools, says Holly, where they hold similar values and attitudes to each other. The rest of us have a long way to go in casting off the long tradition of an alienating school experience. However, not only are new relationships developing and our understanding of them growing (Downey 1977), but experience in schools of these new courses and examinations to support them are also showing us that such approaches are educationally valid for all pupils, as was argued in Chapter 1.

But tradition dies hard. Many teachers still prefer the strongly didactic methods, with their related stock answers and impersonal assessments. (Jeremy Bentham's search for impartiality in examining, centred on the notion of one correct answer for every question and on the production of official 'Question Books' for candidates to learn by heart beforehand, is reflected in the modern practice of preparing booklets for pupils to buy, which give 'model' answers and key facts in various subjects.)

There has been a well-established tradition of relying mainly on written papers in examinations, though 'practicals' have also had an essential place in many subjects. Before about the mid-eighteenth century the *viva-voce* method of examining had been usual, especially in universities. It was used, too, in the latter half of the nineteenth century in the elementary schools under the 'Revised Code'. Here, though, it became too impracticable to assess thousands of pupils this way, besides being only suitable for testing the most superficial knowledge in any case. Oral methods have returned recently to school examinations in some subjects.

However, whilst holding some doubts about the impartiality of written examinations and accepting them as a necessary part of our assessment procedures, most of us would probably agree in some measure with the views expressed by Horace Mann in the middle of the last century. He wrote that essay-type written papers could fulfil the requirements of objectivity which had been the cornerstone of the *viva voce* examination, in that (a) they were impartial; (b) they allowed pupils an hour to set out their ideas and knowledge; (c) a wider range of questions could be given than in a short oral; (d) the teacher had no opportunity of prompting or interrupting a train of thought; (e) they did not permit favouritism; (f) they could allow pupils to *use* facts to develop ideas and arguments rather than to require the simple factual answers of an oral test; and (g) 'a transcript . . . of the state and condition of the pupils' minds, is taken and carried away, for general inspection' (Morris 1961).

Though essays, orals and practicals remain important ingredients of most examinations, there has been a development of a variety of other assessment techniques to meet a variety of *educational* purposes. Certain sorts of knowledge of basic facts can be tested by multiple-choice, 'objective' tests which require different types of fixed responses. Other tests can assess pupils' basic levels of understanding, in a series of short-answer questions. Others can assess pupils' abilities to synthesize different sorts of knowledge in problem-solving or problem-posing contexts, and others can be devised to test critical thinking. 'Prepared questions' can be used, whereby students are given questions several days before the examination, to enable them to think about the issues involved, to gather together ideas, and to revise what they think to be appropriate. Continuous assessment and coursework assessment, including individual projects, can serve our understanding of pupils' abilities for independent learning, research work, and for interrelating knowledge from different fields.

Three 'modes' of examining were developed for the CSE:

Mode 1 examinations conducted by the examining board on syllabuses set and published by the board,
Mode 2 examinations conducted by the examining board on syllabuses devised by individual schools or groups of schools and approved by the board,
Mode 3 examinations set and marked internally by the individual school or group of schools but moderated by the board (Schools Council 1973b).

Mode 3 has often been adopted by those schools which value continuous and course-work assessment as appropriate ways of responding to the individualizing of the curriculum.

All these kinds of assessment can be seen as reflecting wider notions of teaching and learning, and of the sorts of knowledge which can now be reliably examined.

The objective tests and multiple-choice tests may be an efficient way of testing the common or core curriculum in a subject (if such a core can be arrived at), whilst the others can be geared to the free-choice, individually selected curriculum. A full-scale report on examinations in Nuffield 'A' level chemistry shows this wide use of assessment methods, and points to many of the problems of coping with the free element of the curriculum, since 'it is here that students and teachers can express their reaction to the curriculum and the examination, not through questionnaires or committees but by what they actually choose to do or not to do' (Matthews and Leece 1976). Though much more research needs to be done in this area of examining, Nuttall and Willmott have shown that we already have assessment techniques for dealing with wide choices of objectives (Nuttall and Willmott 1972).

We need to remember here the problems of setting up different kinds of objectives in our courses and the associated problems of trying to assess them (Kelly 1977). The kinds of objective in the Nuffield 'A' level chemistry course are classified similarly to those in Bloom's *Taxonomy of Educational Objectives* (Bloom 1956), whereas the skills and abilities promoted by the Schools Council's Integrated Science Project (at 'O' level) are largely based on the ideas of Gagné's *The Conditions of Learning* (1970). But, as Matthews and Leece (1976) admit, we still have some way to go in assessing some of the higher cognitive skills such as the ability to synthesize or to hypothesize. If we want to evaluate aspects in the 'affective domain' we meet with even more difficult problems, as we do, too, in 'aesthetic' subjects. That examination boards and teachers are seriously tackling these more difficult matters is a sign that we are really trying to evaluate some of the more important educational aspects of our courses. It is also an indication that we are seeking ways of being as objective as possible in areas which were hitherto regarded as too subjective to evaluate reliably. Such attempts at assessment in these areas will help to give added status and respectability to many subjects which have been pejoratively termed 'non-academic'.

### *Concern about comparability of standards*

This discussion leads us into a consideration of the comparability of the standards of different kinds of assessment – the matter of the third criticism of examinations. In the search for directions and guidance in the mid-nineteenth century many examinations proliferated. Universities developed their own 'local' and 'school' examinations. Besides these, other bodies came into the field at that time, notably the College of Preceptors (founded in 1846) and the Society of Arts (founded in 1754, and becoming 'Royal' in 1908), which, in 1854 designed examinations for adults in mechanics institutes. In 1878 the City and Guilds of London Institute was founded, with interests similar to those of the Society of Arts which had now widened its concern to include commercial subjects and to encouraging younger pupils to sit its examinations.

These examinations were not always suitable for those who took them, and people found it difficult to judge their relative standards and merits. Eventually a Board of Education Circular (849) in 1914 proposed that a central coordinating body be set up with authority to decide on standards in examinations and to have a general oversight of regional boards without lessening their powers. The Circular also proposed to bring in teachers 'either by representation on the examining body or by a system of consultation' and to enable them to submit their own syllabuses and their own assessments of their pupils' performances, for borderline cases at any rate. Then, in 1917, the Secondary Schools Examinations Council came into being to advise the Board of Education. Throughout the twentieth century the many bodies continued to attract candidates in schools which were, at the same time, also subscribing to the dozens of local 'leaving certificates'. Concern for standards, and for undesirable pressures of these examinations on curricula, resulted in the Beloe Report of 1960 recommending radical changes in examining for those pupils not taking GCE. The Ministry decided that it ought to step in to devise a plan for validating on a national level its own schemes of local examinations. At the same time the Beloe Report advocated setting up a 'research and development unit' to assist the Secondary Schools Examinations Council. The CSE followed in 1965.

These moves, together with those already existing for GCE, helped considerably in easing worries about standards in the external examinations. Examinations by the RSA, City and Guilds and so on rapidly fell out of use in the school sector. But questions remained about the standards between the boards (eight for GCE and fourteen for CSE). In 1964 the Schools Council for Curriculum and Examinations took over responsibilities from the Secondary Schools Examinations Council, with one of its main functions being the coordination of secondary school examinations in England and Wales. It has overall responsibility for national standards and has researched into the comparability of (a) standards between the GCE boards; (b) standards between the CSE boards; (c) standards between the GCE and CSE boards; and (d) standards between subjects within boards. Several other comparability studies have also been made, e.g. between different years (Nuttall 1971; Forrest 1971; Forrest and Smith 1972; Schools Council 1966). The main study was the 1968 Monitoring Experiment which 'revealed no evidence of a lack of comparability of standards in each of the wide range of subjects' (Nuttall, Backhouse, and Willmott 1974). The Schools Council Examinations Bulletin 29 (1974b) also shows evidence of comparability and consistency between the GCE and CSE boards. This is not unexpected when we remember that the same committee discussed the standards in both examinations in deciding to equate a grade 1 pass in CSE to a pass at 'O' level. That same Bulletin reports several other interesting results. Both the GCE and CSE boards show consistent tendencies to mark some subjects more 'severely' or 'leniently' than others;

English language and English literature are more leniently assessed than French and chemistry 'together with physics in the GCE sector and mathematics in the CSE sector'. French and the physical sciences seem to be regarded by pupils and, perhaps, teachers as more 'difficult' than some other subjects, and evidence supports this by indicating that those subjects are taken mainly by more able students.

Questions arise, too, about comparability between the different kinds of assessment, between, say, essay and objective methods. A famous study done in 1935 by Hartog and Rhodes, which does not appear to have been repeated, compared the marking of different examiners of the same essays on two occasions. It showed a remarkable difference of standard between the examiners and between the marking of individual examiners on different occasions (Lewis 1974). But many of us still have great faith in essay-type answers. The report in the Schools Council Examinations Bulletin 29 (1974b) does, however, indicate a far greater consistency in the marking of these answers than did Hartog and Rhodes. Objective tests are easier to validate, though they are usually more difficult to devise. They have the advantage of being properly pretested and made statistically reliable, whereas essay questions do not have this kind of reliability. However, it is probably not as helpful to think of comparing these two kinds of assessment in this way as it is to see them as different but as equally acceptable for different purposes.

Research and development of assessment techniques are going on all the time in order to make them more reliable and to generate moderating procedures to ensure continued levels of comparability. It is worth mentioning that most research in examinations has been towards improving their validity and reliability rather than towards developing new kinds of examinations for different educational purposes. As mentioned earlier, several new developments have been initiated for these latter purposes in recent years. Indeed, examination boards have been the stimulus to curriculum development in some cases, as, for example in new examination syllabuses set up in Design and Technology at 'O' level and 'A' level in London University, which served to promote changes in our notion of education in the craft subjects (Kelly 1977). The search for objectivity and comparability in examinations has given teachers the confidence to be more sure of their ground in curriculum matters, especially in development and innovation.

### *Confusion over the purposes and uses of examinations*

This discussion has revealed that there have been different purposes for which examinations have been developed, and these have not always been understood. Most people tend to see them as a main means of selecting pupils by competition for different, often élite professions or higher education. Many examinations were and are for these sorts of purpose whilst others, set up for different purposes, have become used in these ways. The GCE 'O' and 'A' levels were originally intended to be *qualifying* examinations, to indicate that possessors of certificates had reached a level of attainment to qualify them either for sixth-form courses (as with 'O' level) or for university entrance (as with 'A' level). They had only a pass/fail classification, though later, grades were sent to schools for their internal use. Only the scholarship level papers were designed for competitive purposes. But only a couple of years after its introduction in 1951 the 'A' level began to be used for *selection* purposes by universities, and the Minister agreed to recommendations to introduce different grades in response to pressures to use the 'A' level in the competition stakes for university entrance (Montgomery 1965). This had bad effects on the sixth-form curriculum by forcing extreme specialization, cramming and the 'rat race' mentality upon teachers and pupils alike. Nearly ten years after its inception and after much deliberation the 'A' level was changed to include five grades, A to E, with A and B being used for *predictive* purposes in indicating candidates' suitability for honours degree courses. The Secondary Schools Examinations Council still claimed the examination to be noncompetitive, and that the new grades were merely 'to assess standards of excellence, not to discriminate between rivals' (Montgomery 1965, p. 147).

A similar discussion had gone on in the 1920s and 1930s with the School Certificate and Higher School Certificate, and similar fates had befallen them also. The Norwood Report in 1943 had discussed a new examination (which eventually materialized as the GCE) and stressed its purpose as not being selective or competitive. But it was not to be so in the long run. Throughout the history of examinations there has been a dispute between those who want to avoid competition and those who think that the only fair method is by selection and competition.

There was, of course, a whole period, mainly in the nineteenth century, when 'competitive examinations' were all the rage. They developed for several reasons, one of which was the need to draw on a wider social background of people to fill the ever-growing requirements of a far-flung political and economic empire. Another was that of raising and maintaining high standards in public and academic circles. These and other reasons emphasized the desirability of replacing advancement by patronage with advancement by merit and individual worth. Universities issued degree results with the pass lists which we still have today. The Society of Arts from its earliest days encouraged prizes and awards for industry, and continues to do so. At the same time as the opening up of the academic and administrative worlds, many people were concerned at 'the social menace of a huge academic proletariat', as Sadler wrote in the 1930s, echoing a fear expressed through several centuries (Morris 1961, p. 23). But as R.A.C. Oliver has reminded us, the 'dual function of educational systems – to educate and to assign people to roles – is a perennial source of difficulty' (Oliver 1961, p. 166). Society needs to develop all its human resources, but it also has to cope with the results of these social developments. The proposers and opposers of contemporary efforts at mass education, and the devices for assessing the pupils, still invoke the traditional arguments. Whilst supporters of the proposed common examination at 16+ currently being discussed look for a certificate of *attainment* (in which no one 'fails' but merely has higher or lower levels of attainment), others are concerned about giving adequate incentive and justice to those at the top who are entering the competitive lists.

Morris (1961) has suggested that examinations may be put into four groups: (1) those devised as a means of maintaining standards; (2) those planned as incentive to effort; (3) those planned for administrative purposes; and (4) those as a tool for social engineering. He goes on to point out that examinations designed for one purpose may be *used* for other purposes. The GCE 'O' level, for example, may be used to test the standards of pupils' attainments after a five-year secondary school course. It may also be used as an incentive to stimulate pupils to work and, indeed, was often used in this way after ROSLA in secondary modern schools. Then again, it may be used for organizing different 'sets' in the fourth and fifth forms, and for planning the shape of the sixth forms – an administrative use. It is also used as ammunition by politicians in their views on shaping society in different ways.

### *The lack of teachers' influence on examinations*

A discussion of the uses of examinations brings us to the final part of this review. Teachers and administrators are now putting examinations into a wider context of assessment and evaluation. External examinations are seen as only part of a repertoire of assessment methods which teachers can draw on to improve their courses, to improve their understanding of individual pupils' attainment, and to improve the teaching and learning in schools. The emphasis has now moved to the *teacher* as a central figure in assessment rather than as merely a follower of external examiners' syllabuses. Examination boards are responding encouragingly here. Perhaps the greatest step was that of instituting the CSE in 1965. It brought teachers into direct involvement in examining in a system which had national status and reputation. Previous 'local' leaving certificates had also involved teachers and had often developed imaginative syllabuses, but their comparable standards were suspect. CSE introduced Mode 3, as mentioned before, where schools set and marked their own internal examinations which were moderated by the local board. It encouraged the development and use of a wider range of assessment techniques, some of which were referred to earlier. As well as these, it also enabled teachers to visit schools other than their own in their moderation exercises. (Mode 3 is also available in the GCE but is still only rarely used.) Though the Mode 3 in CSE gave a great opening to teachers, their traditional reticence made them slow to take up the opportunity. Mode 3 is still used in only a minority of cases, and though on the increase accounted for only 14.8 per cent of all the subject entries in CSE in 1972 (Macintosh and Smith 1974). It must be acknowledged, however, that Mode 3 is costly to administer, especially in terms of time and human resources.

An important aspect of 'teacher modesty', as Macintosh and Smith call it, is that teachers have not the training and experience to set examinations that would match up to national standards. Indeed, the time, energy and resources for preparing such examinations are heavy and daunting. Examination boards have been very helpful here in giving practical advice to teachers by, for instance, setting up 'question banks' of validated and tried questions prepared for different purposes, and in giving guidelines to help teachers prepare their examination objectives (Hoste and Bloomfield 1975). Another element in 'teacher modesty' is, perhaps, a tendency in all of us to be very sure of our ground before making any moves. A teacher may, therefore, spend much time polishing up a course only to have his brainchild beaten down by an examination board. What the boards welcome is *early* approaches to them by teachers, so that basic ideas and tentative proposals can be discussed, and advice, support and encouragement given, so that when the teachers' syllabuses are finalized, they reflect their educational aims and the appropriate assessment standards of the boards (Macintosh and Smith 1974). Major changes in Mode 1 syllabuses are subject to relatively slow rates of change which teachers often interpret as inflexibility and as reactionary attitudes to new ideas, but as Wyatt (1975) has explained, it normally must take up to five years before a suggested reform can be effected.

External assessments may be useful to teachers in filling out their knowledge gained from internal assessments, from teachers' reports, pupils' own wishes and interests, parents' hopes and fears. At the moment, and judging from the experience of Nuffield 'A' level chemistry, we can say that external examination boards are better able to give teachers advice on the 'average profile achievement of *all* students and *groups* of students than in attempting to report profiles of *individual* students' (Matthews and Leece 1976). (The profile mentioned here is the breakdown of types of response to answers set on different kinds of objective *within* a subject examination.) Perhaps we shall eventually be able to get useful techniques for giving us reliable information from examination boards on individual students. If so, teachers will have a piece of firm evidence to put alongside their own profiles of the attainments and performances of individuals. Such a profile could be seen, then, as a complex, sensitive, sophisticated monitoring system for the teacher's better understanding of the effectiveness of his teaching and for the pupil's understanding of the efficiency and potentialities of his learning.

## The teacher in the central position

We have arrived now at a view of the teacher as the key figure in pupils' education, as a truly professional person managing the complicated sets of factors that directly impinge on his work with pupils. But this professionalism has implications for the training and support of teachers. Macintosh and Smith (1974) have discussed some of the main implications of these developments. The obvious point in this present context is the continued growth of the links between teachers and examination boards so that the former can draw on special skills and expertise within the boards, whilst the latter can more closely follow the educational aims of the teachers and their pupils. But this link should be part of a wider 'communications network'. There is already a loose, informal network of agencies like Local Education Authorities, their advisers, and their teachers' centres, as well as the Schools Council, HMIs, periodicals, conferences and so on. But a drawback is the diffuseness of the network which results in teachers not really knowing whom to contact for a particular purpose or spending too much time trying to communicate with the right people. Macintosh and Smith would like to see the hub of the network residing with the examination boards, with some of the various agencies being called upon through the boards to help teachers in the schools. This would be a service available to teachers to enable them to make better, informed, professional judgements; to allow them 'to move towards a freer curriculum as they see it rather than as others see it for them' (Macintosh and Smith 1974, p. 79). And as we have already seen, a central aspect of this freer curriculum is the development of appropriate courses for individual pupils, which is, after all, what education is all about. From the mass, gross, insensitive, impersonal methods of examining characteristic of periods in the past, we can envisage the further growth of personalized assessment and its concommitant curricula.

This is not to suggest that we shall lose our concern for 'standards'. Indeed, it will be especially necessary to continue to refine our techniques of assessing students' standards at local, regional and national levels. There is no logical inconsistency between the concepts of individualized assessment and interpersonal standards. What is required is further research into relating them in reliably practical ways. The final evidence of success or failure in educational activities is the evidence of standards achieved.

These developments are to be welcomed from both the educational point of view and that of public accountability of teachers and their work. Public accountability is an important factor, and it is educationally desirable as well as professionally prudent that teachers develop their own professional criteria and standards of accountability before outside bodies impose undesirable ones upon them. The recent establishment (1975) by the DES of the Assessment of Performance Unit (APU) has been seen as a threat to teachers from an outside body, but it could easily become another source of relevant data available to teachers to use according to their own professional judgement.

## The political context of examinations

The outcome of the discussion is more complex than might appear at first. Examinations and their associated curricula are inevitably situated in a political arena. One aspect of this is the concern at all levels of government with the costs of education as a whole. Cost-effectiveness is a proper matter here as with all areas of public expenditure. With the continuing increase in the numbers of examination candidates has come the need to develop those kinds of assessment which can cope with these people reliably and efficiently and for the minimal cost. Traditional essay-type papers are expensive to mark, in both time and money, besides requiring costly moderating procedures in order to avoid charges being made of their being too subjective. The increased use of objective tests such as the multiple-choice papers is linked with computer processing. Though expensive initially in capital outlay, the running costs are far less than for the other labour-intensive marking arrangements. A case could be argued for encouraging the use of Mode 2 examinations, so that the somewhat expensive Mode 3 examining could give way to a system in which teachers' independent use of curricular syllabuses could be examined by the reliably tested, objective means of the examination boards' resources.

Allied to this is the setting-up of the item banks of pretested, validated questions which can be stored in computers and be available to individual teachers or groups of teachers and other examiners for use in internal and external examinations. Not only does this keep down the costs of examining, but also the users of this kind of central facility can better answer those critics who fear the loss of objective standards when more personalized, individualized profiles of assessment are adopted. Indeed, if GCE and CSE boards came together to use a common facility locally, or even nationally, costs would be further minimized and standards made truly reliable (Montgomery 1978).

The resulting centralization of test items and examination syllabuses could be a source of worry to those who value independence and the local control of assessment at school level. It raises, too, the issue of common core curricula and the related issues of the distribution of and access to these curricula. The proper concern of government here for justice and fairness is, in a democracy, effected in the devolving of decision making onto publicly accountable institutions. The Assessment of Performance Unit (APU) set up by the DES is attempting to monitor the standards of groups of children in several areas of development (mathematical, language and science, followed later by a first modern language, aesthetical, physical, personal and social development), whilst the recent HMIs' discussion paper, 'Curriculum 11–16', proposes eight areas of experience which should be common to all pupils.

Graham Byrne Hill, in Chapter 7, gives a closely knit discussion of different views of democracy, in which he traces the place of legitimate decision making at different levels in education. He suggests that the tendency to develop 'democracy as communication' may result in a more suitable way of accommodating the different views of groups in a plural society than is that of participatory democracy.

The employment of both centrally promoted agencies such as the APU and the HMIs in trying to define a common minimal core of experience and the standards of achievement in them, and of democracy as communication where elective curriculum areas are under dispute and review, is valid in this discussion of examinations. Teachers, whether as individuals, as members of a school staff or as organized bodies, are only one interested party in the network of groups which must make decisions about examinations. We recall that the Schools Council, with its teacher majority prior to 1978, had its recommendations for a twenty-point system for grading GCE 'A' level results turned down in 1972 by the Secretary of State, Mrs. Margaret Thatcher, after she had made her own test of the opinions of the interested parties. More recently, just before the general election in the spring of 1979, the then Secretary of State, Mrs. Shirley Williams, effectively put into long-term cold storage the Schools Councils' recommendations for 'N and F' level examinations. Neither of these Secretaries of State judged it appropriate to make a decision which would undermine the confidence held by many people in the 'A' level. Mrs. Williams's reconstitution of the Schools Council in 1978 was clearly a move to reduce the power of the teachers' unions' representatives on that body, and to increase the level of democratic participation and representation.

At primary school level, the abolition of the 11+ has freed the curriculum to some considerable extent but, as in the ILEA for example, headteachers assess their children's abilities in mathematics, English and 'verbal reasoning', by using tests common to the authority's schools. As Rust and Harris (1967) say, however, this is still selection of a sort in that the results, together with other profile evidence, are used for secondary school allocation purposes. They also explain that this examining is in the hands of teachers where, they say, it rightly belongs. Educational and social dangers of this are pointed to in Chapter 7, where Graham Byrne Hill recalls instances of the too great power of teachers' unions in the democratic process and indicates the desirability of developing more rationally the dynamics of democracy as communication.

With the increasing involvement of teachers in the development of examinations over the years, and their maturing professionalism, comes the need for their being more publicly accountable. The power of teachers, or rather the different power of different groups of teachers, is being scrutinized at local and national levels. It may be argued that their authority and, perhaps, their power are stronger now that they are called upon to be more articulate, more responsive and more responsible to the wider community. Public examinations must respond to the needs and purposes of society, which include the educational needs as understood by teachers as professionals. For example, early in 1953, what was soon to be known as the Associated Examining Board (AEB) was set up in response to the calls of interested parties in technical and commercial education to cater for these areas of knowledge in the school sector where, hitherto, they had been neglected at GCE level (Earnshaw 1974). This new GCE board is, then, the only one of the eight which is not of university origin.

Political as well as educational arguments figure significantly in the debate over the common examination at 16+. Moral concern over the access of all students to socially valued courses and examinations is the legitimate interest of government. But this concern is linked with an ideological concern for egalitarianism which worries those people who question the possibility of a single examination system being capable of doing justice to a very wide range of student achievement. Democratic processes must be seen to work out a solution to this matter, in which the educational interest of teachers is a key factor. It may well be, however, as Montgomery (1978) suggests, that the need for examinations at 16+ may decline as more and more students stay on in schools and colleges beyond the statutory leaving age.

Whilst it has been argued that too great an emphasis on the use of public examinations is to be avoided, and that teachers need to develop their awareness of and skill in using other modes of assessment, it is not being claimed that public examinations should be removed altogether, as some people advocate. Democracy of any sort requires the presence of such examinations in its educational system and must prevent moves to promote what would become the anarchy of only school-based assessment, even though considerable advances have been made in making these more reliable and objective (Scottish Council for Research in Education 1977). As in other areas of educational provision, the matter of examinations is necessarily an interest of the state both in mediating the views on the minimum requirements and in settling disputes between conflicting groups which support different status cultures and examinations.

This review of examinations, with its brief discussion of the political dimension, needs to be placed in the broader context of the political influences which are explored by Graham Byrne Hill in Chapter 7 and of the administrative and organizational structures which Wynne Davies analyses in Chapter 6.

## Summary and conclusions

Throughout the long career of examinations we can see the emergence of four broad features:

1 they have always been attempts to influence and to manipulate the work of schools in one way or another;
2 they have often been attempts at remedying the undesirable effects of existing systems once they have become clear;
3 all the innovations have brought their own constraints and limitations;
4 yet nevertheless, the public examinations system is an indispensable part of our educational system.

Various outside bodies have repeatedly held sway over school curricula, especially the universities which are still very influential. The acceptance or rejection of the current 'N and F' proposals for sixth-form courses is likely to rest mainly on the views of universities. Examinations have affected the content and methods of school curricula, as well as the goals of teachers and pupils. Now we are seeing a move towards greater control of examinations and curricula by the teachers who are directly concerned with our children's education. This move should result in teachers being able to give a more professional account of themselves in the public arena.

In conclusion it can be argued that far from being the greatest constraint on curriculum, examinations are already and will increasingly become an important factor in teachers' repertoires of skills and techniques for their own curriculum development. But much work still needs to be done not only in developing the 'communications network' but also in helping teachers to see the possibilities open to them and taking steps to realize them.

We have tried to see examinations in a broader perspective which brings them into a closer, if perhaps contingent, relationship with curriculum. We might go further by suggesting, with R.S. Peters (1966), that education itself is essentially about individuals' development in certain sorts of ways which involve their coming up to some standards of achievement. If so, we can say that assessment of an individual's attainment is a necessary element in 'education', provided that the methods of examination do not conflict with other criteria of 'education', such as the development of knowledge and understanding in as wide a sense as possible, or the avoidance of methods which might lead to rote learning, coercion or the prevention of autonomous intellectual development. Such a positive view of examinations may serve to clarify our understanding of their proper place in curricular matters and to give teachers the confidence to use them in educationally valuable ways.

Rather than being anti- or non-educational aspects of schooling, examinations, properly organized, can be seen as essential to education itself. It is to be hoped that curriculum development, teacher development and examinations development will have a planned, integrated future.

# CHAPTER SIX

# ADMINISTRATIVE AND HISTORICAL ASPECTS

**Wynne Davies**

Issues related to curriculum figure prominently in the current debate on education and among these is the issue of curriculum control. Unease about standards in education, pressure for more extensive participation at all levels of policy making and demands for greater accountability have all tended to focus attention on aspects such as power and control in the education system generally and over the curriculum in particular. Events such as those surrounding the William Tyndale School, the publication of the report on 'The Nations Schools' and the Taylor Report, *A New Partnership for our Schools*, have brought a new sharpness to the debate and have led many to question whether the accepted conventional patterns of power distribution and control are any longer appropriate.

Maclure (1970) and more recently Weaver (1978) have reminded us that the concept of 'control' may be inadequate and inappropriate as a means of describing and analysing relationships between the various elements in the education system, and particularly so in relation to the curriculum. In the language of educational discourse, terms such as 'the freedom of the teacher', 'institutional autonomy' and 'academic freedom' tend to prevail in any discussion of curriculum issues. If by 'control' one implies the existence of uniform policy which is implemented at various levels in the system under the direction of a controller with a clearly defined chain of command and formal channels of communication, then it may well be claimed that in the British educational system curriculum is 'out of control'. The Secretary of State is, by the 1944 Act, required to 'promote, control and direct', but nowhere is the central government more constrained by law, tradition and convention than in relation to the curriculum. Nowhere has the attempt to initiate change according to some form of centre-periphery model met with such limited success.

There is however considerable uniformity in curriculum and in what is actually done in schools in Britain, and evidence of what Becher and Maclure (1978) describe as the 'Public Curriculum'. It contains 'those aspects which embody our education system's shared assumptions about the main things which pupils should do and learn in school' and it 'provides the general accepted framework within which individual teachers and pupils, in particular schools, insert the details which best meet their own needs'. This framework is one which in the main is prescribed formally by official bodies at all levels in the system, bodies such as the LEAs, public examination boards, teachers' associations, and central government departments. This 'Public Curriculum' does not fully encompass all that goes on in school in that a wider interpretation of curriculum would include all those offerings of socially valued knowledge, skills and attitudes made available to students through a variety of arrangements during their time at school. Consideration is given elsewhere to those elements in the social and political context of the school which help fashion, maintain and develop this wider curriculum. Here our concern will be largely with the administrative context and with institutions and groups which have a formal place in decision-making processes. Some of these, like the local education authorities and school managers and governors, have their right to influence and control legitimized by law, while others have become legitimized by convention and tradition. Many operate at points remote from the classroom but their attitudes, values, perception of needs, together with the way in which they order priorities and determine the structure of the system, all have implications for the teacher and the pupil. They influence not only the 'Public Curriculum' but also the terms and conditions under which pupil and teacher attitudes are fashioned and under which teachers and pupils 'fill in the details'.

The first section of this chapter suggests how historically the providers of educational institutions established and maintained control of curriculum. It then illustrates how devices such as codes of regulations, designed initially to enable resources to be allocated to the system, came to be used as a means of exerting influence on curriculum. The nature and extent of this control will be shown to have been constantly changing over the last century, the predominantly local influences of the mid-nineteenth century being counterbalanced by those of the central government in the last thirty years of the century. In the first half of the twentieth century the influence of organized teacher opinion became powerful, only to be challenged in recent years when strong centralizing tendencies seem again to be at work. In this section the part played over this period by bodies such as the Inspectorate and advisory councils and committees of inquiry in fashioning the 'official' view of the curriculum will be briefly considered.

In the second section it will be tentatively suggested that major changes which have occurred at the level of local government over the last decade may mean that crucial decisions on curriculum which will have considerable significance for teachers will in future be taken by local authorities. One implication of this may be that educationists and all of those interested and involved in curriculum maintenance and development will need to sensitize themselves to the new situation so as to be able to relate effectively to local policy makers.

## Curriculum as the responsibility of providing bodies

The clearest formal statement on responsibility for curriculum is that contained in Clause 23 of the 1944 Education Act which places it firmly in the hands of the local education authority. This formally acknowledges the direct link which has existed from the outset between the bodies which provide the school and the curriculum of the school, and recognizes the right of the providers to play a major part in determining what will be taught and the conditions under which teaching will take place.

In the first half of the nineteenth century local providers of early elementary schools defended strenuously their right to determine the purposes of their schools, often refusing badly needed financial aid when it became available because they feared the threat to their control that might come with it. The first state grant of 1833 in support of voluntary schools was to be paid direct to those providers of schools who applied for it and who met the conditions laid down in the Treasury Minute. Thus, the decisions whether to apply for building grant and whether to accept it on the terms offered were made at local level by the providers of the school. When they accepted grant they still contributed to cost on a pound-for-pound basis and thereby safeguarded their right to control.

The curriculum, of the endowed grammar schools was, for the first forty years of the century, governed by trust deeds backed by statute. The restriction that they were only 'for teaching grammatically the learned languages' was removed by the Grammar Schools Act of 1840, and headmasters in conjunction with managers and governors were able, where they wished, to introduce a range of new subjects for the first time. It was in the 1860s that the first formal statement appeared on the relative responsibilities of heads and of governing bodies of public schools and of endowed grammar schools. Both the Clarendon Report (1864) and the Taunton Report (1868) located responsibility for curriculum clearly with the governors.

> . . . What should be taught and what importance should be given to each subject are therefore subjects for the Governing Body; how to teach is a question for the Head Master (Public Schools Commission 1864).

The statement by the Endowed Schools Commission was brief and clear. The governors were to have 'the general direction of the conduct and curriculum of the school', and the headmaster was to control 'internal organization, management and discipline'.

In the last quarter of the nineteenth century school boards supplemented the school provision made by the voluntary bodies. Most of the large boards such as those at Leeds, Hull, Manchester and Birmingham preferred to administer their schools centrally and to retain responsibility for curriculum in their hands. They sometimes appointed curriculum committees to oversee the work of the schools, though other boards delegated this responsibility to managers and governors. When as a result of the 1902 Education Act the county and county boroughs were given responsibility for education, as the new providers they assumed responsibility for school management. Sir Robert Morant, Secretary to the recently established Board of Education, wished to retain strong management bodies at the level of the school as a counterbalance to the growing power of the local authorities. It was only after a bitter struggle with the Board that these authorities established their claim to effective control of their schools. They delegated substantial aspects of school policy making such as those related to curriculum to school governors in maintained secondary schools though, save in the counties, it was up to the local authority to decide whether to appoint managers of elementary schools and what responsibilities, if any, to delegate to them. Voluntary schools naturally retained the tradition of having managing and governing bodies, their composition and powers varying in relation to the status they chose to adopt vis-à-vis the county schools. The power granted by local authorities to managers and governors of the county schools was delegated power, and as such could be withdrawn. Ultimate responsibility and power remained with the LEA and this was to be confirmed by the 1944 Education Act.

It was in this first decade of the century that the new local authorities established their Education Office to administer the local education service, and it was from the struggle with the Board of Education that the office of chief education officer was to emerge as a powerful element. With time, they, as the senior educational advisers to the LEAs, were to play a major part in determining the quality of the education service. As Claire Pratt (1973) has rightly claimed, the 'thrust of innovation' was to come largely from them. It will be suggested later that recent developments in local government will again underline the importance of the local 'office' in relation to curriculum planning as well as to other aspects of local education more usually thought of as being the province of the administrator.

## State aid and the machinery of control

### *Codes and inspection*

Provision of aid by the state to voluntary bodies and later to local authorities was a predominant feature of the development of the English school system. The principle of state support was a source of widespread controversy and the terms on which grant should be offered and received was a cause of constant debate. Much of this was focused on the 'religious question' and on the reluctance of the denominations to concede any control over secular instruction to the state on the grounds that the curriculum was indivisible and that this would soon lead to control over religious education. Almost from the outset there is evidence that state influence on curriculum was exercised through the grant mechanism even though in its original form the grant was designed only to 'aid private subscriptions for the erection of school houses for the education of the poorer classes'. The second half of the nineteenth century saw an elaboration of a system whereby Codes of the Education Department and the Science and Art Department came to influence curriculum. The Revised Code of 1862, in stating specifically the contents of the elementary school curriculum and in relating payment of grant to results achieved in examination, perpetuated a system under which grant was used as a device to induce schools to fashion curriculum in ways determined by the authors of the Code. Though the Code was refined and it became a more sophisticated instrument with time, it was its cramping effect on curriculum, and the legacy of bitterness and hostility that it encouraged, that was remembered after it was abolished in the 1890s.

Less familiar to many today is the system instituted by the Science and Art Department in 1859 in an attempt to encourage the study of science. The Royal Commission on Scientific Instruction reported in 1872 that the system of payment by results had given a remarkable impetus to elementary science teaching and increased the number of students under instruction from 500 in 1860 to 34,000 in 1870 and to over 100,000 by 1890. The Minute of 1859 included only six subjects as grant earning, but by 1897 the number had increased to twenty-five and included subjects such as building construction and naval architecture as well as the basic sciences.

Opposition to state provision of teacher training meant that the college training of teachers was almost exclusively in the hands of the religious bodies to the end of the century. The principle of support for the colleges had however been accepted from the start, originally, as with schools, in the form of building grant. Shortage of cash and a shortage of candidates of good quality were two of the many problems facing those who were attempting to staff the schools. A step towards their solution came with the introduction of the pupil-teacher system in the 1840s and with the establishment of Queens Scholarships to provide the best of these with financial support when on college courses. Grants to students and grants to augment teachers' salaries, together with other forms of financial support, provided the central administration with an instrument through which influence could be exerted. Awards were made only if the recipients fulfilled specific conditions, and soon these conditions came to include many related to curriculum. Syllabuses of the training colleges were prescribed in detail and regularly revised in Regulations from the Department of Education, and through them one can see how restricted was the prevailing view of the needs and the status of those who were to serve in the elementary school system.

The extent to which the Codes actually influenced the work of schools depended to some extent on the effectiveness of government inspection. Appointed to '. . . collect facts and information and to report the results of their inspection to the Committee of Council . . .', they were 'to bear in mind that this inspection is not intended as a means of exercising control'. However, in spite of these instructions issued in the Minute of 1839–1840, the contribution made to educational advance by the early inspectors was considerable. They gave constructive advice, encouraged experimentation, and spread knowledge of good practice. Their influence over teacher education through the examination and certification of teachers was powerful and was retained well into the twentieth century. During the period of payment by results their influence over what was taught in school became tighter and the climate in which they worked became harsher. The considerable achievements of some schools under the system owed much to the initiative of those members of the Inspectorate who helped teachers overcome the rigours of the Code. The contribution of the Inspectorate, then as now, fell short of control, but through their independence of mind and through the quality of their advice, their influence has at times been immense.

### *Fashioning of the 'official view'*

In the absence of machinery of local government, instruments such as the Codes provided a direct link between the administrators at the Education Department and the individual schools and enabled resources to be channelled to them. They became the means by which the clerks and the examiners at the Department were able to ensure that their perception of the needs of the schools, and of the curriculum appropriate to the schools, would prevail. In these circumstances, those who helped to fashion the official view of curriculum as represented by the clerks and examiners had a considerable influence on the life and work of the schools. Observation by the Inspectorate has always helped central government formulate a view on matters such as curriculum, and as 'eyes and ears' of the Department they remain the main formal source of advice. The impact of recent reports such as those on Primary Education (1977c), and on 'Ten Good Schools', suggests that in terms of official policy formulation their influence may be enhanced over the next few years.

Advisory councils and committees of inquiry too have helped in policy making through a long series of reports presented to the central administration over the last century. Their influence on practical policy has depended not only on the quality of their enquiry and advice but on factors such as their timing, the level of priority given to them by the government of the time and the attitude adopted to them by pressure groups in the system.

The impact of the Newcastle Commission Report (1861) was great partly because its recommendations were based on the first extensive survey of the elementary school system. It also had an impact because they were in accord with the prevailing views of the time. More recently the Bullock Committee reflected an underlying concern about the quality of language and in turn stimulated interest and inspired people to act. Over the years other reports have simply been shelved or have been used as delaying tactics. Much depends on the extent to which their recommendations can be reconciled with planning being undertaken in other parts of the system. The central advisory councils were not reconvened after 1967 because it was claimed that they had outlived their usefulness as bodies to inquire and advise, and were simply duplicating work done by other agencies in the system. In the late nineteenth century, when government control was relatively direct and the means of gathering information rather limited, the commissions of inquiry and advisory bodies had a role as informing agencies which was more important than today, when there is a far more sophisticated system of information gathering available. Nevertheless, these still have, as Kogan and Packwood (1974) indicate, a contribution to make. They provide examples of good educational practice and by publishing arguments for change they can help a wider public to identify them. They at times provide the government with the consents of those influential elements in the system whose views are sought on particular issues, and can so help legitimize new thinking.

The means by which these committees are appointed, the range of interests represented on them and the ways in which their terms of reference are determined are some of the many questions that arise in relation to them today. In that these bodies have an influence on the development of attitudes, and on the formulation of policy, they are questions worthy of the attention of the curriculum planner.

## Relaxation and reassertion of central government influence

Tight control of school and college curriculum by regulation, inspection and examination came in the first quarter of this century. Regulations were to give way to guidance by 'Handbooks of Suggestions for Teachers'. The process of emancipation was to reach its climax after the publication of the Hadow Reports of 1926 and 1931, when the emphasis was placed on the freedom and responsibility of the teacher in matters related to curriculum. Two developments were to encourage this.

The first of these was the growing professionalism of teachers and with it their increasing political effectiveness. The main teachers' associations had emerged during the last quarter of the century and had established their right to speak for teachers. Supported by a strong tradition of school management and of powerful headship in the independent sector, they were able to ensure, with the aid of central government, that a considerable amount of effective power to run the schools would be granted to teachers.

The second development was that of growing university involvement in the field of teacher education and of school examinations. The creation of joint boards in 1926 took examination of the 'academic elements' of college courses out of the hands of the Inspectorate and made it a joint responsibility of the universities and the colleges, and after the McNair Report of 1943 validation of courses also became a joint responsibility. The impact of university examination boards on school examinations was growing at the turn of the century but was uncoordinated. The Secondary Schools Examinations Council was set up in 1917 to bring some order to the system, and its history to the middle of the century was one of increasing teacher involvement. Central government influence and control was by no means eliminated but the universities and the teaching profession had come to share power and responsibility on bodies which formally concerned themselves with curriculum, and on these their voice was the dominant one.

The creation of the Curriculum Study Group in the Ministry of Education in 1961 to act as a small 'commando-like unit' to make raids into the curriculum indicated a degree of dissatisfaction with the existing school curriculum and with the attempts that had been made by the teachers themselves to reform it in the 1950s. The study group was to 'try to make the Minister's voice heard rather more often and positively and no doubt more controversially' (Eccles 1960) on what was taught in the schools and the training colleges. The outcry from the profession marked the strength of feeling towards this apparent challenge to the position which had been hard won by teachers over a half century or so.

The outcry led ultimately to the setting up of the Schools Council for Curriculum and Examinations, and on it a teacher majority. This gave recognition to the claims of teachers to be strongly represented on any formal body with responsibility for decision making in the field of curriculum and examinations. The subsequent history of the Council has been well documented and its effectiveness in curriculum innovation and in the field of examinations has been widely questioned and is dealt with elsewhere in this book, the former in Chapter 3 and the latter in Chapter 5.

Recent changes in the composition of the Council, together with rejection of some of the main recommendations put forward by it for the reform of the examination system are indications of the changing attitude towards teacher influence on curriculum. It indicates too a growing pressure for involvement of others who claim a legitimate interest in curriculum, and the recent restructuring of the Council indicates that these claims are being heeded. The setting up of the Assessment of Performance Unit by the DES in 1975 with a renewed interest in testing and in monitoring the system suggests how the balance of control and interest is shifting towards the centre and towards a more clearly interventionist curriculum strategy. The resignation of Sir William Alexander from the consultative committee of the APU in 1977 seemed to confirm the view held by some that the Unit represented a return of the Curriculum Study Group with all that that seemed to imply. For some time the activities of the DES have been primarily with resources and organization, and it has respected the rights and powers of the LEAs and teachers over curriculum. The OECD Report (1975) and the Expenditure Committee Report (1975–1976) on policy making in the DES believed that this separation of organization and resources from curriculum itself was a weakness in our system, and they recommended that they should be more fully integrated. Since the publication of these reports the more positive approaches to curriculum by the Inspectorate and in the Green Paper 'Education in Schools' (1977d) are further indications of change. The changed composition of the Schools Council, and in particular the increase in representation and power of the LEAs and the DES on the Finance and Priorities Committee, again illustrate the changing balance of power. Joint consultation, broad representation of interests on consultative committees and similar bodies will continue to be a major feature of policy formulation in education, but the balance of power and the nature of the responsibilities of these bodies is in question.

The impetus towards the creation of new control mechanisms in education may have been increased by another quite different development in the 1950s and 1960s. This was the development of educational technology which was so rapid in that period. Rapid developments such as those of educational television have provided the educationist with a potentially powerful means of exerting influence, but two decades of experience have in the main indicated the limitations rather than the practical possibilities of the new technology. Decisions about the sorts of programme to be produced and when and how they should be transmitted may effect a very large number of teachers. Decisions of this kind are at the moment taken by networks of committees on which teachers are represented, and decisions as to whether the television sets are turned on in individual schools are left to heads and teachers. At times developments have been checked or reversed because appropriate consultations with relevant groups have not followed accepted conventional patterns. This occurred in the early 1960s when controversy arose over what was claimed to be lack of consultation by the television companies before they announced their first schools programmes. The development at national level, or within a local authority, of a system of educational television, or the investment in some other form of advanced technology, is extremely costly and has an impact on the range of resources available for other purposes. Programme content can be transmitted to a vast audience, programme timing can have implications for school timetable even though the video-tape exists. Given the vast costs involved and the nation-wide implications of any one decision, it may be that the claim that curriculum is too important to leave to the teacher and the processes of learning through technology too expensive to allow absolute discretion to the individual teacher over whether or not to switch on the television set, will lead to renewed pressure for new control mechanisms.

## Local authority responsibility for curriculum

There are clear indications of centralizing tendencies at work in the education system over recent years and these are having subtle effects on decision making on curriculum. Developments in local government which have taken place over the same period may however have even greater significance for curriculum development over the next decade or so. Demands for accountability in relation to the curriculum are directed largely at the control exercised by the teaching profession, but they have also brought home to people generally the fact that responsibility lies formally with the local education authority. Risinghill in the 1960s and William Tyndale in the 1970s raised questions not only concerning the powers and responsibilities of teachers but also those of the local authority and its officers.

Attention was drawn to this responsibility by the Department of Education and Science when outlining in the Green Paper 'Education in Schools' (1977d) what it saw to be the responsibilities of the various partners in 'the proper functions of the education system'. The Green Paper indicated that the DES would seek a review by the LEAs of curricular arrangements in their areas, and the form of this review was set out in Circular

14/77. It was intended to gather systematic information about arrangements in order to 'enable the Secretary of State to assess how far the practice of local education authorities meets national needs, and will assist in the preparation of future national plans. . . . From the information gathered the Secretary of State expects to be able to gather examples of good practice which can be recommended for wider adoption.' The Circular gives some indication of how the central authority views national needs and interests in the curriculum field. It seeks information on arrangements made for attaining balance and breadth in curriculum and for meeting the need to reconcile curricular claims such as those of a multi-racial society, careers education and moral education, with those of the basic skills. Among these basic skills special mention is made of English, mathematics, modern languages, science and religious education, because . . . 'they have given rise to recent discussion and concern', though 'other subjects are not to be considered less important'. The fifty-seven detailed questions posed in the Circular provide a framework within which the local authorities are encouraged to frame their report. These questions deal with general matters such as the procedures and systematic arrangements made by local education authorities to carry out their responsibilities under Section 23 of the 1944 Education Act; arrangements for collating information about curricula offered in schools; the part played by inspectors, teachers and school managers and governors; the help given by the local authority to schools to decide on the relative emphasis they should give to particular aspects of the curriculum. Other questions are more specific and deal with matters such as the authority's policy towards the teaching of French in the primary school, and policy towards the teaching of science to pupils up to the age of sixteen in secondary schools. The emphasis is on local authority responsibility for, and involvement in, curiculum policy, and it underlines the formal statutory requirement that ultimately the LEA is answerable. The Circular however concludes with the declaration that 'any action that may follow the gathering of evidence will be taken only after consultation with local education authorities, teachers and others'. It thus acknowledges the conventional situation in which effective power is delegated by the local education authority to others at the level of the school.

In their response to the Circular many LEAs may assert, as one of the largest of them has, that 'while it delegates oversight of curriculum to governors and managers and control of it to heads, the authority retains ultimate control and reserves the right to give direction on matters relating to powers it has delegated'. Local authorities may be involving themselves more directly in curriculum partly as a reaction to difficulties experienced and discontent expressed about the state of schools and their curricula.

There have however been other developments underway for some time which have created conditions which encourage a shift of decision making towards the local authority. The first of these is the changing role of the CEO and educational administrators within the local authority. They have from the outset had substantial responsibility for educational policy making. Two other developments, the setting up of new management structures and falling school rolls, may result in the concentration of more detailed policy making at the level of the 'office' and the council committee. The fact that these developments coincide with a period of financial stringency would seem to suggest that this tendency will increase.

## Changing role of the Chief Education Officer

The Chief Education Officer has, since the turn of the century, occupied a key position in the education service as head of a team of professional administrators responsible for the day-to-day running of the system. He serves as senior adviser to the education committee and the council on all aspects of education, and coordinates the work of the main groups involved in educational policy making at local level.

The increased professionalism of the teaching force has meant that, particularly since 1944, the CEO has been required to work out a new relationship with the profession quite unlike the paternalistic and authoritarian régimes that were a familiar feature of an earlier age. As Cook (1973) has reminded us, in general the relationship with heads is not that of manager and subordinate but one in which the officer can, sometimes informally and unofficially, exert influence and control, and initiate and encourage developments. Major innovations in education such as the creation of forms of comprehensive school, school camps, community colleges and the teaching of modern languages in primary schools can all be associated with the names of particular education officers. This developmental aspect of their work has for many CEOs always been recognized as a primary responsibility.

The style of administration varies from one authority to another and reflects factors such as the different personalities and interests of the CEO, and the nature and strength of political control. The style is displayed not only in the nature of relationships formed and the degree of openness of the lines of communication between the Education Office and the other elements in the system, but also in the way in which structures are created to support the work of teachers.

Though the distribution of resources to the various sectors of the education service within the local authority is determined to some extent by national legislation, regulation and agreements, a considerable amount of discretion remains at local level and decisions made by administrators can have major implications for the curriculum planner. The nature and scale of the advisory service and its responsibility for allocation of finance, materials and staff to schools can have a crucial bearing on attitudes adopted to curriculum and on possibilities of curriculum change. An advisory service organized entirely on a subject basis may well have a different impact on curriculum from that organized on some other basis, particularly in those many authorities in which the views of advisers carry weight in discussion about allocation of additional resources for school curriculum projects. The provision made for staff development both within and beyond the school depends very largely on the attitudes adopted to it by the local authority and the officers. Opportunities for in-service training, the extent of support provided by teachers' centres, the quality of materials and equipment available to schools are all largely determined at the level of the local authority. The significance of decisions such as these for the curriculum planner is considerable.

Other responsibilities of the LEA, such as that for staffing schools, are equally important. The way in which the local authority officers implement nationally agreed staffing ratios and order their staffing priorities varies from one authority to another. Those which have evolved ways of sensitizing themselves to the needs of schools generally and to the special needs of particular schools are more likely to create a climate supportive of sound curriculum maintenance than those authorities which have not. Whether to delegate to heads the responsibility for appointing staff, or whether to allow flexibility in the allocation of resources through some form of 'alternative use of resources scheme', are other sorts of policy decision taken at local authority level which obviously have an impact on what can be done by the curriculum planner within the school. Perhaps most significant of all is the power of the local authority to appoint heads of schools. Responsible for internal management, they are, in spite of moves in some places towards more participatory forms of internal organization and decision making, still the most important single 'gatekeepers' determining which influences on curriculum will be able to enter the school and to flourish within it. LEA policy on appointment of heads therefore remains crucial.

The local authority is also responsible formally for determining the 'educational character of the school', and for the overall organizational pattern. Over the last ten years central government has increased its control over this area by persuasion or compulsion, but considerable power still remains with the LEA. Whether schools should be single sex or mixed, whether they should be large or small, whether the intake be selective or non-selective and whether or not the pupils should be drawn from a clearly defined neighbourhood are all decisions taken by the LEA. There are constraints upon them when making decisions of this kind, some provided by central government, some by teachers and parents, but the need for sound policy making and administration within the LEA is clear. These are all concerned with creating the detail of a framework within which teachers and pupils interact and within which they in turn make decisions on curriculum.

## New structures and procedures of management

Not least of the constraints upon the Education Department is that it is located within a multi-purpose local authority as one department among many competing for resources. In the past it was generally the largest of these departments and it benefited in many ways from the 'special relationship' it had with the DES. Both formally shared responsibility for education. There were national requirements that had to be met by the local authority, and there were regular channels of communication between the education office and the DES as well as links with it through the HMI. The period from the mid 1940s to the mid 1960s was one of expansion and for the most part one of optimism when there was ready acceptance of the view that investment in education was sound investment. From the late 1950s grant from central government to local authorities was paid as a block grant and this allowed some discretion to the local authorities over allocation of grant to meet local needs. Circumstances in this period were such as to make the claims of the Education Departments strong and their ability to win resources considerable.

More recently, restrictions on spending applied by the central government have been a major constraint on policy making generally but particularly so on education, where expansion has given way to contraction, optimism has been replaced by a degree of pessimism and scepticism about the value of investment in education. This has coincided with changes in the ways in which many local authorities carry out their policy making, management and administrative functions. Many have established some form of corporate management. This implies not merely a change in the structure of management and administration, for in some authorities changes of this kind have been minimal, but also a change in attitude. It implies an attitude of mind which considers the needs of an area as a whole and which orders priorities to meet these needs. It means defining objectives and sub-objectives, and the planning and ordering of resources to achieve those objectives. It requires not only new planning structures to replace the old or to be superimposed upon them, but, in addition, that arrangements be made to monitor progress towards the achievement of objectives and a feedback so that there can be continuous modification of plans and redefinition of objectives where necessary. This is not the place to attempt a consideration of the possible implications for education generally of new systems of planning, management and decision making, particularly as evidence is as yet rather patchy. But already there are indications of how these changes may matter to the curriculum planner.

The existence in many local authorities of a powerful Policy and Resources Committee, as Jennings (1977) and others have shown, has meant that discussion of policy making in education and allocation of resources related to it is no longer largely confined to the education sector and to teachers, administrators and councillors within it. It is now a matter for discussion outside the education sector and subject to decisions taken at a higher level.

The creation of new departments, such as the Personnel Department, with expert staff responsible for formulation and execution of staffing policy throughout the local authority has posed a potential threat to the relative autonomy of other sectors. Resistance to this threat has so far prevented substantial changes being made to traditional procedures, but pressures for change exist. New hierarchies in local administration have sometimes led to a reduction in status of the education officer and his subordination to other officers who have overall responsibility for a number of associated departments. Planning groups drawing their membership from a number of different departments plan detail of projects which may well involve the education service and have an impact on schools. It is too soon to estimate how fully the hoped-for efficiency will be achieved as a result of changes in organization and attitude though events such as those associated with the resignation of the Chief Education Officer of the county of Avon suggest that the teething troubles have in some places been considerable.

The aspect of these changes of most relevance to us here is that they place a heavy emphasis on definition of objectives, ordering of priorities, monitoring of processes and finally on quantifying results. This concern for clarity of objectives, assessment of progress and measuring of results may be appropriate to many branches of local government and even to some of the activities of the education service where waste may be eliminated and duplication avoided. But, as we have seen in earlier chapters, many educationists have expressed their considerable unease about this approach to curriculum planning, believing that the essence of the process of education is not readily measurable according to criteria now being advanced. Conscious of the consequences for education in the past, when measurability of results was emphasized, they fear that the criteria, techniques and language of the planner, if applied to education, will lead to an undesirable emphasis on those aspects which are measurable to the detriment of those aspects which are not.

In the changed situation and changed climate of local authority administration today, the task of the educational administrator in presenting the case for education has in many respects become a more demanding one. The case has to be presented in terms acceptable to others, who, in relation to their own services, may be able to talk more readily and convincingly of objectives and of measurability of results. It may mean that in this situation the claims of some sectors of the education service, such as those most nearly vocational in aim, and others, such as those most clearly designed to promote basic literacy and numeracy, will be promoted more readily than those which are considered to be peripheral. If the 'balance' of the curriculum is to be that which is thought to be educationally desirable by those involved in the service, there would seem to be a need for educationists to be aware of the processes at work.

The escalation of party politics in local government has meant that over the last decade the policy guidelines within which the officers work have in many cases been more closely defined, and the area within which officers have been given discretion to act has been restricted. The comprehensive school issue more than anything else placed educational decision making in a political setting, but there are other areas and issues on which the political parties are divided and when they arise at local authority level their effects can be damaging. Detailed planning of curriculum is of course no part of the responsibility of committees of the local authority, but where party attitudes prevail and where the political party is in a position to ensure that its will prevails, the possibility that constraints and limitations may be placed on the activities of the schools in relation to curriculum should perhaps be considered more seriously than it has in the past. Direct involvement in curriculum decisions other than possibly those which may be politically sensitive or which involve significant moral issues is unlikely. However, in that the curriculum is in the broadest sense political, and that changes in it often seem to imply a threat to deeply held views about relationships, or a challenge to long-accepted conventions about the nature and form in which knowledge should be transmitted, much curriculum decision making is of relevance to the politician. The new patterns of control and the new relationships which are appearing at local authority level suggest that the educationist needs to be aware of the political context within which his proposals are presented.

## Falling school rolls

A second change, and one having obvious relevance to the curriculum planner in the future, is that of falling school rolls. Expenditure cuts make it unlikely that any of the advantages which might come with a falling staff-pupil ratio will be realized, and all the signs are that the adjustment will continue to be painful. Some of the implications of falling rolls are considered here because they involve decisions which are likely to have significance for curriculum and these decisions will be taken by the local authority and not by the individual school. Some of the most difficult decisions, both educationally and politically, will be over school closure. LEAs will be required to work within the guidelines provided by the law, particularly Section 13 of the 1944 Education Act. Local authorities were reminded by the DES in Circular 5/77 of the procedures to be adopted and of the educational and other criteria that should be applied when proposing to the Department that a school should be closed.

It is likely that some form of rationalization that falls short of outright closure of schools will be preferred wherever this is possible. Arrangements for the sharing of facilities, and the provision of joint courses between schools in the way that sixth-form courses are sometimes provided now, are already familiar means of rationalization. Restriction of the range of subjects offered in particular schools is however a solution to the problem that is clearly likely to be seriously considered in many areas in future. This may take many forms, such as the reduction in the number of languages or the range of sciences offered in the secondary school. A restriction of the range of options available to pupils at various stages, and the requirement that choices should be made between courses rather than between subjects, are other possible responses to particular problems posed by falling rolls.

Whatever form the rationalization takes and although decisions on detail will, in many cases, be taken by individual heads of schools, or taken by them in consultation with others, it is the local authority which has the responsibility for meeting the overall needs of the area. This will almost inevitably mean closer oversight of arrangements by the authority. In order to do this there is likely to be, as Hanson (1979) has suggested, much more interest by the LEA in gathering information to help them identify and cost the curriculum. If the authority is to effectively coordinate policy and rationalize provision of education, it is only going to do so if it is fully aware of and sensitive to what is going on within the schools in its area. The quantity and range of information required from the schools by the local authority is already considerable and considered by some heads to be burdensome and not to be increased. Decisions will however be taken, and taken in light of what information the authority has available. It would seem to be in the interest of the school that the additional burden of informing the LEA, and of intensifying the dialogue, should be welcomed in the present situation and the machinery of consultation fully used if the voice of the school is to be heard.

Falling rolls may tend to encourage a concentration on a 'core' curriculum. Staffing of subjects within this would be given priority, with other subjects being seen as peripheral and for which arrangements for retaining or retraining staff would not be so tight. This possibility, mentioned though not approved of by the CEO for Manchester in his speech to the North of England Education Conference (1978), is perhaps less likely than a move towards some reduction of subject specialism in the schools, thereby allowing schools to ease staffing difficulties by employing more general subjects teachers. This might take the form of organizing the curriculum in relation to areas such as the six being considered by the Assessment of Performance Unit. In addition to the major objections to these proposals which many would put forward on educational grounds, the practical problem that most teachers at secondary school level are specialists would seem to suggest a need for a massive retraining programme and a major restructuring of the pattern of education for new entrants to the profession. The present political and economic climate makes this rather unlikely.

Falling school rolls have coincided with a period of particularly severe financial stringency and have made the education service extremely vulnerable when cuts are made in public expenditure. There is already evidence of

LEAs diverting to other purposes funds originally negotiated for in-service education of teachers. There has been a massive cut-back in the scale of initial training of teachers and suggestions that over the next decade the staffing needs of schools can be met, to a greater extent than in the past, by the employment of those returning to the profession. Though much curriculum development is initiated within schools by experienced teachers sensitive to the needs of their pupils, the implications of a fall in the proportion of the teaching force with recent experience of developments in higher education in their subject field and in educational thinking may be serious. Equally damaging may be the effects of the reduction in scale and possibly in quality of the research and development on curriculum carried out in the universities and colleges, sceptical though some may have been of its impact in the past.

The bureaucratization of the curriculum with a hierarchy of major and minor departments within schools was developed in and was appropriate to a period of expansion. These were reflected in the Burnham arrangements and these arrangements may be inappropriate in a period of contraction, as salary structure and career prospects are tied to factors such as pupil numbers. Restructuring will require discussion and negotiation and the outcome will have relevance for curriculum in that decisions regarding development and change may be in some cases influenced more by factors such as their impact on the status of a subject department and the prospects for individual members of staff than by more purely educational considerations.

Competition between schools for the reduced number of pupils will become more pronounced in many areas, suggesting that the need to publicize the school and what it has to offer may become a more obvious feature of the headmaster's art in future than it has been in most state schools in the past. Further restriction of parental choice of school by some form of planned entry limits applied by local authorities are likely to reappear in future government legislation, though not necessarily in the form they took in the 1979 Education Bill introduced by the Labour administration. However attractive the concept of 'freedom of choice' might be, the educational and administrative problems which would arise in areas of declining population would outweigh any political advantages that might arise from granting unfettered parental choice. There will nevertheless be a degree of competition between schools in many areas and one consequence of this may be that schools will be tempted to emphasize those elements in the curriculum which would seem to them to have most immediate local and general public appeal, and to adopt those approaches to teaching and learning which would most readily produce visible and measurable results.

## Demands for participation

The third aspect of the local administrative background that is of relevance here is the demand for 'participation' by groups and individuals seeking a legitimized place in local policy making. Formal pressure groups such as teachers' associations and local authority associations have, through their links with Whitehall, town halls and parliament, contributed to policy formulation, but few others have been allowed such a clearly defined place. Many are now demanding to be allowed to play a part in linking school and community more effectively, and to help open the school to community influences, particularly in relation to curriculum.

Formal involvement of the local community in the affairs of the school has traditionally been through the managers and governors, but research by Baron and Howell (1974) confirmed the general impression that their value as community representatives and as contributors to the local administration of education was a very limited one. The Taylor Committee (1977) believed that managers and governors still had a contribution to make, and in their wide-ranging report they recommended changes which they believed would make governing bodies more representative of the whole community and a more effective aid to local administration. The Committee believed that the recommendations contained in their report would also make it possible for governing bodies to contribute more fully to policy making and to the implementation of policy by the school head and the staff. On curriculum their recommendations were clear and direct. Governors were to help to 'establish the educational objectives of the school . . . share in the formation of structures of learning, care and rules needed to achieve these objectives'. They were to monitor progress in curriculum, and to assist them to do this they were to have some training and have more ready access to advisers and inspectors.

These recommendations, with the threat seemingly posed to teacher professionalism and autonomy, were, more than anything else in the Report, the object of teacher hostility. The struggle to establish a measure of teacher control over curriculum had been a long and difficult one and the reaction of the profession to some of the proposals was not surprising. To reject the proposals out of hand and to resist totally the principles underlying them might however be ineffecive now that the gate to the 'secret garden' is already partly open and many are fully aware that teachers have no formal and legal right to hold the only key. In the present political and economic climate it may be impossible to sustain the present pattern of control. It might also be undesirable. The Report may have underestimated the difficulties of involving governors in detailed planning of curriculum and school organization, but there may clearly be a place for them as a body with power to review and respond to school initiatives on curriculum and other things even though they are not equipped to take initiatives themselves. With the focus of policy making shifting towards the local authority, much would be gained by strengthening the link between schools and their local community. If the voice of the school is to be heard and responded to, the 'other channel' to the administrators and to the local political policy makers which can be provided by a body such as managers and governors may be significant. It can provide a broader base for the legitimization of the claims of the school and support for its policies. Given the changed balance of power at local authority level, the voice of the parent and of the community representative might carry more weight than that of the professional teacher. The problems of establishing a system that effectively allows community views to be expressed are immense, and that of setting up lines of communication to officers and committees can be daunting, particularly at a time when the changes in local authority structure and procedure are so dynamic. Many would claim that the effort needed to overcome these problems would be worthwhile.

## Summary and conclusions

The administrative context of the school is extensive and complex. Decisions taken within it by administrators and politicians, sometimes at points remote from the educational institutions themselves, can have a major impact on what can be achieved within the classroom. The 'administration' is sometimes seen as supportive of teachers, though all too often it is felt to be inhibiting and unsympathetic to their wishes. There have been changes in the nature and degree of control exercised by various elements in the system, as has been suggested, and there are changes under way at the moment which are bringing new attitudes, new priorities and new criteria to the running of the education system at both national and local level. These have significance for curriculum. Some of these changes are alien to the traditions of the education system but one cannot ignore them. An awareness of them would seem to be essential if curriculum planning is to be effective.

CHAPTER SEVEN

# SOME POLITICAL INFLUENCES ON THE CURRICULUM

**G. Byrne Hill**

This chapter discusses some of the political implications of the value pluralism that was noted in Chapter 1. It considers the implications on the one hand of seeing the state as an arbiter between the conflicting interests of groups, and on the other hand of seeing it as the provider of basic services. Both considerations point to the political significance of decisions about curriculum activities and subjects, as distinct from judgements about the manner of teaching, which may more often be considered to lie exclusively within the professional discretion of teachers.

## The role of the state

The politics of the curriculum may be understood as the activity through which state institutions monitor and articulate conflicting views about what children should learn at school. The power of the state may be used either to facilitate the emergence of public agreement about the curriculum or to control the curriculum in the interests of dominant groups. The phrase 'politics of the curriculum' has been used, alternatively, to refer more generally to the seeking of power in relation to the curriculum. This usage, however, may be considered to rob the word 'political' of its distinctive meaning, its reference to the state. 'Political' will be distinguished here from social by having to do centrally with those elements of social conflict and power which bear on the framing and non-framing of policies by the state.

The state can be understood in this context, then, as the institutional arrangements, conventional as well as formal, by which conflicting views of the curriculum are accommodated. These arrangements include those of quasi-government bodies, such as the Schools Council, advisory committees, the university-based examination boards and school governors, in so far as their activities depend upon public finance or formal government recognition. Much decision making is delegated to such bodies, in effect on the condition of good political behaviour. This means that government, local or central, when its requirements or priorities are seriously discounted, may in the last resort intervene to alter the context of delegated policy making. Recent examples of such intervention include the Tyndale enquiry, the granting of a new constitution to the Schools Council in 1978 and the partial implementation of the Taylor Report in the election-aborted Education Bill of 1979.

Political influences upon the curriculum therefore depend upon the different ways in which the state relates to education. If the state's primary function has traditionally been to settle and prevent conflict, its positive function in contemporary societies is to promote justice and, in particular, to provide a basic minimum of welfare as in housing, medical care, social security and education.

Centralized accountability for such politically-defined minima is an almost inevitable constraint upon the curricula of state-provided schools. On this feature of the welfare state, an unexpected degree of common ground has existed between the education spokesmen of the major political parties. Resistance to constraints such as a common curriculum core or to the clear articulation of standards, for example, is fuelled mainly from within the teaching profession and from public bodies, like the Schools Council and the advisory committees which produced the Newsom and Plowden Reports, on which teachers were strongly represented.

This resistance to political influence partly reflects universal tendencies to job secrecy and autonomy. But it may gain strength from the argument that, because the quality of schools depends on the quality of involvement of the teachers in them (Stenhouse 1975; Rutter 1979), teachers should therefore themselves make the most important decisions about the curriculum.

The conclusion does not follow. The ethos of a school and the morale of its teachers may be improved by having unambiguous guidelines in those areas of the curriculum where there is the clearest political accountability, that is, where the state is attempting to provide a minimum of education to which all citizens believe they are entitled.

Beyond a basic minimum, the promotion of welfare, justice and education is not, in pluralist states, exclusive to the state. The welfare state has taken over part of a task that was formerly left entirely and is still left to a considerable extent to voluntary effort (Raphael 1976). Numerous associations and communities seek to promote in very different ways the education, justice and welfare of their members. By necessity, however, this must often be through the state-provided schools. A further task of the state therefore is to monitor and prevent the conflicts that arise betwen interest groups in the contested areas of the curriculum. Such an accommodation was achieved in religious education in the 1944 Education Act. Here the accommodation did not represent part of a political consensus about the basic minimum of education for all children. It was never regarded as such. It was no more and no less than a historic and explicit compromise between conflicting interests in the state.

More usually in the English education system such accommodations between interest groups are achieved by avoiding major decisions at central government level, and by allowing policy to devolve upon or to remain with semi-autonomous, public or voluntary authorities. This has educational advantages in so far as conflicts over curriculum depend upon different views of a good life. To the extent that the vision of a good life should ultimately determine curriculum content, then curriculum content cannot be imposed on people. In the long run the vision must be their own (Warnock 1977).

Political influences upon the curriculum thus reflect the different ways in which the state acts towards education. Firstly, it is responsible for providing a recognized minimum of education for all citizens. Secondly, in the contested areas of the curriculum where questions about what is a good life and what is a good society remain open, the state must settle and prevent conflict between interest groups. It may also take initiatives itself. Where either a consensus is thought to exist or, what may be the same situation viewed differently, where an interest group commands state power, the state may, by manipulating advice and finance, give a positive lead in promoting curriculum change. More often, because of the political risks incurred by decision making in contested areas of the curriculum, central government avoids positive direction. It limits itself to the publication of an even-handed discussion paper and delegates policy to other public authorities.

Thirdly, therefore, the state influences the curriculum through the public bodies to which its responsibility for curriculum is delegated; or, more precisely, through the institutional arrangements which are permitted to articulate the interests of parents, employers, associations and communities outside the school. These arrangements include local elections, education authorities, participation in the government of schools, procedures for consultation at school level and parental choice of school.

## Protected areas of the curriculum

The political influence on the curriculum to which teachers have been most alert as a profession is the attempt of the state to ensure a basic minimum of education. This has led to looser or tighter constraints on teachers according to the degree of public trust that teachers would provide the minimum of education without centralized accountability. In recent years, trust that the educational establishment, unlike other well-unionized public employees, was not primarily concerned to safeguard its vested professional interests has faltered. The implementation of the Houghton Report, markedly improving the structure of teachers' salaries and careers, coincided with the unprecedented intervention in the curriculum of a Prime Minister in October 1976, when Mr. Callaghan spoke at Ruskin College of public anxiety about standards and implied that standards 'were not keeping up with current demands' (Kogan 1978, p. 66). In the following year Mrs. Shirley Williams, the Secretary of State for Education, moved decisively to reduce the power of the teachers' unions on the Schools Council. Its third constitution (1978) showed that the attempt 'to keep political influences away from the curriculum was fundamentally undemocratic' (Becher and Maclure 1978, p. 169).

The Auld enquiry on Tyndale School had drawn attention in 1976 to the accountability of teachers for offering a curriculum that is politically acceptable (Auld Report 1976). In particular, how can groups of teachers be stopped from framing the curriculum according to their own ideological approach to welfare and justice in society, and from disregarding the political guidelines that have emerged through public discussion and accountable institutions? The pressure for an agreed minimum of education may be particularly difficult for teachers to resist when it is linked to teachers' claims for public money, for higher salaries and better resources, and to public support for the legitimacy of teachers' claims to authority over their pupils. The more plural society is, the more clear and acceptable must be the justification of the curriculum, which is the basis of their claims to increasingly threatened authority and to scarce resources.

Both the uncertain authority of teachers and the issue of standards illustrate the inevitability of political influences upon the curriculum. Centralized accountability is a defining characteristic of representative democracy. Tension, therefore, between centralized accountability and professional responsibility is to be expected as normal, rather than regretted as intrusive. They are conflicting imperatives which must be recognized. The alternative, a powerful autonomous bureaucracy, would be no more tolerable in education than in housing or defence.

A common alternative to democracy that is representative, especially when it fails, is participatory democracy. This may wreak havoc, as it did at William Tyndale School, when the more normal accountability to democratically elected representatives breaks down. Participatory democracy, exemplified by the influence of employers, parent participation in the government of schools and parental choice, is both more personal and less predictable in its effects than representative democracy.

W. Taylor has illustrated how vulnerable secondary modern schools were, in the 1950s, to local participatory pressures to develop in the direction of ad hoc examination arrangements (Taylor 1963). This process was aided by the lack of effective, centralized accountability. Teachers' professional susceptibilities may in practice be more carefully respected in arrangements that depend on informed discussion and on open, centralized policy making than by devolved decision-making where the democratic safeguards are participatory.

Such misgivings about some teachers' vested and ideological interests, together with the unsettling consequences of non-interventionist policy, contributed to the recent government initiatives on standards and a common curriculum. The Tyndale Report gave legitimacy to the attempts of the Assessment of Performance Unit, from 1975, to identify standards and to lead thinking on a common curriculum. It brought to an end a period in which 'the education system was allowed to evolve its own consensus about progressivism in the primary schools' (Kogan 1978). A similar crisis of authority developed over the curriculum of those comprehensive schools that were hastily cobbled together after Circular 10/65. The disconcerting backlash of the Black Papers from 1969 was increasingly influential, despite the indifferent quality of their early evidence. Only in 1977 did Baldwin begin convincingly to substantiate some of his claims about the disruption of secondary school curricula by school reorganization. His figures, together with those subsequently released by the DES, showed that at the publicly sensitive point of the percentage of the age group in the public sector of education who gained five 'O' levels (or CSE grade 1) there had been a steady decline from 18.65 per cent in 1971 to 17.14 per cent in 1975 (Baldwin 1977; *Times Educational Supplement* 12 May 1978).

In response to such growing misgivings, Her Majesty's Inspectorate was reorganized in 1974 by the new Chief Inspector, Miss Sheila Browne, to focus on an enquiry into the curriculum. In 1976 a subcommittee of the Expenditure Committee proposed ways of bringing 'trade unionists, employers and ordinary citizens more formally into the education debate' (1976). And in late 1976 the Yellow Book and Mr. Callaghan's speech together heralded a sustained official effort to identify the minimum standards and coherence of secondary school curricula. This development was to include a single examination at 16+ that would be publicly acceptable as proof of achievement, unlike the proposals of the Schools Council (1971) which, even after their revision by the Waddell Committee (School Examinations 1978), were to prove unacceptable to Mr. Carlisle, the new Conservative Minister (*Financial Times* 24 July 1979). The development was also to include a recognized core to individual subjects, starting with mathematics, science and English language, and a government-sponsored curriculum core for the years eleven to sixteen. This core would be a minimum curriculum that could be accepted widely as meeting basic human needs in contemporary society, acceptable perhaps to all groups except those for whom acceptance would imply support for an unjust social order and who therefore reject the very principle of a common core curriculum. For example, 'Curriculum 11-16', a discussion paper from Her Majesty's Inspectorate, recommended that eight areas of experience should occupy two-thirds of the timetable for all pupils to the age of sixteen (Department of Education and Science 1978). The age of sixteen as the limit for a common core curriculum has also been supported structurally by official encouragement, and the rapid spread of sixth-form and tertiary colleges, of which there were already 95 and 15, respectively, in 1978. There is now a marked readiness at both local and central government levels to ensure that 'the secondary school curriculum across the whole of the system has some coherence' (Becher and Maclure 1978, p. 173) and that the statutory minimum of education, which the public (employers, trade unions, parents and pupils) can expect, is clearly defined.

## Public welfare versus 'political' interference

The positive function of the state, to promote welfare and justice, rests on two assumptions. The first is that a priority of government is the pursuit of moral ideals such as the reduction of poverty, ignorance and injustice, the extension of individual responsibility and culture. The second, related assumption is that rationality in planning to achieve these aims is to be taken seriously. Without these assumptions, the positive function of the state lapses. This does not imply that there should or will be consensus about the particular ideals to be pursued which may, for instance, be economic, egalitarian or meritocratic. It implies only that moral ideals will be pursued, ideals which have been politically defined as the result of democratic processes of public discussion, elections and accountable government. In its relationship to such politically defined ideals the curriculum is unavoidably political. Political influences upon the curriculum, articulated and legitimated by the state, are intrinsic to the very notion of the provision of welfare by the state.

In plural societies, however, the pursuit of positive good, beyond a minimum, is largely a matter for the individual and for the many associations and communities which 'seek to promote the welfare and just treatment of their members: the family, religious communities, charitable organisations, trade unions etc' (Raphael 1976, p. 49). The distinction between minimum and non-minimum in relation to the curriculum is illustrated in the 10th Report of the Expenditure Committee (1976) which recommended that the government should act upon the conclusions of the Assessment of Performance Unit's enquiry. It added that its members were extremely anxious to avoid 'political interference in the work of the classroom' (para. 65). The use of 'political' here must be taken as referring to the contested areas of the curriculum which are *not* part of that politically defined minimum (defined through public discussion, elections and representative institutions) which it is the welfare state's duty to determine and to provide. In relation to such contested areas the state's task is essentially negative, to settle and to prevent conflict and to assist the mutual accommodation of conflicting interests; although this does not exclude state institutions from having a point of view upon contested areas of the curriculum and from contributing those views to public discussion.

The line where the basic minimum should be drawn, however, is always uncertain as interest groups try to adjust it to include their objects of concern. An issue which exemplifies the difficulty of distinguishing between an agreed minimum for which the state takes responsibility, and a wider area of disagreement, devolution and local negotiation and choice, is that of egalitarian versus academic curricula. Brian Simon, for example, the influential campaigner for secondary school reorganization, has pressed on successive governments the egalitarian view that the aim of comprehensive education is (or should be) that all children 'experience a common, basic education' and that there should be no formal differentiation of content (Simon 1978). This has been widely associated by others with the view that academic education is anti-egalitarian and that the comprehensive school ought not to be attached to academic values. Egalitarian curricula stress the equality of respect which may exist in a non-competitive classroom where there is cooperation rather than rivalry, and where activities may be avoided which expose divergence of achievement. Academic activities include especially those where there is a premium on memorization, close attention to detail and the cumulative grasp of complex rules. The conflict between expert and egalitarian curricula has not been settled by government or even widely debated, except through the issue of mixed-ability grouping. Both academic excellence and a common educational experience, both intellect and fraternity are widely approved, without recognition of the practical difficulty of reconciling them. Two contrasting views illustrate this difficulty. Lawrence Stenhouse, in a BBC ROSLA broadcast, proposed that the curriculum should be decided in the light of a prior decision about how to group pupils. The problem, he said, was 'to get curriculum elements suitable for mixed classes' (BBC 1972). Iris Murdoch, a socialist, has argued on the other hand that 'comprehensive education does not *mean* non-selective education . . . [the primary school] is the place for a first, and ideally a second and third, foreign language. . . . Greek or Russian begun at the University is a poor device, serious maths probably impossible' (Murdoch 1977).

Academic curricula almost inevitably differentiate between pupils, as the opposition to the teaching of Latin in comprehensive schools has illustrated (*Teachers' Action* Number 10, 1978). In differentiating between pupils, education 'identifies insiders . . . poses barriers to outsiders . . . and reinforces the privileged position of superior status groups' (Collins 1971). Such hierarchy cannot be equated crudely with capitalism. The role of inherited cultural capital in the transmission of inequality between generations is even greater in those societies that have abolished private ownership of the means of production (Karabel and Halsey 1977).

Thus views of the curriculum may be seen as reflecting differences between status cultures. Though class conflicts in welfare-oriented states may have been stilled (Habermas 1976) there remain substantial challenges from underprivileged or aggrieved groups. These include ethnic minorities, groups of working-class boys (Willis 1977) and radical socialist groups that would 'struggle to question, challenge and transform society .... in the classroom' (Gleeson and Whitty 1976, p. 111).

Brian Simon has scorned the notion of the curriculum as a battleground between competing groups for legitimacy. If this scorn were more widely shared, a democratic compromise might have begun to form, to be stabilized and clarified by the government. Even in relation to examinations at 18+, however, this compromise has not occurred, as the unacceptability of the 'N and F' proposals shows.

The conflict between expertise and egalitarianism in the curriculum illustrates a further aspect of the state's influence on the curriculum, the role of government inactivity and non-decision-making, whether deliberate or unintended. A pluralist system in which conflicts are defused by avoidance, or by devolution to local bodies to be resolved in a variety of ways, may still be firmly biased in favour of certain groups and against others. Non-policy-making does not mean the absence of political influences. Institutional practices may themselves have a built-in bias, resulting from the form of organization. The location in universities of secondary school examination boards is one example. Other examples include the local discretion of each school in making judgements about mixed-ability grouping, and in determining its own curriculum.

We may, for example, as Warnock suggests, widely reject the theory of differential education, that a child born in Brixton of West Indian parents should receive an education suitable to his background. In practice many schools acknowledge that a child may emerge with more opportunities in his life style than he might have had if he had sat through classes designed for children who started with far greater advantages. 'How difficult most of us would find it to institutionalize such views: such adjustments are best left to teachers' (Warnock and Annan 1975, p. 99). Through such devolution, the absence of government may be itself an important influence on the curriculum. The example also illustrates again the variety of influences that make the curriculum a battleground for the teaching of status cultures.

The late Labour government sought hard for a consensus between the conflicting egalitarian and meritocratic pressures, through its election-frustrated negotiations for new examinations at 16+. In the meantime, decisions were left, as they have been for many years, to individual schools, guided where they wish to be by local advisers and by the existing examination boards. Policy making has been devolved, fragmented, sensitive and vulnerable in turn to locally identified needs.

The debate over academic and egalitarian curricula is at a point of balance. On one side is the minimum of education which the welfare state is expected to provide on consensual, moral grounds, on grounds of equality of access to knowledge. On the other side is the area contested by different status cultures, where the interests of groups are in conflict and where the state's role may be seen as to settle and to prevent conflict, rather than to determine what is right. It is a recurrent Anglo-American fear that government might seek to determine policy in such essentially contested areas that led the Curriculum Study Group, in 1961, to be 'located in a protected position away from the potential influence of reactionary ministers or permanent secretaries' (Kogan 1978, p. 64). It has also been suggested that a similar apprehension, directed against socialist Ministers, led Lord Eustace Percy in 1926 to omit the curriculum from the elementary code and thus to launch the principle of the school's autonomy to decide its own curriculum (White 1975). Each increase of state power for the public good is a potential weapon against its original purpose.

Which curriculum elements are in that area of welfare that is the responsibility of government and which are to be located in the contested area of interests? In a bitter speech on unemployment at the depth of the Depression, Aneurin Bevan told the House of Commons in December 1934, 'I have never regarded politics as the arena of morals. It is the arena of interests' (Foot 1962, p. 168). Yet his personal influence and the cutting edge of his speeches were strongly moral, and the National Health Service which he created epitomizes the moral consensus on which the provision of a minimum of welfare by the state rests. Bevan based his appeals vigorously on the force of the better argument. It is this force of the better argument which gives legitimacy to the welfare state and to the basic curricula of its schools. In particular, it gives legitimacy to the identification of a core to individual subjects and to the government's articulation of public expectations about the elements of a common curriculum which all children need to be taught. These elements must be seen to rest on the better argument. Compulsory schooling cannot rest merely on a compromise between competing interests, excluding considerations of value, and still be seen as legitimate. Where the initiatives of the state rest on such compromises they may frequently face what Habermas has called recently a crisis of legitimation (1976).

## Contested areas of the curriculum

In English education the settling and prevention of conflict between interest groups has frequently been devolved to quasi-government or locally based structures. They may simply be allowed to continue making policy. Legitimacy is obtained through local discussion and negotiation. Accountability for the curriculum and the political influence of interest groups have focused on the individual school.

The influence of the local education authority on the curriculum is important, as we saw in Chapter 6, in the support that it can give to a school through its advisers and through the allocation of additional staffing and resources. But the resolution by the local authority of conflicts between interests is impeded by the degree of autonomy which each school enjoys over its curriculum. This is based on official memoranda relating to the 1944 Education Act, which have been widely understood to place responsibility for secondary school curricula on school governors. 'The Local Education Authority shall determine the general educational character of the school and its place in the local education system. Subject thereto the Governors shall have the general direction of the conduct and curriculum of the school' (Ministry of Education 1945, Schedule B, Section 8). In particular, local authorities have made only limited attempts to resolve conflicts between interests, preferring to devolve policy making to schools. For example, the Inner London Education Authority, the largest and most professionally staffed of the local authorities, was found in the Auld Report to have 'no policy . . . as to the aims and objectives of the primary education being provided in its schools' (Auld Report 1976, para. 830). In this respect, it is no different from most other local authorities.

In some authorities where the influence of teachers' unions is strong, as in the Inner London Education Authority, lack of policy may be compounded by weakness of political will. The Auld Report notes how ILEA's leaders, ignoring their inspectors' adverse reports, were fearful of antagonizing the teachers and frightened to intervene at Tyndale. The hostility of teachers' unions to local authorities' initiatives on the curriculum is illustrated again by their increasing readiness in recent years to refuse to operate plans which in their view are unsound. In September 1978, for example, Coventry's plan to test all children at twelve and fourteen years was blacked by the National Union of Teachers (*Times Educational Supplement* 19 September 1978).

The limitations of representative democracy at local authority level as a device for resolving conflicts between interests, as well as its occasionally subservient or interdependent relationship with the unions, prompted the appointment in 1975 of the Taylor Committee. This committee concluded, significantly for the curriculum, that 'power in running schools . . . should be equally shared among all those who have an interest in the school's success, . . . all those people on the spot who care about the school and want it to succeed' (Department of Education and Science 1977b). In other words, conflicts between interest groups – for example, between advocates of academic, technological, egalitarian, vocational, locality and religious-based curricula – should be resolved at the level of the individual school. The governors should comprise equal numbers of local authority representatives, elected staff, elected parents and coopted members of the local community. Each school would have its own governors who would be committed to its success.

Some attempts to implement the Taylor Report have been disappointing. In Sheffield, for example, fully representative governors were encouraged to take an interest in the curriculum but did not do so. It was observed that, paradoxically, the formal participation of governors may have increased the power of teachers. Their incorporation into the formal structure of decision making made it more difficult for them to challenge the schools' curriculum policy (Mack 1978). Furthermore, the inner-city schools on the large council estates were served as governors mostly by professional people, thus illustrating one of the eternal consumer verities: most parents do not want to take part in perpetual 'folk-moots' about policy.

Conflicts between interests may be less appropriately settled by giving decision-making powers to school governors than through the professional leadership of teachers who are answerable to the governors. Legal responsibility for the curriculum entrusted to governors is unnecessarily cumbersome, and perhaps ineffective, as a way of giving voice to interests. More appropriate to school governors may be powers like those of the monarch, to be informed, to warn and to advise.

Having to give a full account to observant clients puts some pressure on the provider of a service to take account of their point of view. A full explanation to school governers of the curriculum puts pressure on teachers, firstly, to clarify in their own minds what they are doing; secondly, to give an accurate account, in that many governors will have alternative sources of first-hand knowledge in the children; and thirdly, to justify the curriculum in terms of, and so to take into account, points of view which may be remote from the teachers.

Taking into account points of view of different social groups may be better accomplished through democracy as communication than through democracy as participation in decision-making. Representative school governors may then be seen as a powerful means of ensuring that communication by teachers is accurate, detailed and concerned with what parents, employers and politicians want to know. Democracy as communication may need only the hint of sanctions, to be effective as a means of democratic control, of ensuring the consideration of the interests of the governed: five-yearly elections at national level, and an element of parental choice of school at the level of school government. It was the ability of parents to vote with their children's feet, by sending them to other schools, that caused the local authority to intervene at William Tyndale School. Without such a real sanction, even the right of governors to appeal to the local authority, or to call in its advisers when they are not satisfied, will often sink like a wave into the sand of local bureaucracy. A further sanction in the background is that a school's reputation in the community, which the governors represent, has an important influence on the effectiveness of its teachers' claims to authority.

Democracy as communication is 'the maximisation of a free flow of information and the enhanced guidance of a more positive feedback of information and knowledge between ruler and ruled' (Crick 1968). Feedback to teachers through representative governors' meetings, open evenings, the response to newsletters and the local press are not to be disregarded as influences on a school's curriculum. They have an educative effect upon teachers, and so guide them in resolving the contested issues of the curriculum in ways that may satisfy their clients.

Local democracy as communication may be increasingly influential on school curricula as a result of the biparty policy of requiring local education authorities to provide full information about their schools. After Mrs. Williams failed, through Circular 15/77, to persuade some authorities to give such information, she determined to make it a legal obligation in the 1979 Education Bill. She insisted that parents should know what schools have to offer and must be given information about courses (*Times Educational Supplement* 3 November 1978). Schools should give details of the arrangements for teaching children of different abilities (*Times Educational Supplement* 16 June 1978).

Among the authorities which sought to carry out the spirit of Circular 15/77 were Richmond-upon-Thames and Oxfordshire which, in 1978, published comparative examination results in order to give parents a better idea of what subjects the secondary schools offered. This action was defended by the leader writer in the *Times Educational Supplement* on the grounds that 'it is morally, politically, and professionally indefensible to withold [from parents] information essential to intelligent judgement' (22 September 1978). Such selective publication of information puts pressure on more reticent schools to give the full account of their curricula which is necessary for a fair judgement. It also represents a respect for interested parties outside the school and for their influence upon contested areas of the curriculum, which is markedly different from the way parents are sometimes seen. In 1975, for example, Sharp and Green reported in detail the views of some 'progressive' teachers at Mapledene Infant School, who described parents as incompetent, irresponsible, 'clueless' and uninterested in education (Sharp and Green 1975). Although the withholding of information may help to maintain professional autonomy, if not isolation, its disclosure may lead to closer community involvement and support for the work of teachers.

The dissemination of information may thus have greater relevance for the interests of conflicting groups of parents, employers and politicians than the mechanism of representation. The layman who is concerned about the balance of the curriculum, whether the point of balance for him is academic, egalitarian, vocational, technological, religious or local, 'is constituent of a territory so amorphous that it is impossible to see how he could be democratically represented' (Coates 1977, p. 111). To have influence he needs access to objective information. 'Free public opinion will sooner or later do the rest. If *Which?* reports that a given car is twice as costly and half as efficient as its competitors, then its manufacturers . . . will have to pay attention' (ibid).

The dissemination of information about schools combines powerfully with the significant elements of choice which have slipped through the interstices of public sector education. A smaller number of children in the locality made choice a reality for the parents at William Tyndale School. Respect for the Welsh language and for the positive commitment of Anglicans to the Christian way of life makes choice of school a reality for those who can establish a claim to minority language or denominational status, whatever the basis on which choice of school is actually made, academic, egalitarian or religious, etc. Similar ambiguity attaches to the choice of a single sex or mixed school and to the exercise of a claim based on having a previous child in a school, or on living near a school. The rising efforts to place children in good schools, whatever the criteria of good, can only lead to redoubled efforts by teachers to find out and to offer curricula that link with the interests of different groups. The alternative for a school may be a falling roll.

Mrs. Williams stated, in October 1977, that under new legislation 'a child [should] be admitted to the school of his choice'. Under pressure from the education and science subcommittee of the Labour Party's executive, she subsequently shifted to mere 'recognition of parental choice' (*The Times* 27 January 1978). But this change was more than offset by her increasing emphasis during 1978 on the dissemination of information about the curricula of schools, and on the development of a proper appeal system. Pressures on teachers to recognize and to reconcile the interests of outside groups would have remained considerable, even without the change of government in May 1979.

The possibility of choice may be an essential safeguard, if the consideration of outside interests in the curriculum is not to degenerate into a sham. It is in the many parts of the country where there is now an element of choice that outside influences on the curriculum, both formal and informal, may be most strongly felt. The hazards of differentially falling rolls have become acute in secondary schools only recently, as the effects of lower birth rates in earlier years work through the system. Local authorities have attempted to prevent the downward spiral of less popular schools, to ensure that all children receive the minimum of education which it is the welfare state's duty to provide. But the increasing variety of schools, through their varied responses to outside interests and through their efforts to gain legitimacy and external support, is likely to continue in all places where there is no effective zoning of catchment areas. Where no choice is allowed, however, as Michael (Lord) Young has recently pointed out, 'fee-paying schools may well become more and more popular' and the flight from city to suburb may continue (1979). He argues for alternative kinds of curricula within the state sector, to give parents more of what they want, on an analogy with American experience: schools specializing in languages; schools in which education is linked to contemporary issues; centres for performing arts, mathematics, science and vocational studies.

These varied and sometimes conflicting views of the non-core areas of the curriculum are to be expected, if not encouraged, in the absence on the one hand of a professional consensus and on the other hand of overriding and widely accepted grounds for government direction. In what may be called the voluntary curriculum, different views of the importance of local, vocational, technological, religious, egalitarian and academic criteria struggle to prevail. Should locality-based studies occupy up to half the junior school timetable, and the language of infants be developed through local materials, such as a Scouse language kit, as proposed by Eric Midwinter? Should curricula focus on local customs and cultural identities? Should older pupils of compulsory school age have the opportunity to study in institutions other than schools and to pursue vocational interests within a normal school? Should some schools develop a technological or commercial bias, as Michael Young proposes? Should Sikhs, Moslems and Hindus have the same freedom to teach their moral principles as Roman Catholics and secular humanists, through institutions or curricula which illustrate and give vitality to those principles? Should children of different abilities and interests be taught together in mixed-ability classes in order to learn to live together? How early should children have the opportunity to learn a first, second and third foreign language?

These and similar contested questions about the ends of the curriculum may be best resolved, as at present, largely at the level of the individual school, with the school as the unit of accountability, in an increasingly discriminating and competitive market situation. This links with much recent curriculum development which also concentrates on the school level. As Tony Becher and Stuart Maclure concluded in their recent study of curriculum change, 'eclectic and locally relevant curriculum development is much more likely to penetrate the individual classroom and be accepted by the individual teacher than anything engineered by remote control' (Becher and Maclure 1978, p. 170).

Local, school-based development does not merely defuse the issue of who is responsible for the contested areas of the curriculum. Judgements in such areas commit one morally, and this is often a sufficient reason for denying that only teachers or representative politicians should make them. Both the Assessment of Performance Unit's work on basic standards and the initiatives of Her Majesty's Inspectorate on a minimum curriculum are consistent with pluralism about the ends of education, and with decentralization of decision making abour the vision of the good life which ultimately determines curriculum content.

## Summary and conclusions

It has been suggested that conflicts of interest in society (and what were referred to in Chapter 1 as differences of values) are consistent with and may require a measure of pluralism in school curricula. The state's traditional role as the settler and resolver of conflicts between interests was noted. It was then argued that the legitimate influence of outside interests on school curricula may be both substantial and, at the same time, acceptable to teachers through the working out of 'democracy as communication', toughened in the last resort by sanctions such as parental choice of school.

Pluralism and choice in relation to the 'voluntary' curriculum is compatible, nevertheless, with clear articulation by the state of an acceptable minimum of education, defined by standards and by the coherence of a compulsory curriculum core. Such visible guidelines may be essential in a representative democracy which is committed to a minimum of education and justice for all its citizens. Representative democracy requires that public services be seen by citizens to be adequately provided. Schools in particular need external legitimation if their work is not to be undermined by incomprehension and, sometimes, alienation amongst pupils and parents. They must be seen to provide a minimum which is desirable or acceptable. Only such recognition can justify the compulsory nature of pupil attendance and of public financial support.

CHAPTER EIGHT

# A COMPARATIVE VIEW OF CURRICULUM DEVELOPMENT

**E.J. Nicholas**

This chapter does not attempt to survey foreign countries with the intention of gathering an assortment of interesting ideas or worthy practices ripe for importation to the UK. Nor does it seek to illustrate an argument or press for a particular pattern of necessary change because of foreign developments. Again it makes no suggestion that one country or another is superior or inferior with regard to curriculum matters, i.e. that one or other country 'succeeds' more through its curriculum policies than others and should thus be seen as an exemplar. Further, it is not concerned to apply a physical science paradigm to the analysis of curriculum by using the comparative method to test a hypothesis. The aim here is to highlight our domestic scene and thus help to understand it better by providing an international setting. This can be achieved by seeing the extent to which we in the UK are typical, when compared with some other countries, in our practices; in respect of the reforms we are proposing; in the way we implement them; but, most important, in the way we conduct our curriculum debates. A comparative dimension may make some things previously deemed routine more problematical and thus perhaps in need of either reexamination and rejustification on the one hand or reform on the other. To summarize: James Thurber, when once asked by a newspaperman, 'How's your wife?' replied, 'Compared to what?' We need to take the epistemological stance implicit in his question seriously.

## Common problems

If attention is focused on a selection of First World countries, i.e. certain Western European nations, the USA and the USSR, the literature suggests that they share, and themselves recognize, several general though very difficult curriculum problems. Some of the points made below may be familiar, but for the purposes of this analysis it is necessary to reiterate them in outline. The first problem emanates from the dramatic explosion in human knowledge which has undoubtedly occurred during the twentieth century (Bereday and Lauwerys 1958). A common index of this phenomenon is that it is now estimated that man's scientific knowledge alone is doubling every ten years. Given the sheer scale of this growth, questions arise in many countries, like, 'How can school knowledge be kept up-to-date?' or 'What, out of this knowledge, should children be taught?' or 'What principles can inform our decision to include or exclude some of this knowledge from the school's curriculum?'

A second factor which tends to compound the first is the concurrent explosion in human expectations in respect of education. That is to say that since the early 1950s citizens have increasingly demanded for their children access to more and more schooling, and specifically to those high-status knowledge areas traditionally provided only for the élite. An OECD publication put it this way: '. . . all European school systems are responding in one way or another to the political pressures for greater equality of opportunity and for less specialization' (Centre for Educational Research and Innovation 1972, p. 12). There is a recognition here by the clientele that extended schooling in some subject areas provides the best chance for social and economic mobility and access to the good life.

Arising from this pressure, a third problem emerges, namely that most countries have had to face up to what the curriculum in mass education can, must or might look like. Thus, is mass education a general 'liberal' education for all? If so, where does vocational education appear? Or has the former always implied the latter anyway? Must mass education, to meet the equality principle, mean a common compulsory education for all, and if so, for how long, and what should it include? On the other hand, should the equality principle find expression in treating differing individual needs differently, by organizing an extensive optional or choice-based curriculum? But who is to decide who has special needs? Can the differentiation inherent here avoid élitism? But, how can students with a profound depth of knowledge in what has to be a very limited range of subjects, so necessary for creative and frontier research, be produced without specialization?

A fourth problem logically connected to what has already emerged concerns resources. Even in relatively rich countries the provision of more and better education makes it necessary to find new financial resources, and sometimes this involves difficult priority choices, within the educational sector, and between it and other social services, as we saw in Chapter 6.

A fifth argument poses an even more complex problem and raises yet more dilemmas. The postulation is that the curriculum of schools is insufficiently relevant, mainly to the needs of society and the economy. In short, the majority of children are not provided with the skills, knowledge, experiences and attitudes needed in the world of work which they enter when leaving school. (Neither, incidentally, does the school help them in making realistic decisions about their future employment.) A commonly heard rejoinder to this view is that because of the rapidity of technological change it is impossible to anticipate what knowledge or skills will ultimately be most useful to students, particularly with a forty-year working life in prospect in which they may have to be drastically retrained at least twice. Better, the argument goes, to recognize that the most certain prediction is that the future will see a marked increase in the leisure time citizens are going to enjoy, and the curriculum should focus instead of preparing for this by developing in them worthwhile interests. But the relevance argument does not rest here. It is also suggested (King 1974) that the curriculum in most countries is irrelevant to the needs of individual children, as perceived by them, and thus they become alienated from schooling. Such perceptions are however very varied and may not only be in direct contradiction to what the schools are offering, but to societal or economic requirements as well.

This dilemma illustrates nicely another fundamental difficulty, the parameters of which are very clear and broadly agreed upon. That is that what children are taught should take account of (1) societal needs; (2) individual needs; and (3) the nature of knowledge. Such a statement is all very well, but what weighting should be attached to one or another factor? As will be shown later, various countries proceed with this weighting process differently, depending on local factors which are often subtle and delicate.

A seventh identifiable problem compounds matters further because, it is argued, countries must recognize the consequences of the increasing economic and political interdependence of nation states. This argument is applied particularly forcefully to the EEC context, but also recognizes cross-continental, i.e. First to Third World, relationships, and thus the need to develop curricula for internationalism. Sometimes this is couched in very basic terms like the need for more foreign languages so as to aid the geographical mobility of future labour forces; or in similar vein the need to harmonize curricula, examinations etc. across educational systems. Another version presses for a curriculum for international understanding in which at least a beginning can be made by removing the overtly ethnocentric and nationalistic character of most history syllabuses and geography textbooks (Merchant 1967; Dance 1970).

What has already been said throws up a number of miscellaneous contingent issues which must be mentioned. There are serious implications in what has been said for the work of the teacher: given even the knowledge explosion point, inevitably his or her traditional role as *an* authority becomes less tenable. More seriously, teachers occupy a completely central and quite critical position in the classroom and outside it, negotiating directly with children and others about the very problems outlined here. Sometimes doubts are therefore raised about their claim to be *in* authority. Questions also arise about methods and systems of evaluation and assessment. Given the apparent need for curriculum innovation, there is an obvious need to look at the sources of such innovation and its effective dissemination.

The final problem is probably the most important, for in a sense it overrides all the others. This has to do with questions of politics, control and power. It has already been demonstrated that even one curriculum problem can raise questions to which there are several possible answers which are in turn contradictory or irreconcilable. In practice, some preferred answers are offered and canvassed by a variety of groups or individuals for a variety of motives from the ulterior to the altruistic. Examples of such groups abound, i.e. elected representatives of the central, regional or local political structure, all perhaps in disagreement; employers' associations; trades unions; university authorities; groups of teachers and their associations; professional bodies; parent or community groups – and this list is by no means exhaustive. In this situation, which is applicable to many countries, the curriculum has to be seen as a political matter, and decisions about it emanate from national patterns of power and control.

Both Wynne Davies and Graham Byrne Hill have highlighted this in detail for the United Kingdom in Chapters 6 and 7 of this volume.

In the UK the problems of curriculum are not necessarily couched in quite the above terms, yet it is difficult to deny that many ring true for us. Certainly notions of mass education, curriculum relevance and matters of control, power and incidentally teacher autonomy and responsibility are most germane. A more detailed set of reflections on our domestic scenario is delayed until the final section of this chapter.

## Common trends and solutions

To begin here with the primary level, all countries continue to give a very heavy priority to teaching children the basic skills of literacy and numeracy, i.e. reading, writing and arithmetic computation. Much stress is also put on the physical health and well-being of children and to beginning the process of the socialization of the child away from an exclusive dependence on its family. But in general, as we saw in Chapter 3, the UK primary school appears to have pressed further ahead than any other country, even the USA and Scandinavia, and very certainly the USSR, with 'progressive' classroom practices. This is exemplified in a number of ways – e.g. the informal methods used to teach children basic skills. Such aims are normally achieved elsewhere by more traditional direct, didactic teaching. Again, the UK primary school curriculum tends to be much more extended in terms of content than abroad. Whilst art, music, nature study etc. are given nominal attention, with the exception perhaps of the USA, very little time is devoted elsewhere to the wide range of activities, from science, environmental studies or history to thematic topic work, all of which are familiar features of most schools here. Similarly, comparatively speaking, we are unorthodox in our use of time and space and the way we group children for learning purposes. Whilst some English critics have tried to call a halt to these developments and urged a 'return to basics', many foreign experts, notably the Americans, (e.g. Silberman 1973), have urged that their countries follow in our steps. Another feature to be noted is that the process of the assessment of children in most countries is limited to the testing of their attainment in the various curriculum areas. Objective testing does occur in the USA, but is rarer in Western Europe and positively rejected in the USSR. Finally, at the end of this stage of schooling, Western European countries have followed the earlier lead of the USA, Sweden and the USSR in deferring selection as late as possible via the establishment of some form of 'common' secondary school, which has vital curricular implications.

This provides a useful bridge to a consideration of common developments at the secondary level. In all countries there has been a noticeable, even dramatic, decline in classical studies (Latin and Greek), perhaps to make room for the increase in the attention given and time devoted to mathematics and the sciences. But more noticeable has been the trend to establish a required common curriculum for all children, ranging from the three years of the orientation cycle in France, to five years in Sweden and seven years in the USSR. Often these curricula are established at the central Ministry of Education level (e.g. France, Sweden, USSR, Denmark – though in this last case they are advisory rather than mandatory in character). The Soviet Union's requirements are probably the most extensive in scope, specifying as they do: (1) what subjects must be taught, per hour, per week; (2) the syllabus for each subject, including the sequences of topics to be covered; (3) the textbooks which have to be used; (4) the teaching methods to be applied; (5) the tests or examinations for assessment purposes. However, France comes close to this degree of detail, and even in the USA, the State, or Local, School Boards of Education commonly lay down requirements that all children have to be taught some subjects, and specify precisely what texts and textbooks must be used.

In general the justifications proffered for these developments are twofold: first, that the state, for security and cohesion reasons, has the right to demand of its intending citizens a mastery of a basic core of knowledge; second, that selection or sorting is endemic to curriculum differentiation and such a process runs contrary to equality of educational opportunity. On the surface there is a remarkable similarity about what is included everywhere in the compulsory, core list of subjects. They are, in descending order of commonality: mother tongue and its literature; mathematics; natural and physical science; modern foreign language(s); history; geography; art; music; P.E. It is also significant that this curriculum can be described thus, using the very orthodox labels of descreet subjects. Notions of integration or combined studies are not unheard of, say, in the USA, or perhaps Scandinavia, but they are uncommon elsewhere and are often provided late as an elective, often for the least able. In the Soviet Union they are rejected totally, though the need for children to see the relationships or interconnections between disciplines is admitted and sought.

Another interesting trend is the way in which many countries have set about solving the explosion of knowledge, even the relevance, problems. What they have done is to identify the central skills, concepts, ideas and methods of particular subjects and to teach these to children, rather than continuing with an encyclopaedic cover of all the known knowledge of a particular field. This principle has informed, not only the UK science and mathematics projects (e.g., Nuffield, SMP etc.) and the Schools Council's project in history, but also the changes in subject content in France, under Haby, the USSR's new syllabuses and the various curriculum projects of the 1960s and early 1970s in the USA.

Developments in the UK are not wildly unlike what has been identified here. The move to comprehensive secondary schools, our usual practice within them of having a more or less common curriculum for all children in the first two or three years, followed by electives on top of more limited core subjects, bear comparison with the above. However, in terms of control over content, teaching methods etc., the considerable powers exercised by external agencies in other countries makes an enormous qualitative difference, including the area of terminal examinations. Without doubt, comparatively speaking, the autonomy of teachers in the UK in all aspects of curriculum matters is, at present at least, very much greater than anywhere else.

## The significance of varying epistemological traditions and styles

It is hoped that what has been outlined so far has some value and interest. In summary, the claim is that in recent years, owing to important political, economic and social changes, the school curriculum, particularly at the secondary level (what it is, should be and so on), has emerged as a major problem for most countries. The parameters of the problem, and certain solutions, are agreed. But this stress on similarities glosses over important differences between countries and it is these which will refine our analysis and make the particular situation of the UK much clearer.

To this end, the remainder of this chapter focuses exclusively on four foreign countries: the USSR, the USA, France and the GFR. This selection is not arbitrary. Obviously these countries represent very different political, social, even cultural systems; but they are also the sources and epitomes of three different, significant and influential epistemological styles. The USSR (1) we can call Marxist/Leninist; the USA (2) Pragmatic; France, the GFR and the UK, taken together (3) are manifestations of a classical European tradition. Each of these styles has characteristic, idiosyncratic and thus differing approaches to questions concerning the nature of society, man and knowledge which we have already seen are currently the critical elements in the analysis of the curriculum and its development. It is the differences here which will decide local variations.

Put diagramatically the above proposition looks like this:

Varying Epistemological Styles
1. Marxist/Leninist
2. Pragmatic
3. Classical European

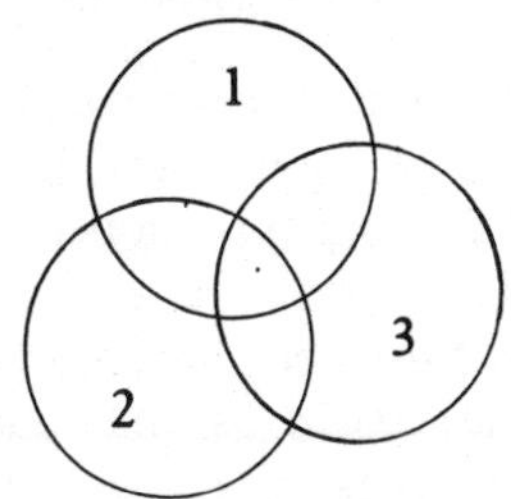


The common ground explored in the first sections of this chapter is indicated by the area where all three circles overlap. Other degrees of similarity are where two circles cross each other. But it is now necessary to provide an outline profile of the areas of real difference.

## *Marxist-Leninism – the USSR*

Arithmetically speaking, most of the children in the world who attend school do so in countries which are organized on Marxist principles. The Soviet Union is discussed here because it is the oldest socialist system, and has undoubtedly been a most influential model, not only for Eastern European countries, but for nations elsewhere. Space precludes a survey of the shifts of emphasis and reinterpretations of Marx for society, and thus education, since 1917. Anyway, the central general ideas concerning the role of schools and what they must teach has remained pretty constant among Soviet educators. Currently they can be paraphrased through the following theoretical propositions.

> Education is first and last a political matter.
>
> The political purpose of schools is to act as the main agent in the production of the new Communist society of tomorrow.
>
> This requires them to meet the needs of society, current and future, and must therefore involve them in inculcating into future citizens the skills, knowledge, attitudes and behaviour which are and will be needed.
>
> The processes of teaching and the quality of learning are critical for they have to be such as to guarantee the thinking, understanding,

self-disciplined Marxist man. Thus, for example, processes which generate mere blind rule-following behaviour, characteristic of indoctrination, should not, in theory, be permitted.

In these terms, the curriculum of the school is extremely broadly defined, involving not only the acquisition of subjects and knowledge, but also, for example, proper ethical and moral actions by pupils.

Within this broad spectrum of the curriculum, the content of the knowledge segment has to be and is selected for impartation on grounds of societal needs.

It follows, too, that all pupils need to acquire these abilities – not merely for equality reasons, but for the New Society to be born. And, that with very few exceptions, (i.e., those who are measurably physically impaired), they are capable of doing so.

The Communist Party is invested, as the vanguard cadre, with the duty of leading the process to Communism; as such it has the right to retain absolute control over educational matters, including the curriculum, its definition and content.

Given these ground rules, many of the dilemmas facing other countries disappear. Soviet educators would claim that their orientation has always had to be towards mass education; far from having to cope with a pressure of increasing demand for schooling, they have positively fostered it. Currently their version of it involves ten years of compulsory schooling, with a required core curriculum for everyone. This consists of three years of Russian, mathematics, plus some art, music, nature study and P.E. in the primary classes, followed by seven years of Russian, mathematics, history, geography, biology, physics, chemistry, foreign language, P.E. and a little astronomy and technical drawing at the secondary level. It is interesting that Western visitors tend to find the teaching methods used in these subject areas very traditional, normally involving (1) recapitulation of the last lesson or homework often via questioning; (2) exposition of new material by the teacher, maybe using demonstrations or visual aids depending on the subject; (3) setting of homework exercises on the new work. This diadacticism, however, fits their notion of instructing or informing the young; the model of childhood here is of inferiority, passivity, being made expert.

Again they have no difficulty in this context in describing the role of the teacher, the agent of education, as quite unambiguously *in* authority and *an* authority. Further, the issue of control does not occur, for this is vested in the Party. They would also claim that a Marxist version of internationalism has always featured heavily in Soviet schools. Most of this stems from the overwhelming preponderance given to the societal determinant in shaping the curriculum and the selection of its content. This governs also the other familiar curricular mechanisms of the school, like the rules of behaviour for pupils, the youth movements, the parents' committees etc., all of which are carefully constructed with societal goals in mind.

Residual problems do exist however. Concern is expressed, for instance, about the indirect effects of the teaching methods which can result in school life being defined by children as tedious, and also raising questions in their minds of relevance to work and life. But without doubt the most acute difficulty arises over the implications of the knowledge explosion. Their epistemology suggests that Communist citizens will need to know everything about everything. Partial solutions to this crisis have been found by extending compulsory education; or teaching more efficiently – e.g. the recent collapse of the time devoted to primary class work from four years to three. A more permanent cure may be forthcoming in their proposal, already mentioned, to teach those skills, concepts, methods etc. central to given subject areas, instead of a complete coverage of all the known knowledge of the field. Arising from this difficulty is another, namely how to provide children (some or all?) with a real depth of specialist understanding in one or two subjects given the overwhelming demands already made upon them by the extensive core curriculum. What is more, this specialization is necessary for at least some, as a prelude to higher education, which in turn will produce the creative frontier researchers that the economy needs. Some policies involving specialization, like the special schools for the brilliantly gifted begun by Kruschev, have not been extended, for they were seen as politically unacceptable, carrying too many élitist overtones. Their current answer involves the following steps: (a) allowing children to study optional subjects for anything up to twelve lessons a week, usually after eight years (age fifteen) at school, though occasionally after six years (age thirteen); (b) moving to a professional trade school, which continues teaching the core curriculum but also provides an extensive preparation for a particular industrial or commercial trade, the notional target clientele for these institutions being about one-third of a given age group; (c) each ten-year school will shortly be designated as being specially equipped to teach in depth one of the orthodox school subjects. Again about one-third of an age group will be encouraged to specialize in such subjects, if necessary by moving to another school should the one they attend currently be offering an inappropriate option.

Quite clearly this policy involves differentiation and selection and thus an agency of the division of labour, for routes to, say, higher education or semi-skilled work, will result from the pursuance of some options or none at all. Extensive adult education does ameliorate, or make less inevitable, the life and work chances consequent upon these choices. But in the end the argument is that they have to face quite honestly society's needs for a differentiated workforce, all of whose contribution is, theoretically, equally valued.

### *Pragmatism – the USA*

The American pragmatic epistemological tradition is less easy to describe than Marxist-Leninism, for, as might be expected in a more pluralistic society, it is less coherent and explicit. Also it does not derive exclusively from one authoritative writer and his interpreters, though undoubtedly John Dewey was a seminal influence. However, propositionally its elements look like this:

> Schools in twentieth-century America were encouraged to play the central role of homogenizing the children of vast numbers of diverse immigrants into being Americans. In this process they served necessary societal needs in inculating into children the common agreed values, ideas and information of a liberal American democracy.
>
> However, quite the most important feature of being an American was to be free – *from* poverty, persecution, etc. and *to* pursue individual happiness. This American Dream, as Myrdal (1944) put it, was that any citizen had maximum opportunities to achieve anything; the path from log cabin to White House, or its equivalent, was readily negotiable, given hard work, ingenuity and perhaps a little luck.
>
> Any wealth or power élites established were based on individual merit and thus just; entry to them was open to anyone.
>
> The schools and what they taught had to be seen as servicing to the full the needs of the individual, in his or her pursuance of freedom and social

mobility. The pragmatic answer to 'What knowledge is most worthwhile?' was 'That which is most *use* – to the individual's perceived purposes'. (This tradition finds great difficulty in understanding the notion of knowledge for its own sake, for intrinsic worth.) Apart from basic national defence reasons, societally determined needs were not to override those of individuals who after all collectively formed society.

In this tradition *knowing how* is taken more seriously than *knowing that*. As a result far more subjects were granted full status – witness the range and type of electives offered in an American high school, or the wide range of vocational undergraduate programmes at colleges, even universities. Thus traditional European academic disciplines, strong on propositional knowledge, were not necessarily placed at the top of a hierarchy of respectable subjects. Similarly, boundaries between subjects were far less firm, permitting integration based on an eclectic selection of knowledge depending upon the goals of a particular course.

Control over schools and what they taught, in this context, could not but be localized, possibly at the state level, better still at the local school board level; certainly not at the federal government level.

The recent wave of radical critics of American education (notably Gumbert and Spring 1974) confirm this broad outline. Whilst they argue that what has been described above is a set of fradulent and manipulative arguments, used by corporate capitalism to legitimize the status quo, their strictures evidence its existence and resilience.

It is now possible to show how this epistemological style can find answers to some of our general problems.

The knowledge explosion issue can be solved by using the criteria of usefulness and relevance to the individual's needs to select what is to be taught. This also permits any increased aspirations to be met. The high school curriculum, based on a small common core plus a very wide range of electives and aided by the credit mechanism, is therefore a coherent version of mass education.

It is also worth noticing how the 'equality' problem was couched and discussed. In the process of the establishment of the Coleman Report on inequality of educational opportunity, and the subsequent furore about it, the almost exclusive concern was with providing the disadvantaged with a staggered race, i.e. giving them a fair start. With the possible exception of

Jencks (1975), there was almost no questioning of the validity of the race metaphor; but clearly within the American tradition, this is a solution to the equality problem. It was the federal government which was to ensure this equal start via legislation, e.g. the Civil Rights Acts, and the provision of money – for instance to finance the compensatory education movement. There was considerable resistance to these developments founded on the argument that such federal intervention was unconstitutional in that it infringed state and local rights in educational matters. This is an important example of the way issues of control and power are debated in the American context.

In very recent years, federal activity has declined, relatively, so that the residual curriculum debates in the USA have become more muted. However some unresolved difficulties remain and can be traced back to the crucial events of the 1960s. The USSR's Sputnik successes were a serious challenge to the general viability and success of American society, which in turn produced a telling impact on her prestige internationally. Critics (e.g. Trace 1971) rapidly raised trenchant attacks upon the inadequacy of the educational system. In short, they argued that children in general just did not know enough; further, the system produced insufficient scientific experts to man the necessary counter space programme. Yet, ironically, the logical implication of this argument was that children would have to be taught more of those subjects traditionally seen as being 'academic', i.e. mathematics, the physical sciences, modern languages etc. The pressure of this demand implied a considerable tightening of tracking procedures and a stiffening of high school graduation requirements. A powerful 'back to basics' movement also emerged.

In addition there was a proliferation of federally and independently funded projects which sought to redesign and improve subject syllabuses (Project Physics); discover very able youngsters (Project Talent); and other schemes to improve teaching efficiency. These latter invariably adopted an 'objectives' model, and used an overtly behavioural learning theory.

These influences persist today, but are in collision with the traditional American pragmatic style. The societal needs argument based on national defence and prestige needs, pressing for academic and intellectual vigour, runs counter to the well-established individual needs and useful knowledge notions. Another current strand in the curriculum argument is understandable in these terms as well. Those who present deschooling arguments or advocate the voucher system are restating, in novel forms, conservative or traditional ideas. They seek to return to individuals and families their lost freedom and liberty over the content of education by curtailing the powers of government and other societal agencies to prescribe content. In general it would seem that the traditional curriculum, and the justificatory arguments sustaining it, are likely to win through.

### *The European tradition*

Many of the assumptions regarding what constitutes worthwhile knowledge in the European tradition are derived from the Renaissance, and can be traced through the eighteenth-century Age of Reason and to nineteenth-century notions of the liberally educated gentleman. A summary of the propositions underpinning this tradition might go as follows:

> Objective knowledge exists which should be pursued for its own sake; the search for wisdom, truth, beauty etc. is the highest form of human activity.
>
> Some forms of knowledge are much more worthwhile to pursue than others, because they form the necessary foundations for eventual enlightenment. Such knowledge is essentially intellectual, propositional (knowing that), often rational and invariably referred to in terms of the mental discipline of a subject.
>
> Over time, shifts and extensions have taken place in the definitions and parcelling of this kind of knowledge. The original list of, say, classics, philosophy, mathematics, the fine arts plus modern languages was augmented by the inclusion of history and the sciences and then more recently, and reluctantly, the social sciences. This list of subjects constitutes the respectable, high-status knowledge of the European tradition and is what is meant by the term *Bildung* in German and *Culture Generale* in France.
>
> It follows that other types of knowledge – knowing how, the knowledge of the economy, the workshop, etc. – are disparaged and situated low down in a hierarchy of subject areas.
>
> Only some people were capable of being initiated into this esoteric world. Initially it was assumed that the few would be the children of upper-class families, but in this century the need for a meritocratic selection basis as a substitute for birth has been admitted.

> The German gymnasium, the French lycée, and the English grammar schools are the institutional manifestations of these assumptions. In addition the Arbitur, the baccalaureat, and English university matriculation requirements are exact statements of what this prestigious knowledge looks like in school knowledge terms.

There are two other points worth drawing attention to. The first is that in Europe the university was and is the key institution, in that its existence and purpose was explained in the above terms. As such it was the major agent of generating and replicating the kinds of knowledge identified above. Further, its influence upon the selective secondary schools' curriculum was enormous, not least because of its examining role, as we saw in Chapter 5. Second, it was and is assumed that the few who could demonstrate that they were successful initiates into this world of mental esoteric knowledge should also be those recruited to élite occupations, be they commercial, political, administrative or professional. The list of overtly 'vocational' university courses (medicine, dentistry, law, theology, engineering) was quite restricted. In fact therefore the pursuit of highly theoretical knowledge for its own sake is translated into, and cashed for, vocational, economic, status and power rewards.

As with Marxism and pragmatism this European epistemological style has shaped the way in which the general curriculum problems identified earlier have been recognized and analysed (if at all) in various countries. Similarly it has conditioned the kinds of change which have been introduced. Thus, in the Western European countries selected for discussion, developments can be seen to be qualitatively different from those in the USA and USSR. To illustrate this a brief description of trends in France and the German Federal Republic needs to be provided.

In France there has been a great deal of activity in the educational sector over the past two decades, much of which has been designed to have important consequences for the curriculum. An extended three-year orientation cycle, involving a common curriculum for all children attending common secondary schools, has been established. This represents a concession to democratization, and a reiteration of the well-established French tradition of a meritocratic basis for differentiation. But in fact this policy at best only involves delaying the selection of children and this is explicitly admitted. What it perhaps achieves is the injection of more justice or fairness into the process. But the basically élitist tradition has not been jettisoned; what is more, despite the reforms, traditional underachievers like children from working-class homes continue to be underselected for high-status baccalaureat courses. Extensive revisions have been made by the Ministry of Education to the syllabuses in various subjects taught at all schools. The purpose has been to update school knowledge and to make it more relevant to the needs of future citizens and workers. This is the way the 'societal needs' argument has been recognized and met. A particular example of this process has been the extension of the possible baccalaureat courses open to the gifted. There are now five of these: A, B, C, D and T, so that the original classics-, modern languages- and mathematics-based courses have been augmented by science- and technical studies-centred tracks. Hence the French manpower needs in these latter fields have been recognized, and the old lycée tradition has been extended and marginally modified to include those subjects in demand in the economy. Yet the process remains consistent and congruent with traditional views of knowledge and the number of people capable of acquiring it.

In fact, very few changes have occurred in the German Federal Republic, and for this reason it is a singularly interesting case in terms of this analysis. Some Länder, usually those under Social Democratic control, have established 'comprehensive' secondary schools, but even here the majority have been multi-lateral in organization with children ascribed to different curriculum tracks on entry. Thus, in general, the Gymnasium tradition and bipartism continues to be the clear norm. The content of some Abitur subjects has been revised, and again science- and mathematics-centred courses have been extended, though these always existed in Germany. Undoubtedly the key to an understanding of the West German situation is that popular pressures for mass education based on radically different principles and procedures, i.e. the explosion of aspirations argument, have been very muted and have thus not created any need for change.

The main explanation for this must be seen in one central element within German education, namely vocational education. This has always been taken very seriously indeed, and continues to be readily available to all children. It follows that there are very real compensations offered to those children not selected for the Gymnasium, and its Arbitur courses, for they can see their long-term destinations in one of many trades. Further, with the Federal Republic's postwar economic successes, the financial rewards in most of these jobs has been very considerable. Again, this vocational education provision has meant that the economy's manpower needs have been very adequately met at the skilled and semiskilled levels. In short, then, *Bildung* for some, plus vocational education for the rest, has proved a perfectly viable equation to solve the social, political and economic needs of the state, and its citizens.

## Curriculum development in the United Kingdom

It is now important to try to identify carefully and exactly what this international analysis highlights with respect to Britain: otherwise there is the risk of the frustration endemic to all types of voyeurism.

As Geva Blenkin has already demonstrated in Chapter 3 of this volume, there has been a great deal of activity on the curriculum front in England and Wales over the last two decades. A very considerable literature has been produced concerned with the analysis of problems, contributing to a vociferous debate of general issues concerned with aims, purposes etc. At the next level initiatives from official bodies, notably the Schools Council, have taken the process further by recommending in some detail planned change in what should be taught, whilst various curriculum centres have taken yet another step in that they have made recommendations regarding teaching strategies and produced materials for use in classrooms.

However the simple model implied above – problem analysis to recommended changes, to implementational actions by teachers at the chalkface – sometimes called the 'centre to periphery model' (Kelly 1977) – is not all that has occurred. Local authority advisers, and most especially teachers in specific schools or departments have also been very active. They have usually proceeded from first principles, producing their own analyses and discussions of problems, their own materials and developed teaching techniques, even methods of assessment quite autonomously. Naturally many have been influenced by seminal writings and also ideas have been adapted to local situations.

We have already seen that some English developments appear to be quite similar to trends abroad. Thus our institutional framework has changed like most countries and common secondary schools accepting all children, irrespective of ability, etc. have been established nationwide. Similarly, at the level of the content of subjects, many syllabuses have been reshaped according to interesting new principles. New subject areas like drama, theatre or film studies, social studies, environmental studies, integrated studies and many others have been introduced to extend the choices open to secondary school pupils. Undoubtedly the CSE examination system has also been a very significant development, partly by providing extrinsic goals for children with average attainment, but also via the Mode 3 system, as we saw in Chapter 5, in allowing teachers more scope to develop courses directly relevant to the local needs and interests of their children. Superficially, all of this seems similar to the central features of the American high school, i.e. an elective system and localized certification procedures. Justificatory arguments relating to the explosions in knowledge and human aspirations plus a thrust in the direction of more equality of educational opportunity through meeting children's individual needs and interests have been woven into the whole process. The trends have often been really radical in intent.

But even in examples like the above, similarities of degree, direction and pace have been more apparent than real. What must be shown is how, comparatively speaking, the English situation is in fact different, more complex and more confused than in most countries. As a beginning, two obvious examples may suffice.

First, a move to mixed-ability grouping with a common curriculum for all children in, say, years one to three is claimed to be a common trend in our schools and it is also argued that similar procedures have been adopted in many other countries. This shift has been recommended on several grounds, including that of an alternative version of equality, i.e. deferred selection through the non-labelling of children, plus equal access for all to certain central knowledge areas. But where other countries have introduced such groupings, e.g. the USSR, the USA and, some would argue, in modified form, France, it is always associated with some kind of grade system. Thus the attainment of children of a given age can be tested and set against the established achievement norms for such pupils. And so clear measures exist, usually applied nationally, as indices of when pupils have satisfactorily completed a given year, i.e. grade. (Incidentally there are implications here also for the performance of a given teacher.) Again set against the nationally or regionally established required common curricula of the USSR, France or Germany, which contain very rigorous and detailed statements regarding content, and even methods of teaching and textbooks, the developments here in England under this guise are so localized and variable that they are in no sense comparable. This is compounded further by our localism in examining – a role performed by the Ministry of Education in France, by national testing systems in the USA and by detailed external surveillance mechanisms including inspectors in the USSR and the GFR.

Second, in all the countries under discussion, the educational system, sometimes through specially planned and designated institutions within it, generates and caters for an élite. But with the possible exception of some institutions in the USA, our major forcing houses of such pupils, i.e. the private public schools, are completely anomalous, for their clientele is overwhelmingly composed of children (statistically mostly boys) with parents with the wealth to purchase their education. It is true that those pupils have to demonstrate a basic academic ability by passing the Common Entrance examination, and for entry to some public schools a great deal more. In curriculum terms, however, it is significant that the content requirements in the Common Entrance, by including classical and modern languages, effectively exclude any child who has proceeded through the state's primary schools. In short, whilst one system of schooling, i.e. the maintained sector, has, perhaps, attempted to change in democratic directions, an alternative system has been retained, for the few, based only partially on meritocratic criteria. Yet this system still provides the majority of successful entrants to our most prestigious universities, and thence to positions of wealth and power in occupational terms. Abroad, where overt élitism has been retained, at least some attempts have been made to develop a more logical basis for selection and to apply the implied rules for acceptance or rejection as fairly as possible.

The character of the English curriculum scene becomes even more complicated when viewed through the conceptual spectacles of epistemological styles. We are undoubtedly the the inheritors of the European tradition outlined earlier, and the assumptions about man, knowledge, even society contained within it are still pervasive. The tradition is still highly influential so that those curriculum reforms that have been attempted, often with radical intentions, have in fact been diluted or nullified. An interesting indication of the truth of this claim is that the curriculum debate in the UK has been conducted in fact very largely in terms of the nature of knowledge. Richard Pring's excellent and influential book, *Knowledge and Schooling* (1976), is an interesting case in this respect. The broad spectrum of English approaches to knowledge – a perfectly proper starting point for any curriculum analysis – is discussed carefully. The book takes in the R.S. Peters/ P. Hirst version and the critique of this position provided by M.F.D. Young and other sociologists; it considers pragmatism, notions of integration of knowledge, even child-centred approaches to knowledge. Significantly, however, there is only one reference or mention given to what we have described as the 'societal needs' determinant of curriculum (pp. 52–53), and then in rather grudging, disparaging terms.

Our over-preoccupation with the nature of knowledge debate has had the following results:

(a) Despite the attention given in some of the literature to individualism and child centredness, we still overwhelmingly accept the assumptions regarding the potentialities of children and how they can be categorized implicit in the IQ's bell-shaped curve. Teachers and others retain its fundamental tripartism, and constantly tend to 'see' children, of whatever age, in A, B, C terms (Keddie 1971). Through this process the old Platonic assumptions about children prevail.

(b) Knowledge remains highly hierarchized on a high-to-low-status continuum. We 'frame' knowledge (Bernstein 1971), using criteria recognized, though not invented, by Hirst, and we then ascribe worth to given bounded subjects according to their pure, intellectual, mind-forming qualities. This claim can be substantiated conceptually; but it can also be demonstrated through focusing on school practices. Subjects like mathematics, the sciences, modern languages, English, history, music, art and more recently georgraphy and economics have high to medium status. Subjects like Design and Technology, social studies, home *economics* (once known as domestic *science* as a first attempt to acquire respectability by parasitic association) are low in prestige. They do not lead to further study at the higher education level; indeed some are not admitted as being sufficiently respectable to merit examination at ordinary level of the GCE. The full implications of this situation for those children who opt for, or are consigned to, low-status courses are too often smudged over. These optional courses may well have been developed to try and meet the individual needs and interests of children. But in our climate of hierarchized knowledge, we cannot also promote mobility or access to power through knowledge, the other version of equality, by this system. In the USA options or electives of all kinds abound, but subject hierarchies are far less apparent; the credit system permits early choice errors to be rectified, and irrevocable selection is considerably delayed by a much more porous higher education system whose courses are far less restricted than ours. In Europe, where knowledge is as hierarchized as in England, they are at least overtly admitted; all children are theoretically given a chance to see if they can acquire the higher forms, and, most important of all, the implications for those who fail are recognized and alternative routes provided. This leads us to a closely connected point.

(c) Given the above hierarchies, it is perhaps not surprising that, in the English curriculum, scant attention is paid to overtly vocational knowledge. In this respect, too, we are, however, highly anomalous, for in each of the other countries discussed, the schools' curriculum organization does provide for vocational preparation, especially for the non-academic. Witness, in the USSR, the professional trade schools; in the USA, the elective system which includes courses of very direct vocational relevance; in France, the assignment of children to clear tracks past age fourteen, ending in various forms of examination which lead to various ordained trades or occupations for those who pass; and the highly successful and mandatory vocational provision of the GFR. It should also be stressed that in each case the preliminary sorting of children and the consequent provision is open and explicit.

The absence of overtly vocational education in England means three things. First, children not studying high-status subjects may be following interesting courses, but their post-school interests are not necessarily being fostered in ways which they can directly perceive, which may be the reason why many become disaffected. Second, the economy is not being provided with a potential workforce which has already acquired some knowledge appropriate to their workplace. Employers complain about this; teachers respond that this is not the school's purpose; yet no very clear, unambiguous or consistent statements about what exactly it is are forthcoming. Third, meanwhile the fact is that vocational sorting does occur, but covertly.

Finally, we must focus upon another feature of the English situation, in which, again, we are highly idiosyncratic and which may be the most significant phenomenon of all. Mention has already been made of the relative autonomy of teachers in England. The matrix on p. 171 can be used to demonstrate this point. It attempts to map out the possible agencies etc. who could or do limit the freedom of teachers in various ways.

Thus, in the USSR and France central governmental ministries completely remove from the teachers control over *what* is taught, how much of it, even *how* teaching and examining are conducted. Much the same effect is achieved in the GFR by the regional Länder Ministries of Education. In the USA locally elected school boards, the PTAs, even powerful textbook companies impinge critically on how teachers are able to operate. These examples are by no means exhaustive, but are sufficient to support the claim that, comparatively speaking, the teacher in England enjoys a greater degree of autonomy than the teacher in any other country.

The reasons for this situation are partly accidental, partly historical, in that, due to our knowledge tradition, full freedom of manoeuvre in professional matters was provided for people who were experts in some brand of esoteric knowledge. A teacher was provenly *an* authority; as such he or she

THE WEB OF EDUCATIONAL FORCES ACTING ON THE TEACHER

| | EXTERNAL | | INTERNAL | |
|---|---|---|---|---|
| | NATIONAL | LOCAL | FORMAL | INFORMAL |
| AGENCIES | Government ministry<br><br>Advisory and administrative<br><br>Examining boards<br><br>Teacher associations<br><br>The law | Regional or local authorities<br><br>Their advisory and administrative agents | Type or level of school<br><br>Governing body<br><br>Headteacher<br><br>Authority or responsibility structure<br><br>Bureaucratic style<br><br>Career structures<br><br>Decision-making system<br><br>Subject taught | Staff views of 'teaching' (general consensus, or significant subgroups).<br><br>The 'politics' of the workings of the formal structure |
| | | TEACHER | | |
| CLIENTS | Parents<br>The PTA<br>Public opinion<br>Employers | | Children (a) individuals (b) classes (c) formal school groups (e.g. houses, tutor groups) (d) extra-curricula groups (e) informal peer groups. | |

was given the complete rights of being *in* authority. It was also argued in Chapter 6 that this autonomy was hard-won by teachers in the UK.

It can of course be argued that teacher autonomy is one of England's outstanding strengths, since it ensures vitality in that either responses to necessary change are rapidly forthcoming, or novel initiatives and improvements are constantly initiated locally. On the other hand, matters of enormous importance depend upon the quality of teachers, as individuals and as a group. Quite specifically, children are at the mercy of the degree of imagination, enthusiasm, efficiency and competence of their teachers and the curriculum strategies that they decide to plan, implement and evaluate. It may in fact be the case that the problems of our curriculum scene, discussed above, are too complex for teachers to be expected to solve, for it is they who will have to do so, given their present powers. Conversely, it may be that some of the problems cannot be solved until the freedom of teachers, especially the inadequate ones, is curtailed, for autonomy can also be obstructionist. Of course this begs the question, 'If teachers are not to decide, who shall?' Similarly it is not enough to require teachers to be responsible without specifying, 'Responsible to whom?' Even the Taylor Report's accountability formula (1977) to answer these questions is too bland, for it will not itself be able to resolve head-on collisions of interests between the assembled parties. Thus we still have some way to go in our attempts to provide acceptable answers.

## Summary and conclusions

This chapter has attempted to discuss the school curriculum comparatively. Trends common to several countries were recognized. But through the use of the analytical device termed 'epistemological styles', attention has been drawn to the complexity, indeed confusion, in the English situation. This state of affairs has meant that many recent innovations have at best been cosmetic. Further, our idiosyncracies are largely the consequence of our failure to face up quite explicitly to the incongruities between the resilient and still pervasive assumptions within our epistemological tradition on the one hand, and attempted changes on the other. One solution would be at least to apply our ground rules consistently, logically and openly. For radical change to be achieved, then new ground rules have to be generated and widely accepted. No one could pretend that this latter course would be easy, for it involves an attack upon the justificatory and legitimizing bases for the existing distribution of power.

# CHAPTER NINE

# IN CONCLUSION

We think we have in this book opened up new issues in the debate about curriculum or, at least, have offered fresh perspectives on issues that have been under discussion for some time.

Inevitably, many themes have recurred and have been taken up and worked over by several contributors and it is worth concluding by picking some of these out for final comment. This may prove not only a worthwhile exercise in itself but also an aid to the attainment of the kind of coherence that has been the aim throughout.

The discussion of values with which Chapter 1 began and which was the theme of the first three chapters led inevitably to a discussion of value pluralism and the impact of competing ideologies, and this theme has been a recurring one. For we saw in Chapter 8 how different ideologies lead to quite different approaches to curriculum planning and we noted in Chapter 7 some of the political problems they raise.

One major problem, as the first two chapters reveal, is that of the appropriate form of educational provision for pupils from 'working-class' backgrounds or, to express it differently, the kind of curricular offering that is most likely to lead to educational equality. For the problem of values raises immediate questions concerning the validity of different sub-cultures within society and the implications of pluralism for education are far-reaching. As a consequence, each of the first three chapters devoted a good deal of attention to the influence of considerations of social class on curriculum planning. Emphasis was placed on the need for teachers to be aware of the implications of their assumptions about social class, and especially about language codes, in order to obviate or at least to reduce what Richard Hoggart called 'the wastage of human beings in our society'. Each of these chapters, from a different point of view, concluded that the 'gentling' process of earlier times is no longer acceptable or justifiable, if indeed it ever was, and that we ought to make demands on all pupils of a kind that will be likely to promote education for all in the full sense, to develop every individual's capacities, to broaden his experience and the range of opportunities open to him, that we ought not to be 'sloppy' in our thinking about the education of such pupils but as rigorous as we are in our thinking about education generally.

Each of these chapters in its own way also suggested that, in order to do this, attention must be focused on education as a process rather than as a body or series of bodies of knowledge, on its principles rather than on its content. There are many different routes to education and, if we attempt to drive all pupils, regardless of their cultural origins and background, along just one of these, many will continue to fall into the ditches on either side of the road.

A second aspect of this approach to education and to curriculum planning, or perhaps a second line of argument in support and justification of it, is that which derives from the work of the developmental psychologists which was examined in Chapter 4. For that work has led to a recognition of the importance of an understanding of conceptual development. It is the development of understanding at progressively more sophisticated levels that fosters education. Such development is facilitated by a concern for the ways in which pupils learn and come to understand, and this in turn requires that they be given opportunities for learning of an active kind and that we adopt 'open' rather than 'closed' systems of learning. Such learning cannot be confined to bodies of knowledge defined in advance by teachers or too clearly circumscribed, since it again necessitates a recognition of the existence of many routes to education and of the fact that education is a highly individualized and personal matter. This is also a device by which, as we saw in Chapter 8, the USSR has tried to deal with the 'explosion of knowledge', replacing the attempt to teach all of the rapidly expanding bodies of knowledge with the development of an understanding of appropriate concepts.

This in turn raises important questions concerning the validity of a scientific approach to curriculum planning and the difficulties, indeed the errors, of that approach comprise another recurring theme, being especially to the fore in Chapters 1, 3 and 4. Again, what is at the root of the opposition to this style of planning is that no kind or amount of scientific research can resolve those questions of value that are at the heart of all educational debate. Once we recognize that education is centrally concerned with that which is intrinsically worthwhile, we must realize that science cannot tell us what that is.

There is a second reason, however, for asserting that educational planning can never be merely scientific planning. Education, as we have just seen, is essentially a matter of individual development and a scientific approach to it can only provide us with goals of a universal kind. If education is a matter of developing capacities, it will require an active or open style of learning and the capacities it will be concerned to develop will include such things as the exercise of individual judgement, an ingredient that is absent from those studies of animal learning that provide the basis for the scientific approach to the planning of education. It is this, as much as the problematic nature of values, that makes the approach to educational planning by a careful prespecification of behavioural objectives incompatible with the notion of education itself, as several contributors have shown.

It will be clear, therefore, not only that particular value positions and the allegiance to particular schools of psychology bring with them certain constraints on curriculum planning, but, more importantly, that the variety of positions that it is possible to take up with equal validity brings its own kinds of constraint. What it is crucial to appreciate, however, is that currently, as we tried to show at the beginning of this book, the general thrust of these developments is pushing teachers towards the adoption of a broader view of education and away from narrow conceptions of schooling or training. For it is suggesting the desirability of open rather than closed systems of learning, of active rather than passive approaches to teaching and of individualized rather than universal curriculum planning, all of these again recurring themes of this book. It is this that we are arguing is creating particular kinds of constraint on the planning of the curriculum.

Response to this changing view of education or even to the differing demands made by different views has one fundamental requirement and that is freedom for the teacher to make professional decisions, to plan educational provision, on his own responsibility. The development of the capacities of each pupil according to his individual needs will require a degree of sensitivity of provision that cannot be met by external planning of a universal kind, no matter how careful and scientific that might be.

Such an approach to educational planning, however, is clearly at odds with and is likely to be inhibited by those other constraints that we have discussed here, those imposed by administrative structures and arrangements that are external to the school and largely beyond the influence of teachers. That these constraints will often be in conflict with those educational principles we have also outlined is another recurrent theme of this book.

The historical survey of the struggle for control of the curriculum, with which Chapter 6 began, revealed quite clearly how that control had at first rested in the hands of the public providers of schools and had only slowly and after a long and determined battle been transferred into the hands of the teachers. We also saw, however, in looking at the practices of other countries in Chapter 8, that such teacher control of the curriculum is unique to the United Kingdom. Furthermore, several contributors have demonstrated in some detail how this control is currently being eroded and clawed back from the teachers. Events like those at the Risinghill and William Tyndale schools, where teachers have been adjudged to have misused their powers in relation to the curriculum, have led to a change of attitude and to pressures for greater external control. Economic stringency and a reduced budget for all those services provided by local authorities are leading to similar demands in an attempt to ensure that scarce resources are not wasted but are put to best advantage. And circumstances beyond any kind of public control, such as falling school rolls due to a lowering of the birthrate, are also resulting in decisions being made outside the school that have important implications for curriculum. In short, the pressures are growing for the accountability of teachers to external bodies, as the frequent references in many chapters to the Taylor Report and the Assessment of Performance Unit indicate.

Several contributors have alerted us to the dangers of this. In particular, they have stressed the risk of a reduction in our conception of education and in the scale of our educational ambitions for our pupils. In other words, they have pointed to the conflict with that developing view of education we discussed earlier. For the main thrust is likely to be towards a return to the 'scientific' planning of educational provision and an emphasis on those aspects of schooling that are most easily identifiable and recognizable by outsiders. Attention was drawn in Chapter 3 to that narrowing of horizons in early childhood education that is resulting from a growing preoccupation with short-term objectives. The discussion of the influences on curriculum of public examinations in Chapter 5 also emphasized the dangers of settling in our teaching for those things that are readily measurable. Consideration in Chapter 6 of the pressures resulting from falling school rolls and changes in the organization of local government led also to the view that teachers are likely to be under increasing pressure to concentrate on those aspects of their work which 'show' most clearly and are most easily assessed. Several contributors have made reference to the system of 'payment by results' and this is no coincidence. The dangers of a return to something resembling that system are apparent and real. The constraints created by such factors as these are at odds with that developing concept of education we considered earlier.

Increased demands for public accountability can lead to all of these ills. However, most contributors have also seen potential advantages if such demands can be handled properly. The discussion of examinations in Chapter 5 revealed not only the dangers but also the possible merits of a properly constructed examinations system. In particular, it was shown that such a system could lead to that very individualizing of education that earlier we had argued to be desirable. It need not lead to the reintroduction of a narrow approach to educational planning based on a limited range of objectives. In Chapter 6, too, it was argued that the involvement of people other than teachers in curriculum planning need not be seen as a disadvantage, particularly at a time when the battle for a fair share of scarce resources is likely to be a hard one. Parents, politicians and others may well be able to fight that battle more ruthlessly and more effectively than teachers could themselves, so that, provided that they can be seen as or can be persuaded to be allies, their presence in such debates could be of positive advantage.

The message, therefore, is plain. It is necessary to recognize the existence and the growing strength of these constraints, but we need not see them as inevitably detrimental to our purposes or as unavoidably holding back the tide of developing educational ideals. If handled aright, they can become a gain to educational provision. The crucial point, however, is that teachers should be aware of the kinds of constraint that are being imposed on their work and of the reasons for them, so that they may hope to be able to deal with them in the most effective manner. Accountability should not be seen as a threat to teachers but, as we saw in Chapter 7, as a necessary facet of any kind of activity in a democratic community, whether we see democracy as participation or as communication. What is important is that we should strive to achieve the right system of accountability and, in order to do that, it is necessary that we understand not only what is at stake but also the many and varied factors that impinge upon educational decisions. Teachers need a clear concept of education; they also need an understanding of the nature and sources of the pressures to which they are subject. Only then can they hope to promote the education of their pupils, since only then will they be able to exercise some influence on these pressures in order to ensure that they be made to forward education rather than being allowed to control and inhibit it. This is another dimension of the truism that all curriculum development is teacher development.

These, then, are the major themes of this book. If it has done nothing more, we hope it has alerted teachers to the pressures that are applied to their work and which form the setting within which all curriculum planning and development must go on. If it has also revealed the tensions between these pressures, then that too is well and good. If it has thus, in improving the teachers' understanding of the context in which their responsibility for the education of all of their pupils must be exercised, increased their control over it, every contributor will be well pleased.

# BIBLIOGRAPHY

**Adorno, T.W., Frenkel-Brunswick, E., Levinson, D.J. and Sandford, R.N.** (1950) *The Authoritarian Personality*, New York, Harper & Row.

**Andersen, H.H. and Brewer, H.M.** (1946) Studies of Teachers' Classroom Personalities, *Applied Psychology Monographs of the American Association for Applied Psychology*.

**Archambault, R.D.** (ed.) (1965) *Philosophical Analysis and Education*, London, Routledge & Kegan Paul.

**Ausubel, D.** (1963) Is drill necessary? The mythology of incidental learning, in Ausubel, D. (ed.) (1969).

**Ausubel, D.** (ed.) (1969) *Readings in School Learning*, New York, Holt Rinehart & Winston.

**Baldwin, R.W.** (1977) The Dissolution of the Grammar School, in Cox, C.B. and Boyson, Rhodes (eds.) (1977).

**Bantock, G.H.** (1963) *Education in an Industrial Society*, London, Faber.

**Bantock, G.H.** (1967) *Education, Culture and the Emotions*, London, Faber.

**Bantock, G.H.** (1968) *Culture, Industrialisation and Education*, London, Routledge & Kegan Paul.

**Bantock, G.H.** (1971) *Towards a Theory of Popular Education*, in Hooper, R. (ed.) (1971).

**Baron, G. and Howell, D.A.** (1974) *The Governing and Managing of Schools*, London, The Athlone Press.

**Becher, T. and Maclure, S.** (1978) *The Politics of Curriculum Change*, London, Hutchinson & Co.

**Becker, H.S.** (1952) Social class variations in the teacher-pupil relationship, *Journal of Educational Sociology* 25(4) pp. 451–465, reprinted in Cosin, B.R. *et al*. (eds.) (1971).

**Bell, R., Fowler, G. and Little, K.** (eds.) (1973) *Education in Great Britain and Ireland*, Bletchley, Open University Press.

**Bennett, N.** (1976) *Teaching Styles and Pupil Progress*, London, Open Books.

**Bereday, G.Z.F. and Lauwerys, J.A.** (eds.) (1958) *Year Book of Educa tion: The Secondary School Curriculum*, London, Evans.

**Berlyne, D.E.** (1960) *Conflict, Arousal and Curiosity*, London McGraw-Hill.

**Bernstein, B.** (1967) Open Schools, Open Society? *New Society* 14 September 1967.

**Bernstein, B.** (1971) On the Classification and Framing of Educational Knowledge, pp. 47–69 in Young, M.F.D. (ed.) (1971).

**Bernstein, B.** (1973, 1974, 1976) *Class, Codes and Control*, Vol. 1 2nd edition (1974); Vol. 2 (1973); Vol. 3 (1976), London, Routledge & Kegan Paul.

**Blackie, J.** (1976) *Inspecting and the Inspectorate*, London, Routledge & Kegan Paul.

**Bloom. B.S.** (ed.) (1956) *A Taxonomy of Educational Objectives*, Vol. 1, London, Longman.

**Bloom, B.S.** (1965) Mastery learning and its implications for curriculum development in Golby, M. *et al*. (1975).

**Blum, A.F.** (1971) The Corpus of Knowledge as a Normative Order: Intellectual Critique of the Social Order of Knowledge and Commonsense Features of Bodies of Knowledge, pp. 117–152 in Young M.F.D. (ed.) (1971).

**Blyth, W.A.L.** (1965) *English Primary Education: a Sociological Description, Vol. 2: Background*, London, Routledge & Kegan Paul.

**Blyth, W.A.L.** (1974) One Development Project's Awkward Thinking about Objectives, *Journal of Curriculum Studies* 6, pp. 99–111.

**Bobbitt, F.** (1918) *The Curriculum*, Boston, Houghton Mifflin.

**Bolam, D.** (1971) Keele Integrated Studies Project 1968–71, in Schools Council (1971).

**Bowlby, J.** (1950) *Child Care and the Growth of Love*, Harmondsworth, Penguin Books.

**BBC** (1972) ROSLA Series, Programme 8: *Towards a Common Curriculum*, London, British Broadcasting Corporation.

**Bruner, J.S.** (ed.) (1960a) *The Process of Education*, New York, Vintage Books.

**Bruner, J.S.** (1960b) The Functions of Teaching, *Rhode Island College Journal*, reprinted in Morse, W.C. and Wingo, G.M. (eds.) (1971).

**Bruner, J.S.** (1961) The Act of Discovery, *Harvard Education Review* 1961.

**Bruner, J.S.** (1966) *Toward a Theory of Instruction*, New York, Norton & Co.

**Carroll, J.** (1963) A Model of School Learning, *Teachers' College Record*, 1963.

**Cashdan, A.** (ed.) (1972) *Personality, Growth and Learning*, London, Longman with Oxford University Press.

**Centre for Educational Research and Innovation** (1972) *The Nature of the Curriculum for the Eighties and Onwards*, Strasbourg, OECD.

**Charters, W.W.** (1924) *Curriculum Construction*, New York, Macmillan.

**Clegg, A. and Megson, B.** (1968) *Children in Distress*, Harmondsworth, Penguin Books.

**Coates, K.** (1977) *Beyond Wage Slavery*, Nottingham, Spokesman Books.

**Collins, R.** (1971) Functional and Conflict Theories of Educational Stratification, *American Sociological Review* 36, pp. 1002–1019.

**Cook, D.** (1973) in Kogan, M. (1973).

**Cosin, B.R.** *et al.* (eds.) (1971) *School and Society*, London, Routledge & Kegan Paul with Open University Press.

**Cox, C.B. and Boyson, Rhodes** (eds.) (1977) *Black Paper 1977*, London, Temple Smith.

**Crick, B.** (1968) Them and Us: Public Impotence and Government Power, *Public Law*, Spring 1968, pp. 8–27.

**Curtis, S.J.** (1948) *History of Education in Great Britain*, London, University Tutorial Press.

**The Daily Telegraph**, 2 April 1979. Report by Izbicki, J.

**Dance, E.H.** (1970) *The Place of History in Secondary Teaching: A Comparative Study*, London, Harrap for CCCCE.

**Davies, I.K.** (1976) *Objectives in Curriculum Design*, London, McGraw-Hill.

**Dearden, R.F.** (1976) *Problems in Primary Education*, London, Routledge & Kegan Paul.

**Delamont, S.** (1976) *Interaction in the Classroom*, London, Methuen.

**Devlin, T. and Warnock, M.** (1977) *What must we Teach?*, London, Temple Smith.

**Douglas, J.W.B.** (1964) *The Home and the School*, London, MacGibbon and Kee.

**Downey, M.E.** (1977) *Interpersonal Judgements in Education*, London, Harper & Row.

**Downey, M.E. and Kelly, A.V.** (1975, 1979) *Theory and Practice of Education: An Introduction*, 1979 2nd edition, London, Harper & Row.

**Eggleston, S.J.** (1973) Guidance and examination – central components of educational technology, *Cambridge Journal of Education*, Easter, 1973.

**Eisner, E.W.** (1969) Instructional and expressive educational objectives: their formulation and use in curriculum, pp. 1–8 in Popham *et al*. (1969).

**Erikson, E.H.** (1950) *Childhood and Society*, New York, Norton & Co.

**Flanders, N.A.** (1970) *Analysing Teacher Behaviour*, New York, Addison-Wesley.

**Flavell, J.** (1969) *Studies in Cognitive Development*, Oxford, Oxford University Press.

**Foot, M.** (1962, 1975) *Aneurin Bevan*, Vol. 1, London, Paladin.

**Forrest, G.M.** (1971) *Standards in Subjects at the Ordinary Level of the GCE, June 1970*, (Occasional Publication 33), Manchester, Joint Matriculation Board.

**Forrest, G.M. and Smith, G.A.** (1972) *Standards in subjects at the Ordinary Level of The GCE, June 1971* (Occasional Publication 34), Manchester, Joint Matriculation Board.

**Friere, P.** (1970) Cultural Action for Freedom, *Harvard Educational Review*, Cambridge, Mass.; also Harmondsworth, Penguin Books 1972.

**Friere, P.** (1972) *Pedagogy of the Oppressed* tr. from Portuguese by Ramos, M.B., London, Sheed and Ward; also Harmondsworth, Penguin Books 1972.

**Fuchs, E.** (1968) How teachers learn to help children fail, *Transactions* pp. 45–49, reprinted in Keddie, N. (ed.) (1973).

**Gagné, R.M.** (1970) *The Conditions of Learning*, New York, Holt Rinehart and Winston.

**Gleeson, D. and Whitty, G.** (1976) *Developments in Social Studies Teaching*, London, Open Books.

**Golby, M., Greenwald, J. and West, R.** (eds.) (1975) *Curriculum Design*, London, Croom Helm with Open University Press.

**Goldsmiths' College** (1965) *Report of the First Pilot Course for Experienced Teachers: The Role of the School in a Changing Society*, London, Goldsmiths' College.

**Goodman, P.** (1962, 1971) *Compulsory Miseducation*, New York, Horizon Press 1962; also Harmondsworth, Penguin Books 1971.

**Gordon, P. and Lawton, D.** (1978) *Curriculum Change in the Nineteenth and Twentieth Centuries*, London, Hodder & Stoughton.

**Guilford, J.** (1950) Creativity, *American Psychologist* 1950; reprinted in Cashdan (ed.) (1972).

**Gumbert, E.B. and Spring, J.H.** (1974) *Superschool and Superstate: American Education in the Twentieth Century 1918–1970*, New York, Wiley.

**Habermas, J.** (1976) *Legitimation Crisis*, London, Heinemann.

**Halliwell, H.F.** (ed.) (1966) *Nuffield Chemistry Introduction and Guide*, London, Longmans/Penguin Books.

**Hanson, J.** (1979) How an LEA should plan for contraction, *Education*, 9 March 1979.

**Harris, A., Lawn, M. and Prescott, W.** (eds.) (1975) *Curriculum Innovation*, London, Croom Helm.

**Hartog, P. and Rhodes, E.C.** (1935) *An Examination of Examinations*, London, Macmillan.

**Hilgard, E.R.** (1964) *Theories of Learning and Instruction*, Chicago, University of Chicago Press.

**Hirst, P.H.** (1969) The logic of the curriculum, *Journal of Curriculum Studies* 1, pp. 142–158, also in Hooper (ed.) (1971).

**Hirst, P.H.** (1975) The curriculum and its objectives – a defence of piecemeal planning, pp. 9–21 in *Studies in Education 2. The Curriculum. The Doris Lee Lectures,* London, University of London Institute of Education.

**Hogben, D.** (1972) The behavioural objectives approach: some problems and some dangers, *Journal of Curriculum Studies* 4, 1972, pp. 42–50.

**Hoggart, R.** (1957, 1958) *The Uses of Literacy*, London, Chatto & Windus 1957; also Harmondsworth, Penguin Books 1958.

**Hollins, T.H.B.** (ed.) (1964) *Aim in Education: The Philosophic Approach*, Manchester, Manchester University Press.

**Holly, D.** (1973, 1974) *Beyond Curriculum*, London, Hart-Davis-MacGibbon 1973; also St Albans, Paladin 1974.

**Holt, J.** (1969, 1970) *How Children Fail*, Harmondsworth, Penguin Books 1969; also London, Pitman 1970.

**Holt, J.** (1970) *The Underachieving School*, London, Pitman.

**Homme, L.E.** (1966) Contiguity theory and contingency management, *The Psychological Record* 1966.

**Hooper, R.** (ed.) (1971) *The Curriculum: Context, Design and Development*, Edinburgh, Oliver & Boyd in association with the Open University Press.

**Hoste, R. and Bloomfield, B.** (NFER) (1975) Schools Council Examinations Bulletin 31 *Continuous Assessment in CSE: Opinion and Practice*, London, Evans/Methuen Educational.

**Hoyle, E.** (1971) How does the curriculum change? A proposal for inquiries *Journal of Curriculum Studies* 1, pp. 132–141; also in Hooper, R. (ed.) (1971).

**Illich, I.D.** (1971a) *The Celebration of Awareness*, London, Calder.

**Illich, I.D.** (1971b) *Deschooling Society*, London, Calder.

**James, C.M.** (1968) *Young Lives at Stake*, London, Collins.

**Jencks, C.** *et al*. (1975) *Inequality: Reassessment of the Effects of Family and Schooling in America*, Harmondsworth, Penguin Books.

**Jennings, R.E.** (1977) *Education and Politics*, London, Batsford.

**Karabel, J. and Halsey, A.H.** (1977) *Educational Research: A review and an interpretation*, in Karabel, J. and Halsey, A.H. (eds.) (1977).

**Karabel, J. and Halsey, A.H.** (eds.) (1977) *Power and Ideology in Education*, Oxford, Oxford University Press.

**Keddie, N.** (1971) Classroom Knowledge, pp. 133–160 in Young M.F.D. (ed.) (1971).

**Keddie, N.** (ed.) (1973) *Tinker, Tailor: The Myth of Cultural Deprivation*, Harmondsworth, Penguin Books.

**Kelly, A.V.** (1977) *The Curriculum: Theory and Practice*, London, Harper & Row.

**Kelly, P.J.** (1973) Nuffield A level biological science project, pp. 91–109 in Schools Council (1973a).

**Kerr, J.F.** (ed.) (1968) *Changing the Curriculum*, London, University of London Press.

**King, E.J.** *et al.* (1974) *Post-compulsory Education: A New Analysis in Western Europe*, London, Sage Publications.

**King, E.J.** (ed.) (1978) *Education for Uncertainty*, London, Sage Publications.

**Kogan, M.** (1973) *County Hall, LEA*, Harmondsworth, Penguin Books.

**Kogan, M.** (1978) *The Politics of Educational Change*, London, Fontana.

**Kogan, M. and Packwood, T.** (1974) *Advisory Councils and Committees in Education*, London and Boston, Routledge & Kegan Paul.

**Kohlberg, L.** (1966) Moral education in the schools: a development view, *School Review* 1966.

**Labov, W.** (1972, 1977) *Language in the Inner City: studies in the Black English Vernacular*, Philadelphia, University of Pennsylvania Press, 1972; also Oxford, Blackwell 1977.

**Lawton, D.** (1973) *Social Change, Educational Theory and Curriculum Planning*, London, University of London Press.

**Lawton, D.** (1975) *Class, Culture and the Curriculum*, London, Routledge & Kegan Paul.

**Lewis, D.G.** (1974) *Assessment in Education*, London, Unibooks.

**Lowe, R.** (1867) *Primary and Classical Education*, Edinburgh, Edmonton and Douglas.

**Lippitt, R.** *et al*. (1947) The Dynamics of Power: a field study of social influence in groups of children, in Maccoby *et al*. (1963).

**Maccoby, E.E., Newcombe, T.H. and Hartley, E.L.** (eds.) (1963) *Readings in Social Psychology*, London, Methuen.

**Mack. J.** (1978) What's the point of strong school governors? *New Society*, 7 September 1978.

**Macintosh, H.G. and Smith, L.A.** (1974) *Towards a Freer Curriculum*, London, Unibooks.

**MacIntyre, A.C.** (1964) Against Utilitarianism, pp. 1–23 in Hollins, T.H.B. (ed.) (1964).

**Maclure, J.S.** (ed.) (1970) *Studies in the Government and Control of Education since 1860*, History of Education Society Conference 1968, London, Methuen.

**McCreesh, J. and Maher, A.** (1976) *Preschool Education: Objectives and Techniques*, London, Ward Lock Educational.

**McPhail, P., Ungoed-Thomas, J.R. and Chapman, H.** (1972) *Moral Education in the Secondary School*, London, Longman.

**Matthews, J.C. and Leece, J.R.** (1976) Schools Council Examination Bulletin 33: *Examinations: their use in curriculum evaluation and development*, London, Evans/Methuen Educational.

**Merchant, E.C** (ed.) (1967) *Geography Teaching and the Revision of Geography Textbooks and Atlases: report of four Council of Europe Conferences*, Strasbourg, CCCCE.

**Midwinter, E.** (1972) *Priority Education: An Account of the Liverpool Project*, Harmondsworth, Penguin.

**Montgomery, R.J.** (1965) *Examinations*, London, Longmans.

**Montgomery, R.J.** (1978) *A new examination of examinations*, London, Routledge & Kegan Paul.

**Morris, N.** (1961) An historian's view of examinations, in Wiseman, S. (ed.) (1961).

**Morse, W.C. and Wingo, G.M.** (eds.) (1971) *Classroom Psychology* 3rd edition, Illinois, Scott Foresman.

**Murdoch, I.** (1977) The Blackboard Jungle, *New Statesman*, 21 October 1977.

**Myrdal, G.** (1944) *An American Dilemma: The Negro Problem and American Democracy*, New York, Harper & Row.

**Nuttall, D.L.** (1971) Schools Council Working Paper 34; *The 1968 CSE Monitoring Experiment,* London, Evans/Methuen Educational.

**Nuttall, D. and Willmott. A.S.** (1972) *British Examinations: techniques of analysis*, Slough, NFER.

**Nuttall, D.L., Backhouse, J.K. and Willmott, A.S.** (1974) Schools Council Examinations Bulletin 29: *Comparability of standards between subjects*, London, Evans/Methuen Educational.

**Oliver, R.A.C.** (1961) Education and Selection, in Wiseman, S. (ed.) (1961).

**Open University Language and Learning Course Team** (1972) *Language in Education : a Source Book*, London, Routledge & Kegan Paul for Open University Press.

**Open University School and Society Course Team** (1972) *Sorting Them Out: Two Essays on Social Differential*, Bletchley, Open University Press.

**Pask, G. and Lewis, B.** (eds.) (1972) *The Curriculum: Context, Design and Development Unit 9*, Bletchley, Open University Press.

**Peters, R.S.** (1965) Education as Initiation, pp. 87–111 in Archambault (ed.) (1965).

**Peters, R.S.** (1966) *Ethics and Education*, London, Allen & Unwin.

**Piaget, J.** (1973) *Main Trends in Psychology*, New York, Harper & Row.

**Popham, W.J.** (1969) Objectives and Instruction, pp. 32–52 in Popham, W.J. *et al*. (1969).

**Popham, W.J., Eisner, E.W., Sullivan, H.J. and Tyler, L.L.** (1969) *Instructional Objectives, American Educational Research Association Monograph Series on Curriculum Evaluation No. 3*, Chicago, Rand McNally.

**Pratt, C.** (1973) in Kogan, M. (1973).

**Pring, R.** (1973) Objectives and innovation: the irrelevance of theory, *London Educational Review* 2, 1973, pp. 46–54.

**Pring, R.** (1976) *Knowledge and Schooling*, London, Open Books.

**Raphael, D.D.** (1970, 1976) *Problems of Political Philosophy*, London, Macmillan.

**Raynor, J. and Grant, N.** (1972) *Patterns of Curriculum*, Bletchley, Open University Press.

**Rist, R.C.** (1970) Student social class and teacher expectations: the self-fulfilling prophecy in ghetto education, *Harvard Educational Review* Vol. 40. No. 3., pp. 411–451.

**Rosen, H.** (1972) *Language and Class: A Critical Look at the Theories of Basil Bernstein*, Bristol, Falling Wall Press.

**Rust, W. Bonney and Harris, H.F.P.** (1967) *Examinations: Pass or Failure?*, London, Pitman.

**Rutter, M., Maugham, B., Mortimore, P. and Ouston, J.** (1979) *Fifteen Thousand Hours*, London, Open Books.

**Schofield, A.J.** (1977) *Pastoral Care and the Curriculum of a Comprehensive School*, unpublished M.A. dissertation, University of London.

**Schools Council** (1965) *Raising the School Leaving Age;* Working Paper No. 2, London, H.M.S.O.

**Schools Council** (1966) *Examining at 16+: the Report of the Joint GCE/CSE Committee*, London, H.M.S.O.

**Schools Council** (1967) *Society and the Young School Leaver:* Working Paper No. 11, London, H.M.S.O..

**Schools Council** (1970) *The Humanities Project: An Introduction*, London, Heinemann.

**Schools Council** (1971) *Choosing a Curriculum for the Young School Leaver:* Working Paper 33, London, Evans/Methuen Educational.

**Schools Council** (1972) *With Objectives in Mind: Guide to Science 5–13*, London, Macdonald Educational for the Schools Council.

**Schools Council** (1973a) *Evaluation in Curriculum Development: Twelve Case Studies*, Schools Council Research Studies, London, Macmillan Education for the Schools Council.

**Schools Council** (1973b) *GCE and CSE* (a pamphlet), London, Evans/Methuen Educational.

**Schools Council** (1974a) *Schools Council: the first ten years 1964–1974*, London, the Schools Council.

**Schools Council** (1974b) *Comparability of standards between subjects*, Examinations Bulletin 29, London, Evans/Methuen Educational.

**Schools Council** (1975a) *The Whole Curriculum 13–16:* Working Paper 53, London, Evans/Methuen Educational.

**Schools Council** (1975b) *Examinations at 16+: proposals for the future*, Examinations Bulletin 23, London, Evans/Methuen Educational.

**Schools Council** (1978a) *Examinations at 18+: resource implications of an N and F curriculum and examination structure*, Examinations Bulletin 38, London, Evans/Methuen Educational.

**Schools Council** (1978b) *Examinations at 18+: the N and F Studies:* Wor-

king Paper 60, London, Evans/Methuen Educational.
**Schwebel, M. and Raph, J.** (eds.) (1974) *Piaget in the Classroom*, London, Routledge & Kegan Paul.
**Scottish Council for Research in Education** (1977) *Pupils in Profile*, SCRE Publication 67.
**Sharp, R. and Green, A.** (1975) *Education and Social Control*, London, Routledge & Kegan Paul.
**Silberman, C.E.** (1973) *The Open Classroom Reader*, New York, Vintage.
**Simon, B.** (1978) Problems in Contemporary Educational Theory: a Marxist approach, *Journal of Philosophy of Education* Vol 12, pp. 29–40.
**Sinclair de Zwart, H.** (1969) Development Psycholinguistics, in Flavell, J. (1969).
**Skinner, B.F.** (1959) *Cumulative Record*, New York, Appleton-Century-Crofts.
**Skinner, B.F.** (1965) Why Teachers Fail, *Saturday Review*, October 1965; reprinted in Morse, W.C. and Wingo, G.M. (eds.) (1971).
**Skinner, B.F.** (1968) *The Technology of Teaching*, New York, Appleton-Century-Crofts.
**Sockett, H.** (1976) *Designing the Curriculum*, London, Open Books.
**Stenhouse, L.** (1970) Some limitations of the use of objectives in curriculum research and planning, *Paedagogica Europaea* 6, pp. 73–83.
**Stenhouse, L.** (1975) *An Introduction to Curriculum Research and Development*, London, Heinemann.
**Taba, H.** (1962) *Curriculum Development: Theory and Practice*, New York, Harcourt Brace & World.
**Taylor, C.W.** (ed.) (1964) *Creativity: its educational implications*, New York, Wiley.
**Taylor, P.H.** (1968) The contribution of psychology to the study of the curriculum, in Kerr, J.F. (ed.) (1968).
**Taylor, W.** (1963) *The Secondary Modern School*, London, Faber & Faber.
*Teachers' Action* No. 10 (1978) London, Publications Distribution Cooperative.
**Thompson, E.P.** (1963) *The Making of the English Working Class*, London, Gollancz.
**Thorndyke, E.** (1913) The Psychology of Learning, *New York Teachers' College Record*, New York, Columbia University Press.
**Thorndyke, E.** (1932) The Fundamentals of Learning, *New York Teachers' College Record*, New York, Columbia University Press.
**Torrance, E.P.** (1964) Education and Creativity, in Taylor, C.W. (ed.) (1964).

**Trace, A.S.** (1971) *What Ivan Knows that Johnny Doesn't*, New York, Random House.

**Tyler, R.W.** (1949) *Basic Principles of Curriculum and Instruction*, Chicago, University of Chicago Press.

**Vaizey, J.** (ed.) (1975) *Whatever Happened to Equality?*, London, British Broadcasting Corporation.

**Walker, R. and Adelman, C.** (1975) Interaction analysis of informal classrooms, *British Journal of Educational Psychology* 1975.

**Walton J.** (ed.) (1971) *The Integrated Day in Theory and Practice*, London, Ward Lock Educational.

**Warnock, M. and Annan, N.** (1975) Equality in the Schools, in Vaizey, J. (ed.) (1975).

**Warnock, M. (1977)** *Schools of Thought*, London, Faber & Faber.

**Weaver, Sir Toby,** Open University Course E222 The Control of Education, Unit 2 *The Department of Education and Science: Central Control of Education?*, Bletchley, Open University Press.

**Wheeler, D.K.** (1967) *Curriculum Process,* London, University of London Press.

**White, J.P.** (1968) Education in Obedience, *New Society*, 2 May 1968.

**White, J.P.** (1973) *Towards a Compulsory Curriculum*, London, Routledge & Kegan Paul.

**White, J.P.** (1975) The end of compulsory curriculum, in *Studies in Education 2. The Curriculum. The Doris Lee Lectures,* London, University of London Institute of Education.

**Whitla, D., Hanley, J.P., Moo, E.W. and Walter, D.** (1970) *Man-A Course of Study: Evaluation Strategies,* Washington D.C., Education Development Center.

**Wickens, D.** (1974) Piagetian theory as a model for open systems of education, in Schwebel, M. and Raph J. (eds.) (1974).

**Williams, R.** (1958) *Culture and Sosciety 1780– 1950,* London, Chatto & Windus.

**Williams, R.** (1961, 1965) *The Long Revolution,* London, Chatto & Windus 1961; also London, Pelican Books 1965.

**Willis, P.** (1977) *Learning to Labour*, Farnborough, Saxon House.

**Wilson, P.S.** (1971) *Interest and Discipline in Education,* London, Routledge & Kegan Paul.

**Wiseman, S.** (ed.) (1961) *Examinations and English Education*, Manchester, Manchester University Press.

**Wyatt, T.S.** (1975) The GCE Examining Boards and Curriculum

Development, in Schools Council (1975b); also in Harris et al (eds.) (1975).

**Young, M.F.D.** (ed.) (1971) *Knowledge and Control*, New York, Collier Macmillan.

**Young, M.F.D.** (1973) On the politics of educational knowledge, pp. 70–81 in Bell, R. *et al.* (1973).

**Young, Michael** (1979) Alternative forms of comprehensive school: the American example, *PRISE News*, Spring 1979.

**Government Reports and other official publications referred to in the text – listed in chronological order.**

**Report of the Commission appointed to inquire into the state of popular education in England** (The Newcastle Report) (1861).

**Report of the Commissioners appointed to inquire into the revenues and management of certain schools and the studies pursued and instruction given therein** (The Clarendon Report) (1864).

**Report of the Schools Inquiry Commission** (The Taunton Report) (1868).

**Royal Commission on Scientific Instruction and the Advancement of Science** – Second Report (1872).

**Board of Education** Circular No. 849, July 1914.

**Board of Education** (1926) *The Education of the Adolescent* (The Hadow Report on Secondary Education), London, H.M.S.O.

**Board of Education** (1931) *Primary Education* (The Hadow Report on Primary Education), London, H.M.S.O.

**Board of Education** (1938) *Secondary Education with Special Reference to Grammar Schools and Technical High Schools* (The Spens Report), London, H.M.S.O.

**Board of Education** (1943) *Report of the Committee of the Secondary Schools Examinations Council: Curriculum and Examinations in Secondary Schools* (The Norwood Report), London, H.M.S.O.

**Ministry of Education** (1945) *Administrative Memorandum No. 25*, in Department of Education and Science (1977d).

**Central Advisory Council for Education** (1954) *Early Leaving*, London, H.M.S.O.

**Secondary Schools Examinations Council** (1960) *Secondary School Examinations other than the GCE* (The Beloe Report), London, H.M.S.O.

**Central Advisory Council for Education** (1959) *15 to 18* (The Crowther Report), London, H.M.S.O.

**Central Advisory Council for Education** (1963) *Half Our Future* (The Newsom Report), London, H.M.S.O.

**Central Advisory Council for Education** (1967) *Children and Their Primary Schools* (The Plowden Report), London, H.M.S.O.

**Department of Education and Science** (1975) *A Language for Life* (the Bullock report), H.M.S.O.

**Department of Education and Science** (1975) *The Report of the Committee into the Payment of Non-University Teachers* (the Haughton report), H.M.S.O.

**Organisation for Economic Co-operation and Development Report on Planning in the D.E.S.** (1975), Paris.

**Tenth Report of the Expenditure Committee** (Session 1975–76) (H.C. 621), *Policy Making in the Department of Education and Science*, London, H.M.S.O.

**Inner London Education Committee** (1976) Report of the Public Enquiry into *Teaching Organisation and Management of William Tyndale Junior and Infants' Schools* (The Auld Report), London, ILEA.

**Department of Education and Science** (1977a) *A New Partnership for our Schools* (The Taylor Report), London, H.M.S.O.

**Department of Education and Science** (1977b) A New Partnership for our Schools (The Taylor Report), the official shortened version, *Times Educational Supplement* 23 September 1977.

**Department of Education and Science** (1977c) *Primary Education in England and Wales. A Survey of H.M. Inspectors of Schools* London, H.M.S.O.

**Department of Education and Science and the Welsh Office** (1977d) *Education in Schools: A Consultative Document* (Green Paper) Cmnd 6869, London, H.M.S.O.

**Department of Education and Science** (1978) *Curriculum 11–16*, London, Department of Education and Science.

**School Examinations Steering Committee** (1978) *Report on Proposals for Replacing the GCE O-level and CSE Examinations by a Common System of Examining* (The Waddell Report), London, H.M.S.O.

# Index

**The Harper Education Series** has been designed to meet the needs of students following initial courses in teacher education at colleges and in University departments of education, as well as the interests of practising teachers.

All volumes in the series are based firmly in the practice of education and deal, in a multidisciplinary way, with practical classroom issues, school organisation and aspects of the curriculum.

Topics in the series are wide ranging, as the list of current titles indicates. In all cases the authors have set out to discuss current educational developments and show how practice is changing in the light of recent research and educational thinking. Theoretical discussions, supported by an examination of recent research and literature in the relevant fields, arise out of a consideration of classroom practice.

Care is taken to present specialist topics to the non-specialist reader in a style that is lucid and approachable. Extensive bibliographies are supplied to enable readers to pursue any given topic further.

Meriel Downey, General Editor

*New titles in the Harper Education Series*

**Mathematics Teaching: Theory in Practice** by T.H.F. Brissenden, University College of Swansea

**Approaches to School Management** edited by T. Bush, J. Goodey and C. Riches, Faculty of Educational Studies, The Open University

**Linking Home and School: A New Review** 3/ed edited by M. Craft, J. Raynor, The Open University, and Louis Cohen, Loughborough University of Technology

**Control and Discipline in Schools: Perspectives and Approaches** by J.W. Docking, Roehampton Institute of Higher Education

**Children Learn to Measure: A Handbook for Teachers** edited by J.A. Glenn, The Mathematics Education Trust

**Curriculum Context** edited by A.V. Kelly, Goldsmiths' College

**The Curriculum of the Primary School** by A.V. Kelly and G. Blenkin, Goldsmiths' College

**The Practice of Teaching** by K. Martin and W. Bennett, Goldsmiths' College.

**Helping the Troubled Child: Interprofessional Case Studies** by Stephen Murgatroyd, The Open University

**Children in their Primary Schools** by Henry Pluckrose, Prior Weston School

**Educating the Gifted Child** edited by Robert Povey, Christ Church College, Canterbury

**Educational Technology in Curriculum Development** 2/e by Derek Rowntree, The Open University

**The Harper International Dictionary of Education** by Derek Rowntree, The Open University

**Education and Equality** edited by David Rubinstein, Hull University

**Clever Children in Comprehensive Schools** by Auriol Stevens, Education Correspondent, The Observer

**Values and Evaluation in Education** edited by R. Straughan and J. Wrigley, University of Reading

**Middle Schools: Origins, Ideology and Practice** edited by L. Tickle and A. Hargreaves, Middle Schools Research Group